ON THE UP

THE STORY OF SHARRINGTON F.C.

David Montgomery

Escafeld Press

On the Up – The Story of Sharrington F.C.

Copyright © 2019 David Montgomery

Cover design and images copyright © Escafeld Press
Footballer graphics: courtesy of: all-free-download.com
Cover font: Heavyweight: © 2001 Nerfect Type Laboratories
and Britton Walters

The moral rights of the author have been asserted.

ISBN 978-1-9996440-8-6

Escafeld Press

For the trips to see Brownie the pony. For feeding the pigeons. For all the stories, the laughs and the lifts. For the help and advice you have given me as I have grown up. For the money. For the endless patience, kindness and love. For being the most wonderful Dad I could ever wish for, this is the best thing I could do for you.

The author: David Montgomery

SHARRINGTON F.C

TUESDAY, SEPT. 16TH

KICK-OFF AT **7.30**

SHARRINGTON

v.

ALDWAY

ADMISSIONS 77/78 SEASON:

SEASON TICKETS:
(STAND) £13.50
(GROUND, COVERED) £12.00
(GROUND) £10.00

PER GAME:
(STAND) £1.25
(GROUND, COVERED) £1.00
(GROUND) £0.75

BULMER, MORRRIS & CO, PRINTERS, REYNOLDS STREET, SHARRINGTON

Chapter 1

'Well, Jack,' said a despondent Sid Parkin the Sharrington F.C. Secretary. 'We've amassed a mammoth three applications for the manager's position. One from old Ted Meersbrook who was recently sacked from relegated Seamingway, the second from a Mr. Norman Collins, who is team trainer at Third Division Ranchley Athletic and the last one from a local crank by the name of Tony Davidson.'

Sid, who was a quietly spoken man, small in stature, greasy black hair and always wore the same sports jacket, started to laugh as he read from Davidson's application form. 'He says he has no experience as a football manager but has studied the game closely, has followed Sharrington F.C. during the past two seasons, is confident that he can build the club up from the depths of the Fourth Division and establish a good team spirit with future success.' Sid tossed the form into the out tray in a contemptible manner and sarcastically remarked 'Quite impressive predictions to say the chap's a qualified driving instructor. Don't some folks have a nerve eh, Jack?'

Sharrington was an industrial town with a population of 120,000. It was positioned in the north west of the country, fifteen 20 miles to the west from where the two main country's motorways intersected. It was a popular railway town with many direct lines running through the centre of the main industrial complex.

Jack Elliott, the club's chairman for the past 15 years, was sitting slumped in an old torn leather chair behind an equally antiquated oak desk in the manager's office. Jack was the backbone of the club. He was a pleasant character with an abundance of smile lines around his eyes, a well-trimmed grey moustache which matched his neatly cut grey hair. He usually wore as he did on this occasion a brightly coloured cravat. He looked up at Sid in disbelief and mumbled: 'What a depressing position this club is in, Sid. After three seasons in the Fourth Division we have had to fight off relegation on each occasion, we have seen the back of three indifferent managers, the result being…' he paused '… an apathetic team, a ground only one-eighth full every other week, a debt to the bank of £50,000 and a season due to start in 5 weeks, without a manager. What a mess to be in! Ask Peggy to make us a cup of coffee, Sid, and then we'll discuss this matter.'

After five minutes, Peggy Hollingsworth, who was employed by the club as programme seller, telephonist, typist, post girl and canteen worker, came into the manager's office with two cups of coffee and a specialist's report on Barrie Trippett, the team's midfield player. She placed the cups of coffee on the desk and waited to hear Jack Elliott's reply.

'Oh no! As if we don't have enough problems,' exclaimed Jack.

'What's wrong Jack?' asked Sid hesitantly.

'It's a medical report from Dr. Ericson on Trippett's injured right ankle. The prognosis suggests that his playing career is over, as the treatment to the damaged ligaments has had no remedial effect. He is also of the opinion that the ankle will never be completely sound again.'

'Just our luck. One of our best players as well,' commented Sid.

'I suppose he knows already,' asked Jack hopefully. Peggy did not know whether the doctor had told Barrie but said that judging by the expression on his face when he handed her the report, she guessed that he did. 'Better send the lad in, Peg. I ought to at least confirm what he knows already.' Peggy left the office and after a few minutes came back with Barrie Trippett. 'Come in, Barrie,' said Jack, hoping not to sound too patronising.

Barrie walked towards the old oak desk and remained standing. He was about 5'9' tall, dark curly hair, broad shoulders with a good athletic physique. He was injured in only the second game of the season against Braman and had not played for the remainder of the season. He was a good midfield player and had played previously for Trackerton Rovers and Brookhouse Athletic in Divisions One and Two respectively. He had been transferred to Sharrington F.C. only two seasons ago for £15,000 by ex-manager, Pete Gosling, to help give the club a little more experience. Barrie was now 32 years old and it was apparent that he knew his career was over.

Jack Elliott sat upright, placed his glasses firmly on the bridge of his nose and said solemnly, looking at Barrie, 'I'm sorry to have to say this Barrie but Dr. Ericson's report suggests that your playing career is over due to the seriousness of the ankle injury.'

Before Jack could continue Barrie said quite slowly and deliberately, 'I guess I have known for a long time now that I would never play competitively again. I was always behind with the exercises the Doctor set me and I cannot turn the ankle, as I know I should be able to. I suppose I've had too many knocks over the seasons. Ah well, I feel better in some respects now I know the Doc's final opinion.'

Jack Elliott felt himself staring at Barrie and admiring him for the manner in which he had accepted the Doctor's report. Quickly Jack looked back at the report and in a serious voice told Barrie how he would be a great loss to the club.

Barrie said he would go home and think the matter over. As Barrie turned to walk towards the door Jack Elliott suddenly said, 'Discuss it with your wife by all means but before deciding anything about your future report to my office at 10 o'clock tomorrow morning.'

After Barrie had gone. Sid asked Jack what he had meant and what he had got in mind.

'Well you know, Sid, a thought just crossed my mind as I was listening to Barrie and I think he could be a big help in assisting us select the right manager for the club. For a start Paddy Graham has not proved himself as a coach during the last two seasons and, apart from that I heard that he's not happy with this club. I therefore propose to dismiss him and bring Barrie Trippett in as a replacement. Barrie's always been well respected by the players and, in the circumstances, I think he would make a good coach. If he accepts he will have an idea of the type of manager, he and the players would be pleased to work for. I feel that the players are basically good enough to get us out of this division and if Barrie comes in as coach and we can get the right manager the club could make an extra effort to give us that final push into the top three places and promotion.'

As much as Sid admired Jack's total belief in the club he felt as though he had heard this conversation too many times before, but although his ideas always seemed to make sense, Sid could never recall the club having any success during his ten years reign as Secretary.

'There's not much to pick from Jack,' said Sid looking at the three names on the list again. 'I know we haven't, but I think we should give the chaps an interview yes even the crank Davidson,' remarked Jack, looking somewhat pleased with himself.

'You've got to be kidding,' said Sid looking up with disbelief.

'There's nothing to be lost in an interview. It's good public relations Sid. Let's get them arranged as soon as possible, I've got to go out now, I'll see you later.'

Sid quickly contacted the three applicants for the manager's position and arranged them all to attend for an interview during Monday of the following week. Sid had assumed all would be there at the times he stipulated over the telephone, but as he had left a message on an answering service phone at Tony Davidson's Motoring School he really hoped deep down that Davidson wouldn't make the 4 o'clock appointment.

Although Sid had held the Secretary's position for ten years, as one season after another passed by, his interest in the job deteriorated. He also felt quite strongly against the Chairman granting a crank an interview. Particularly a crank who had no football management experience. Even Sid had played the game and although he was never in the top flight he felt it was essential to have played the game at a reasonably high standard before attempting to manage men with experience and ability. How could an outsider with apparently no football experience manage men like Bond, Henderson and Turner from the team? All three were vastly experienced and totalled over 30 years of playing the game competitively. As he had spoken to Meersbrook and Collins personally he smiled to himself when he thought that even if this Davidson fellow did get the message he had left at the Driving School he would be too apprehensive to attend. He laughed out aloud at the thought of Sharrington F.C. calling his bluff.

'What are you laughing at Sid?' enquired Peggy returning to the office.

'Oh nothing Peg,' said Sid as he moved uneasily away from the desk. 'I've just fixed up those interviews for the manager's position. Will you make a note for all the directors to be present on Monday? The interviews are spread over the whole day.'

'Righto, I'll attend to it straight away if you give me the names and times of appointments.'

'The details are in the blue book by the phone. See you, Peg. I'm off home.'

Chapter 2

On the morning of the interviews, the three directors Flannagan, Boothroyd and King strolled into the office block in single file. Flannagan was the major influence on the board of directors. He was a stocky, rotund chap with a bald head. He always wore dark coloured suits and a trilby hat. He had a ruddy complexion and an air of authority in his manner. He was a typical self-made man and owned the local abattoir.

Boothroyd was a tall thin middle-aged man with a dapper moustache. He was the local fruiterer and Flannagan's "yes man." Whatever Flannagan said Boothroyd always seemed to give the same opinion.

Steven King was the new blood to the club. He had been on the board for only eighteen months following his father's death. He had also taken over his father's business position as head of the family's painting and decorating firm. He was smartly dressed and a likeable chap, in his mid-thirties and keen for the success of Sharrington F.C.

The three men entered the tiny boardroom, passed the empty trophy cupboard and sat in their regular positions around the walnut panelled table, which was in the centre of the room. Flannagan in the centre, Boothroyd to his right and King on his left. On the opposite side of the table underneath the window sat Jack Elliott, who had the same contented smirk on his face as he had done the other day in the office. The expression seemed to be saying 'I know something you don't know.' There was the empty manager's chair to the right of Jack and also one at the end of the table near the doorway. Peggy Hollingsworth entered the room behind Mr. King and sat at Jack Elliott's right-hand side to take the minutes of the meeting before the interviews began.

Jack Elliott spoke first. 'As you know gentlemen we agreed verbally Friday evening to appoint Barrie Trippett as the club's trainer and also to dismiss Paddy Graham from that position. I can now report that Graham accepted our decision and has left immediately with one month's salary. He told me that he intends to return to Ireland and start afresh over there. I am also pleased to inform you Trippett has accepted the trainer's post with great delight. It seems a good move for the club and I'm sure we will benefit from his experience. I should therefore like to know if you have any objections in his sitting in on the interviews today to help us on some of the finer points.'

'I have no objection, Jack,' said Flannagan. 'And you can quote me on this, Mrs. Hollingsworth, but I'm glad to see the back of that Graham fellow, disliked him intensely.'

'Me too,' chirped Boothroyd in a mouse-like manner. 'It's a good idea to have Trippett on the panel. Nice fellow and a damn good player before that injury.'

'It's O.K. with me,' said King quite calmly. 'Let's get the chap in and get on with the proceedings.'

'Thank you, gentlemen. Peg will you send Barrie in first and then the interviewees as and when they arrive.' Peg returned with Barrie and all five men discussed the main topic of the day and impressed upon one another what they were looking for in the new manager.

During the morning the panel interviewed both Ted Meersbrook and Norman Collins before retiring for lunch.

'Well let's grab some lunch chaps before the third interview at 4 o'clock,' said Jack Elliott picking up his paper. Peggy provided a buffet lunch whilst they discussed the two candidates.

Just as Flannagan put a sandwich in his mouth he blurted, 'Fancy old Meersbrook applying for this job. His recent record does not hold water. Relegation with three clubs in the past five seasons. What's he trying to do – send us into the part-time league?'

'He doesn't look strong enough to take on a managerial post,' replied Boothroyd.

'Nice old fellow, but I think we can all agree that he's not what the club is looking for,' concluded Jack Elliott. All the panel nodded in agreement whilst tucking into the late buffet lunch.

'What did anyone think of Norman Collins,' enquired Boothroyd as he was waiting for Mr. Flannagan to finish with the salt.

'I think it's a move in general that he's after,' said Trippett. 'He was at Ranchley when I played there about eight years ago. As he said he's been with the club in the same position but under different management for the last fourteen years. I think he's just hoping to get his foot on the next rung of the ladder, but if Ranchley haven't recognised his ability then I don't think he's going to make the grade now.'

'Well put, my thoughts entirely,' said Flannagan.

'All I can say is that he is the better one of the two but he wouldn't get my vote for the job,' said Steve King.

After lunch had been cleared away the panel awaited Tony Davidson. Sid Parkin kept looking at the clock in reception hoping he wouldn't arrive. Flannagan quite outspokenly commented that he was surprised Jack Elliott had agreed to give this fellow Davidson an interview. 'The chap's only thirty-four years old, and no experience in the management game.' Boothroyd nodded in approval with everything Flannagan said; the others remained quiet.

On the stroke of 4 o'clock, however, a well dressed, young, blonde-haired fellow about 6'2' tall knocked on the reception door and introduced himself to Sid Parkin as Tony Davidson. Sid was taken aback. Tony Davidson was nothing like Sid had imagined him to be and suddenly felt quite humble. Sid immediately escorted him to the interview room and introduced him to the panel before returning to the main office.

'Sit down, Mr. Davidson,' said Jack Elliott. Davidson sat down in an upright manner and concentrated totally upon Jack Elliott. 'As you will appreciate Mr. Davidson we get a considerable amount of people from outside the game who request the opportunity of running Sharrington professional football club. Can you tell us why you applied?'

Davidson smiled and looked around the five members of the panel before saying confidently, 'Yes, sir. I applied for the manager's position of Sharrington F.C. because I am satisfied I could organise the whole operation of the club with the view of achieving a respected club with future success. I am aware my experience is limited but I have the capability of managing people and obtaining good results. My knowledge of the game is not so limited. I used to play for Sprannon Albion in the First Division ten years ago but had to leave the game owing to a break in my right thigh. As the injury was so serious and as I was 24 years old, I decided to leave the game and obtain alternative employment.' Davidson spoke so clearly that his voice seemed to have hypnotized the five members of the panel. There seemed to be a long silence after he had finished speaking. No one was aware that it was the Tony Davidson of ten years ago. Steve King quickly remembered him to be on the verge of an international cap prior to his injury. Flannagan was immediately impressed thinking only of how quickly he could let the press know who was the new Sharrington F.C. manager. Boothroyd was not aware of his past fame, but felt in awe of Davidson's presence. Barrie Trippett now remembered where he had seen him before and was already excited at the thought of working under his directions. Jack Elliott was aware that his colleagues had now realised that Davidson was no crank, just as he had done in the office the week before.

Questions were bombarded upon Davidson during the one-hour interview and all were dealt with proficiently. His answers were unhurried and his enthusiasm flooded out when he revealed his ideas for the club. After the interview had been closed and Davidson had left, the vote was taken. So impressed were the directors and the chairman that it was a unanimous decision in favour of offering the vacant manager's position to Tony Davidson with the proviso he gave total concentration to the club and sold up or took a sleeping partner capacity in the driving school.

Within four days Sharrington F.C. had a new manager who agreed to their proposals and terms.

Chapter 3

On the following Monday Tony Davidson arrived at the ground to commence his duties as the new Sharrington F.C. Manager. Ever since his appointment had been announced by the club the local press had hounded him for his reasons and comments on joining Sharrington. They had run several stories on his playing career and obtained several famous managers' viewpoints on his return to football in a managing capacity. Although quite a few people had forgotten what happened to Davidson after his serious injury everyone were complimentary of his ability from his playing days. The press were also quick to point out the new manager's lack of recent experience in the game and in addition they commented on the great risk the club were taking in appointing a star of some ten years ago.

Davidson would not be drawn by the press into any controversial topics but repeatedly told them that he was grateful to Sharrington F.C. for giving him an opportunity to prove that he could raise the standard of the club and give the supporters a long awaited share of success in the forthcoming seasons. He was sometimes deliberately evasive to the press questions but his standard quote would be: 'Don't label me a failure already, just give me one season to let the results show you and the supporters that I intend to take this club to a higher standard of football than it has ever been used to in its whole history.' He glowed with confidence and his charisma really made people believe that he was no "flash in the pan." On one occasion, only two days after his appointment he told a reporter of the *Globe* that people had better start ordering season tickets for the First Division now as by the time four or five seasons had elapsed there would be no room in the ground for any late comers! The press would really make him the 'laughing stock' if there were no signs of improvement in the early part of the season, but before that time they and the whole town were judging him on his confidence and his past record of a professional footballer. There was no doubt at all that he had intrigued the town of Sharrington and everyone waited eagerly for news of developments.

Jack Elliott was waiting to welcome Davidson to his office, along with Sid Parkin, Barrie Trippett, Flannagan and club captain Graham Bond. As Tony Davidson finally left the pestering press outside the ground, Jack Elliott introduced him to the waiting reception and, after a warm welcome all round, he directed Davidson to the manager's office.

'Well Tony, I know you'll be eager to start planning your early days at the club, but can I just remind you that I should like to be kept in touch with any policy decisions you have in mind. I know you're extra keen but remember we agreed that there were to be no sweeping changes without the directors O.K. Just before I let you get on with your job Tony, don't forget the weekly meeting with myself, the directors and Barrie every Tuesday evening. All the best Tony I have confidence in you lad but if you are unsure about anything don't hesitate to get in touch.'

'Thank you Mr. Elliott, I'll not forget and I promise I'll keep you up to date with any policy decisions I intend to make,' said Tony. 'By the way I've already prepared my plans for the first week and straight off I would like to meet the players and this afternoon I should like all the backroom staff to be in my office at, say, 3 o'clock. I will prepare a weekly plan of where I will be at all times for the first four weeks until the season starts and issue a copy to you, Sid and Peggy.' Tony produced a copy of a plan and handed it to Jack Elliott. As Jack read the details Tony said in his usual confident manner, 'Don't worry Mr. Elliott I'll not let you down.' Jack Elliott smiled reassuringly and invited Tony to the dressing rooms to meet the players. He pinned the manager's plan on the office notice board and led Tony through the ground, leaving Sid, Peggy and Flannagan to glean the manager's preparations for themselves. The list read as follows:

Mon	18.7.77	10.00	Meet players - inspect ground	3.00	Meet backroom staff (office)
Tue	19.7.77	10.00	Attend training session	2.00	Office for paperwork etc.
Wed	20.7.77	10.00	Attend training session	2.00	Extra training session
Thu	21.7.77	10.00	Visit practice ground with players	2.00	Players meeting (dressing room)
Fri	22.7.77	9.30	Attend training session		Office all afternoon
Sat	23.7.77		Meet and travel to - v - Beckham Town		- v - Beckham Town (friendly)
Sun	24.7.77		Players meeting		Office/prepare next week's chart

'If his management of the players is as good as his detailed preparations Mr. Flannagan, I think your decision of appointing him will not be a regrettable one,' said Peggy as she inspected the detailed plan on the notice board.

'I'll stick by this fellow Peggy. Just something about him. Confident chap. He won't go far wrong, the club neither. Liked the look of him soon as I set eyes on him. Give him time to settle down and there will be no looking back. We'll be fighting clubs off him by the end of the season, just you mark my words,' bellowed Flannagan as he was transfixed in studying the plan.

'I hope you're right,' muttered Sid. 'It would be sad for the club if he failed now. We'd be classed as a joke club who employed any Tom, Dick or…'

'Don't be so pessimistic, Sid,' thundered Flannagan, before Sid had finished speaking. 'What have we to lose? We've tried almost everyone else. A bit of new blood will do the club good. New ideas. Plenty of scope. Good results and plenty of confidence amongst the players. If we hadn't set this Davidson chap on, we'd have been left with either old Meersbrook or one pace Collins. What chances would we have had then eh? Relegation to non-league football that's what,' continued Flannagan.

'Aye, perhaps you're right,' said Sid, in a meek voice.

'Of course I'm right. I want to see some success at Sharrington before I resign my position and this is the fellow to do it.' Flannagan said no more to Sid. He just turned away and walked out of the building.

Sid was left wondering whether he should give Davidson a little more confidence as he felt as though he was the only one around who lacked any faith in him.

Chapter 4

Jack Elliott led Tony Davidson past the barren concrete terraces and the main stand towards the players' tunnel, which led to the dressing rooms. As the two stood looking around the ground, Eddy Connelly, the club's groundsman, was busy attending to the playing area in preparation for the new season. The pitch was well-grassed and looked in good condition. Eddy started to take a 'top cut' off the pitch with the old mower, which left not only grass cuttings on its way up and down the ground but also a trail of blue oily smoke. Eddy was unconcerned with the noisy, smelly mower and also the two onlookers, as he religiously manoeuvred the contraption to the best of his ability. The ground was covered on the stand side only, the other three sides, two of which were behind each goal and the other on the opposite side to the stand, were open to the elements. The stand was constructed mainly of solid oak, creosoted girders, which supported a flimsy corrugated roof. Jack informed Tony that the stand seated only 1,500 people and as far as he was aware it had not developed any leaks since its construction some 20 years ago. It was a compact little ground which required little, if any, attention due to there only being one structure as such. The terracing and standing areas only required sweeping and due to the low attendances over the years there was no evidence of wear and tear. When the ground was full it was said to have an attendance of 24,000. Jack said that on wet match days all the crowd congregated either in the stand or under it, which meant that only one side of the ground, was populated. He quickly joked that the Sharrington players hoped for rain on home games so as to get 'one up' on the opposition who were not used to playing to a crowd who gathered all down one touchline only, and nowhere else. This usually meant that if the ball went out of play on any of the empty sides of the ground, the players would have to jump over the small concrete partition to retrieve it. Apart from the stand needing a coat of paint, it was of an average standard for a lowly Fourth Division club, and, compared to some grounds in the same league it was like Wembley; although the most noticeable feature of the ground was the absence of floodlights.

At the top of the players' tunnel, which was under the centre of the stand side, three pokey brick buildings confronted Tony Davidson. Jack Elliot explained to him that the one on the left was the home team dressing room, the middle one was the laundry room and officials' changing room and the building to the right was for visiting sides.

Although Tony had been a spectator at the ground on many occasions he had never realised that the dressing room facilities were so bad. To make his impression worse there was an overflow of water coming from a hole, where presumably once there had been a spout, in the wall of the middle building. This was far worse than he had ever imagined. He knew his job was going to be difficult today but the condition of the home team dressing room, where he would meet his playing staff for the first time, did not give his confidence a stimulated boost.

Jack Elliott held open the outer door and as Tony walked into the grubby interior changing room all the players stopped talking and laughing and stared at the man they knew was to be their new manager. The quiet remained for a few seconds until Jack Elliott officially introduced Tony to the players.

'Well lads, I'd like to introduce you to your new manager, Tony Davidson.' There were a few hello's, hi's and nods from the group of players. Tony acknowledged the introduction and walked to the centre of the room and sat on the corner of the medical table. As soon as everyone was giving him their attention he started to address the players with confidence. 'Before I get to know each one of you personally I want to tell you of my ideas for Sharrington F.C. and what my policy towards you all will be from now and for as long as I remain manager of this club. As you'll all be aware I played for Sprannon Albion some ten years ago before I was forced to quit the game due to a serious injury. I felt cheated because of that injury which has left me keen for success. I know ten years is a long time to be outside the game of professional football but now I feel the time is right for me to take this managerial opportunity. Although I have not played for ten years I have been involved in coaching junior clubs and learning the development of the game at professional level. Now that Sharrington have given me the chance to prove myself, taking into consideration the risk they have made by employing me, I intend to live up to the predictions, which no doubt you will all have read about in the press, I've made on the future success of this club.

'I have seen you all play but that was from a spectator's point of view and I want everyone of you to impress upon me your own ability. On no account will I pre-judge any of you. I can assure you that the training will be hard both physically and skilfully and to put the cards on the table before we start, anyone who fails to meet the standard, which I set for training sessions, is no good to Sharrington.

'The club has been floundering far too long at the foot of the Fourth Division and let's face it lads if you can't make it with this club just what does the future hold for you. You are all on trial again but the players who show me that they are prepared to learn, work hard and first of all get Sharrington into the Third Division will get my total support on all matters.'

Every player gave Tony Davidson their concentration, but there were few smiling faces. His speech had hit them straight between the eyes. They had all read the press reports but thought that they were in for an easy time. Davidson had made it clear that a life of ease was the last thing they were going to get. He was out for respect from the start and they had all got the message without any doubt at all.

Davidson concluded his speech with: 'If we can work together and get good results I know you'll all get your appetite back for the club. Money is tight, as you know; therefore, I am relying on each of you to help the club towards success. If you don't pull your weight I will seek replacements who will. Finally lads it's Christian names for me, so the same applies for you and now you all know a little bit more about me let's get to know a bit about you. Now then, Graham, are you going to introduce me to my team or not? I've done too much talking for one day.'

Tony Davidson took a further hour walking around the dressing room with Graham Bond, the captain, speaking to all the players individually. His attitude was more light-hearted during these discussions, and after meeting everyone he told all of them to have the rest of the day off but report back to the ground at 9 o'clock the next morning ready for their first training session.

The manager had made the start he had hoped for.

Chapter 5

On the same afternoon, Tony Davidson introduced himself to the backroom staff, which consisted of Sid Parkin, Peggy Hollingsworth, Eddy Connelly and Mrs. Bryant. The meeting was held in a very relaxed atmosphere and Tony discussed many aspects of the club with them, both from the past and also his predictions for the future. Mrs. Bryant and Eddy were particularly impressed that they had been asked to the meeting. They had both been with the club for twenty years in the capacity of washerwoman and groundsman respectively and, as far as they were aware, it was the first time they had been formally introduced to the club manager.

At the end of the meeting, Tony returned to the dressing room to meet Barrie Trippett to discuss the training routines.

'Ah! Here you are, Barrie. I would like to go over these training routines with you.'

Both men sat down on the bench, which was attached to one of the dressing room walls, and studied the details. 'First of all, Barrie, I want to build up the players' stamina. Plenty of long distance running, heart strengthening exercises, and weight training. Once we have killed them off with that after two or three weeks I would like to introduce plenty of variety, both in exercises and skills. But all the time, Barrie, I want hard work and I want you to be firm with each of them, as from the first session tomorrow. I know that won't be easy after playing with the lads for the last two seasons but I'm pleased that you were appointed trainer and I'm going to be joining in from the start. I think this will help us all but don't forget, Barrie, you will be doing all the organising of training. I will only give you guidelines to start with but you will be responsible for the weekly work/training sessions.'

As the two men talked in detail about all aspects of training the telephone in the officials' room rang out until Tony answered it.

'Tony Davidson here.'

'Oh hello, Mr. Davidson, I'm sorry to trouble you on your first day at the club but I would like to have a word with you regarding the transfer of your centre forward, Greg Hanby. My name is Alan Tomlinson, manager of Ravenhead Athletic, the Second Division club. Our club have watched this lad for the latter part of the last season and as Sharrington F.C. were without a manager it was difficult for me to approach their club chairman. Whilst I can appreciate your apprehension at our request particularly when you have been given little opportunity to get to know your staff I thought I would contact you to let you know Ravenhead are prepared to make an offer of £15,000 for Hanby should you wish to consider the deal and if you would contact.'

'Excuse me Mr. Tomlinson, if you don't mind, I am in an important meeting at the moment and whilst I was not anticipating dealings on the transfer market so soon I can assure you that no player will be leaving Sharrington F.C. in the immediate future. I will need the opportunity to see what staff I have but your interest will be recorded, and no doubt if your club feel sure that Hanby is the player they require would you put your requirements in the form of a letter.'

'Certainly Mr. Davidson, you'll be hearing from us and by the way the best of luck, Goodbye.'

'Goodbye Tomlinson,' said Tony as he slowly replaced the telephone receiver. Tony paused for a moment and then continued: 'That was Tomlinson, from Ravenhead Athletic. Tells me he wants young Hanby for £15,000. What a scoop that would be for him, wouldn't it? I think he was trying to catch a raw recruit in office who'd agree to a bit of cash to ease the financial situation.'

'£15,000 for Hanby! He must be joking! That lad's got the skill they need all right but he could be worth a fortune to this club in a couple of seasons. He's only 24 years old now,' remarked Barrie with astonishment.

'Not just a fortune to the club, Barrie, but he could be an integral part of the team. If Hanby adds a bit more work rate to his skill then as far as I'm concerned he's not for sale, even to the league champions Passondale. I remember this lad from the games Sharrington played last season. If I remember rightly didn't he come from the local club Low Grove on a free transfer at the beginning of last season?'

'Yes, he did, and after a slow start he eventually came good towards the end of the season. I used to see the scouts from other clubs discussing him, as I watched our games from the stand. In fact I know Ashton from the First Division approached Pete Gosling about him but Pete was a shrewd judge of young players and told them to come back when they could clear Sharrington's £50,000 overdraft. They wouldn't pay that much for him and he knew it. I hope he will be your type of player, Tony. I know the lad's keen to learn but he does soon lose interest if he is up against a hard tackling team.'

'We will see what happens, Barrie. Getting the players to respond is the next hurdle I will have to get over. I felt the introduction went O.K. but now I want to see the lads working hard and willing to take the club up the league,' said Tony reflectively.

'I'm sure the lads will be behind you, Tony. Most of them want success and will be prepared to work for you, but if I can give you a little bit of advice, there are two players who may give you a lot of trouble both directly and indirectly and although I'm not going to influence you by revealing their names, once you realise who they are, and you will in time, you must get rid of them at all costs.' Barrie seemed extremely serious as he spoke to Tony about this.

'Don't worry, Barrie; I'll spot the trouble-makers. They'll not come between me and the players who are prepared to give everything for this club. I know we can do it, Barrie, and we will work well together. I'm sure our ideas for the club will be compatible.'

He confirmed to Barrie that he'd arranged with Jack Elliott for a plumber to fix the incessant overflow and for Steve King to arrange for some of his own men to repaint the dressing rooms before the season started. 'Good idea,' said Barrie. 'At least all the visiting sides will be impressed with the surroundings as they're recovering from defeat.'

'I just hope you are right about the last part, Barrie,' commented Tony.

Chapter 6

The club only had 14 professional players now that Barrie Trippett had had to retire from the game, due to his injury. Some players had only played for one other club before joining Sharrington F.C, but the majority of players had "worn more colours than Lester Piggott" during their playing careers.

Tony Davidson knew that he was expecting too much to gain success with his current squad of players but the problem did not unduly bother him as he had groomed a number of young amateur players to a high standard whilst he had coached locally. If his existing players failed in their approach to the game he was convinced he could introduce some of these young players to the club without too much difficulty.

All the players arrived at the ground by 9 o'clock on the following day and were quickly changed and eager for their first training session with their new boss. Tony and Barrie entered the dressing room and greeted the players with the announcement that training for the morning would involve three laps of the pitch, road running for three miles, a further lap of the pitch, which was to be followed by weight training and exercises, underneath the stand.

The players had been warned, but they didn't think it would involve so much long distance running. Tony led the players around the first lap with Barrie Trippett bringing up the rear. Both Tony and Barrie were shouting encouragement to the players but after three laps had been completed it was apparent to Tony that the players were not used to this type of training. As the players walked from the finishing position on the third lap to the main roadway outside the ground, Tony heard the first rumblings of dissatisfaction from a few of the players. He quickly split these players up before leading them again on the road running stage of the morning's training session. After a mile of hard constant running and jogging, the distance from first man, which was now Steve Fisher the midfield player, to last man, Dick Henderson the centre-half, was approximately 200 yards. By the time the last players arrived back at the ground the first batch of players; Fisher, Sanders, Docker, Bird and Bond were completing their running in the training programme. Tony Davidson was running with the tail enders: Henderson, Poole, Smith, Hanby and French, and all the time he was giving encouragement and telling them to concentrate on their running and less on their talking.

Finally, when everyone had finished, Tony instructed them to go and have a hot bath but to stay at the ground for extra training in the afternoon. The players were tired and disgruntled about the extra training session but did not complain directly to Tony. As the players all soaked in the communal bath a few comments were heard by Barrie Trippett as he attended to Alan Hawkin's injured calf muscle.

'That's it then is it: six miles every day. Tell you this lads if we don't make it as pro footballers we could join the British marathon team,' said Tommy French sarcastically.

'Give the fellow a chance, Tommy. He told us it would be hard work and when you think about it where did we get before with all the soft training sessions we used to do with Pete and Paddy,' said young Simon Docker, bravely.

'At least we got to kick a ball. Isn't that what it's all about,' interrupted French.

'As I said, Tom, give him a chance. It's only his first week,' replied Docker quickly.

'Yeah, I agree,' muttered Basil Sanders, breathlessly. 'He's really got you lads all keyed up, ain't he. Lambs to the slaughter you'll be, once he sees you are doing everything he says. I've come across this type of chap before. He'll burn you all up within a couple of weeks and you'll be running around on match days like a man after a mirage,' said Henderson butting in with his usual pessimistic comments. 'It's about time you hung your boots up, Dick, if that's all you feel about a challenge. You've really seen the last of any hope for this club, and if I was the new manager I'd be tempted to give you a free transfer to… well any club with a sense of humour,' said the joker of the club, Alan Smith

'You've some need to talk you're funnier with a ball than me,' quipped Henderson.

'Maybe so, but I heard Davidson asking old Barrie to get a bath chair for Henderson tomorrow or else he will skive his last lap due to it being too dark,' joked Smith. Although the players were physically tired they laughed along with Smith when they saw Henderson give up the argument and climb out of the bath in disgust.

During the afternoon the players completed three more laps of the pitch, lifted weights and carried out an assortment of general physical exercises for an hour. After another long hot bath the first day's training session was behind them. Feelings were mixed but the general attitude to the training was encouraging for Tony, but particularly for Barrie Trippett who felt he had gained respect from the majority of players. All the players left the ground looking tired. Barrie did not tell Tony what the minority of players had discussed as he hoped their attitudes would change for the better. He knew he couldn't interfere too much with

Tony's management of the club and realised that in time he would find out the players concerned for himself.

Chapter 7

The rest of the week's training continued but after three more exhaustive sessions Tony informed his team on Friday lunchtime to report to the ground at 6.00 p.m. for a hot bath and massage. He also told them that his arrangements for the friendly match against Beckham Town would be announced.

At 8.00 p.m. whilst the players were all relaxing in the dressing room Tony said: 'I want to thank you lads for the effort you have given me this week and although we have not spent much time with a ball in training. My main intention is to get you all fully fit before the season gets underway. As you know there is a friendly match at Beckham Town tomorrow. At this stage I am not too concerned with results but performances. You have all played together before and I expect total concentration, a 100% work rate and a performance of a team rather than of individuals. I don't want to see players showing off, nor do I want to see them criticising their fellow teammates. This is your first opportunity to show me why I should select you as a regular Sharrington player. Every player will get an opportunity to play in the game tomorrow but the team to start the match will be...' Tony paused and carefully unfolded a sheet of paper which he was holding and read out:

In goal	Alan Hawkins	
Right back	Graham	Bond
	(Captain)	
Left back	Allan Smith	
Right half	Steve Fisher	
Centre-half	Collin Bird	
Left half	Tommy French	
Outside right	Basil Sanders	
Inside right	Graham Poole	
Centre forward	Greg Hanby	
Inside left	Simon Docker	
Outside left	Sammy Chaddock	

Substitutes will be:

In goal	Tony Braddock
Centre-half	Dick Henderson
Centre forward	John Turner

'Yes, lads,' Tony continued. 'I know the positions are old-fashioned but I am insistent that our defence will not be square at any time and that

Sharrington will play with two wingers. The style of play is changing and, in my opinion, it is the most practical and complete system for all round football. Yes, it's back to 2, 3, 5 and whilst I don't expect you to play the roles efficiently I will give you some guidance as to how I expect you to perform them tomorrow.'

Tony continued his talk by illustrating his demands on the blackboard and after a further two hours of tactics, encouragement, and questions and answers, the players were told to go home, get a good night's sleep and report to the ground tomorrow at 11.30 a.m. for the journey by coach to their near neighbours and much improved Third Division club, Beckham Town.

Without any surprise to Tony or Barrie, Grant Evans, the local newspaper reporter of Sharrington F.C. had emblazoned the weekly Saturday edition of the *Sharrington Echo* with headlines of:

'NEW MANAGER REVERTS TO THE OLDEN DAYS TO SEEK SUCCESS.'

The article was told quite truthfully, although in places it was obviously sceptical of Tony Davidson's methods and it made the game against Beckham Town to be either the downfall or success of Sharrington's new, but inexperienced, manager.

The article created an even greater interest in the loyal supporters' conversation and it was expected that, as the friendly match was only eight miles from Sharrington, it would attract a large following.

Saturday arrived. All the players were punctual and smartly dressed. The manager and trainer were confident. A final team talk was arranged before the players boarded the coach at 12.00 – the kit was packed in the skip. The Sharrington's first choice colours were red shirts, black shorts and red socks. The boots, balls, first-aid equipment and other items were loaded onto the bus. The day was bright, warm and humid, and as the coach drove away Tony Davidson realised that although he had tried to emphasise that he was treating this game as an opportunity to understand his players' footballing ability he also realised that the result of this game would mean so much to the directors, the supporters, the reporters and Sharrington F.C, as a club who had taken a gamble and employed an inexperienced manager.

Chapter 8

The pre-match excitement was snowballing to more like a cup match rather than a friendly. The team were ushered through the visiting supporters outside the players' entrance and towards the dressing room. Only four days prior to this game Beckham Town had played against First Division opposition at Rondale and, according to local reports, played extremely well and were unlucky not to win after Rondale had equalised in the last minute to make the score 2-2. The home crowd were keen to see their team's first home game, and particularly as it was against neighbours Sharrington.

As 3.00 p.m. approached and the players were changed, Tony Davidson called for his team's attention. 'Right lads, don't expect miracles today. Just remember, play as a team and give encouragement to each other. Listen to Graham for instructions. Play it hard, no arguing with the referee and on no account must any player let his head drop if things don't go right. Now get out there and let's start this Sharrington season with something to build from.'

The players wished each other luck and walked out of the dressing room and down the players' tunnel.

Tony, Barrie and Jack Elliott followed the team down the tunnel and were surprised at the crowd which had turned up for the game. Jack estimated there to be at least 10,000 in the ground. As they walked along the touchline towards the trainers' dugout, Tony felt as though he was walking along a gangplank. The reactions from the crowd were, in the main, critical, but Tony knew, or at that moment in time hoped, his team would play with enthusiasm and prove themselves to the crowd.

Beckham's ground was larger than Sharrington's and held about 30,000. The stand was almost full and the majority of supporters showed blue and white for the home team. Beckham had finished fourth in the league last season and missed promotion by three points. Their manager Sid Blake had predicted his team would get promotion this season by attacking football. Tony Davidson thought words are always just words and it depends upon the type of psychology used in expressing them as to whether the listener is affected or not. But from the kick-off Beckham took the game to Sharrington and, to say the least, showed their superiority in every department. Sharrington players looked sluggish compared to the sprightly Beckham forwards, but the red shirts stuck at the task of defending and, although they had conceded five corners in the first twenty minutes, the score line remained at 0-0. Sharrington had rarely ventured into attack but the crowd were too interested in the state of the game to consider it a foregone conclusion.

On the half hour Beckham took the lead with an excellently worked goal. The move involved five players and after a one-two on the edge of the goalmouth, centre-forward Alan Reynolds hit a hard low left footed volley passed Sharrington's goalkeeper, Alan Hawkins. The crowd were delighted. Even the small hardcore of Sharrington supporters applauded the well-taken goal. Tony Davidson commented to Barrie Trippett that the goal was well worked, but almost immediately he substituted Collin Bird for Dick Henderson.

'Now then Dick this is where your experience will help us. I want you to mark Reynolds out of the game.' Henderson didn't need telling again, in fact he seemed eager to impress his new boss. Barrie thought Tony would see that Henderson was a "troublemaker" in the club, but he could only wait to see what impact, if any, Henderson made on the team.

Beckham continued to flow forward. They hit the post, crossbar, and Steve Fisher had cleared the ball off the line. Just before half-time Beckham's inside left, Cross, did a sole run of 40 yards only to be robbed of the ball on the penalty spot by a great save from Alan Hawkins. At half-time, with Sharrington skilfully outplayed, Beckham led 1-0.

During half-time Tony Davidson told his team that they should try and get the ball out to either Basil Sanders or Sammy Chaddock on the wings and for Hanby or Docker to be watching for a cross. He congratulated the defence, told them the goal was a beauty but to continue to fight for possession and where possible to counter attack. He attempted to ease the tension by saying he would settle for a draw but he stopped mid-sentence as he could see how tired his players were due to the excessive training sessions. He felt a little sorry for them, as he knew they were trying to help him but it was patently obvious half the team were not up to the standard he required. All he could do was encourage, and encourage he did. He substituted goalkeeper, Alan Hawkins, for Tony Braddock and told Hanby to be ready to come off for John Turner after fifteen minutes of the second half. As the players trooped out for the second half Tony Davidson joined the directors in the stand.

The second half began and, albeit in much the same vein as the first half, Tony Davidson could admire his team for the way they challenged for possession of every ball, tried to play as a team and to his instructions. In the 75th minute, David Peacock, the Beckham's team inside right, scored with a well timed header from a right wing corner and eight minutes later as the Sharrington players fought gamely but ineffectively,

Reynolds scored a simple goal after a defensive mix up in the Sharrington defence. Bravely the visitors played to the final whistle but what Tony Davidson had secretly feared came true, a decisive defeat of 3-0, and although their approach to the game had been spirited he realised that he would have to find new players if he was to achieve his pre-season predictions for Sharrington F.C.

Chapter 9

On the following Tuesday after the friendly game at Beckham Town, the weekly meeting was held in the Sharrington boardroom and comprised of Jack Elliott, Flannagan, Boothroyd, King, Trippett and Davidson. Peggy Hollingsworth was on hand to record the minutes.

As Jack Elliott was the chairman he wasted no time in opening the meeting, as it was clear that all those present wanted to air their views without any further delay. The previous minutes were taken as read and Jack Elliott quickly raised the topic of the game at Beckham.

Eddie Flannagan came straight to the point by asking Tony Davidson for his comments as manager. Tony was half expecting being put on the spot, particularly as the local and national reports had been far from complimentary with the Sharrington performance. The national newspaper, the *Daily Globe* were downright critical of the Sharrington directors for employing an ex-player who hadn't contributed to professional football for over ten years and then allowing him to revert to old-fashioned playing styles.

Tony Davidson coolly rose to his feet after hearing Flannagan's request and in the same vein as he had talked to them at his interview he was clear and precise in his speech.

'Mr. Chairman, gentlemen, my immediate feelings both during the match and after the final whistle was that the Sharrington players had given their utmost to impress both myself and the club. Taking into consideration the extra, hard training the players endured last week and the obvious lack of regular match practice I commend the way in which our players played against Beckham Town.'

The other members of the committee meeting were nodding in agreement; although, one or two looked as though they were about to add some reservations, when to their complete surprise Tony Davidson continued with his speech in a more direct and powerful manner.

'After saying that, gentlemen, it will not do for me at all. It is perfectly plain that Sharrington F.C. needs at least six new players before this club start to win, never mind have success. I do not feel that this is a hasty statement after being at the club for only one week. The club is in dire straights and has no time to delay in transferring the following players…'

Flannagan and Boothroyd were sat with their mouths wide open as Tony Davidson continued: '…Tony Braddock, Collin Bird, Tommy French, Dick Henderson, Basil Sanders and John Turner; and, before you interrupt me, gentlemen, I received a written offer today from Ravenhead Athletics for young Greg Hanby. They were prepared to buy him at their price of £15,000 and I would seriously recommend we, as a club, agree to his transfer, but I would add that I feel I could increase their offer to £25,000 or £30,000.

Just as the manager was about to continue Flannagan slapped his fists onto the table and sprang to his feet exclaiming: 'Hold on a minute, hold on! One minute you are congratulating your playing staff for their effort last Saturday and the next you are recommending half the playing staff should be disposed of, and, to cap it all, you say our "star" forward of last season should go to Ravenhead. I can't allow such drastic changes. I know the players are not as skilful as some, but we have to at least meet our fixture list and, as the start of the season is only three weeks away, how do you propose we do that with only half a team left?'

'With respect, Mr. Flannagan,' answered Tony, 'if you hadn't interrupted me I was leading onto my proposals to cover my earlier comments. On no account, gentlemen, do I wish to override your decision but I now feel that unless the club follows my line of action the town of Sharrington will have another mediocre season in Division Four. I want success for me, the club and the supporters, and I don't do things rashly. After Saturday's game at Beckham, I saw that no matter how much effort the team gave me during the season, things would work out no better than normal for the club. There are only three weeks left to the start of the season and I want to channel my efforts into players who can give success to this club. Boothroyd interrupted this time with a plain and almost sardonic question to Davidson: 'How do you propose to get the players to give the club success when we have no money to buy them?'

'Once again Mr. Boothroyd I have planned the possibilities to this problem,' Davidson quickly replied. 'If I can get to the point – as you know, I ran a junior football team prior to joining Sharrington F.C. and I give you my word that I could easily get six replacement players of eighteen years of age to join this club on, firstly, a part-time basis until they prove to you that they are worthy of signing professionally; and, secondly, that they are, in my opinion already much better footballers now and likely to be in the future than the six players I mentioned to you a short time ago.'

Tony Davidson was now pouring out his feelings to the committee in such a forceful manner.

'And to conclude; with regard to the transfer of Greg Hanby, whilst I can see your concern for this player, I consider I can buy a replacement centre-forward for £10,000 and a player who would give valuable experience to the young players and also one who could do a valuable job for this club. The extra £20,000 I may get from Hanby's sale could, of course, go towards clearing two-fifths of that overdraft.'

Tony Davidson thanked them for listening patiently and asked them, with the interests of the club at heart and not forgetting their reasons for employing him, to seriously think about his plans and give him their overall acceptance.

Jack Elliott stood up and said: 'Well Tony I respect your outspokenness but must ask you to leave the room whilst we discuss your view points.' The manager smiled and nodded to the committee and left the room. Barrie Trippett followed Tony out of the room, as he was also not allowed a vote on the matter.

Steven King stood up as soon as both men had left and said: 'I want to start by saying no man who intends to be successful is ever popular and as I have enormous faith in his managerial qualities I suggest we all give him our full confidence to carry out the preparations he has just informed us of. I know the man has Sharrington at heart and you can see he is fully aware of our predicament and doesn't want to waste any time in delaying the club on the road to success. He gets my vote. What do you think Eddie?'

'I'll tell you what I think,' said Flannagan, sternly, 'for the first time in my life at this club I've seen a man stand up and tell us a numerous amount of things he knew we wouldn't like. He's got guts, I'll say that for him. I know he has the club's interest at heart and all in all we've taken a huge gamble by employing him from the start. I personally cannot see how a team half full of teenagers can get us out of this division, but I'll tell you all this, if we don't give him our support we will never get this club out of Division Four. As you say, Steven, he's certainly not going to be popular and the press and supporters are going to make all our lives a misery if he gets his way but we employed him, I believe in him, he seems to have planned carefully and he will get my vote also,' shouted Flannagan.

'What do you say my old shadow, Boothroyd?' continued Flannagan with an air of humour in his voice.

Boothroyd seemed startled and unsure. 'Well, well.' He paused. 'I was surprised with his attitude and the way he seems to want changes so quickly but whilst I am not going to enjoy the public outcry which will result from his plans, and as my vote is of no real importance now, I will, albeit apprehensively, give him his desired wish and make the vote 3-0.

'Wonderful, gentlemen, I am so pleased,' said Jack Elliott. 'I think you have all made such an important decision. We can only have faith in him now. The changes are revolutionary as far as this club is concerned, but whilst I accept that it won't be popular in the town, particularly if Hanby's transfer goes through, it will also show that some action is being taken to try and lift us out of this league. Peggy, call Tony and Barrie back in and let's give them the good news. We can then get cracking on what methods he has in mind to put these changes into practice and what we are supposed to do for a team for our friendly, tomorrow, at Anstar Heath.'

Chapter 10

Tony Davidson had first of all, after the meeting, approached the six replacement players and offered them all part time professional contracts, all of which had been eagerly accepted. He had signed the following players within two hours of leaving the meeting:

Alan Bates	(goalkeeper)
Stephen Holland	(centre-half)
Mike Thomas	(wing half)
Graham Hart	(outside right)
Tony White	(wing half)
and Paul Cracknell	(inside right)

Each player had played for Tony Davidson's junior team and all were eighteen years old. They all had regular jobs but each player was anxious to make a career of football.

On the Wednesday morning the six players who Tony Davidson had suggested were to be put on the transfer list were told individually before the news was announced to the press. Although the manager had not relished this job, only French and Henderson criticised his decision and told him they would only be too pleased to leave. Tony Davidson realised these two players and Turner would be difficult to transfer owing to their reputation and age; however, he told them he would make enquiries for them all. He realised that unless all the six players were transferred quickly it would be difficult to start a new club atmosphere.

As expected, by Wednesday lunchtime, the manager's proposed changes shocked the town of Sharrington. In some respects the feared outcry at the possible sale of Greg Hanby was cushioned when Hanby was quoted as saying, 'I am pleased Ravenhead have shown an interest in me and if their offer is acceptable I will look forward to playing in the Second Division with them.'

As Sharrington had previously arranged a friendly against Anstar Heath, a local junior team, during Wednesday afternoon the situation at the club was chaotic. The six replacement players were unable to play; therefore, Tony Davidson picked the following team:

Alan Hawkins
Graham Bond

Allan Smith
Steve Fisher
Dick Henderson
Tommy French
Basil Sanders
Graham Poole
Greg Hanby
Simon Docker
Sammy Chaddock

and stressed to his squad that although the recent changes had made life a little difficult for the club he expected a good all round performance from every player. He said, 'Anstar Heath will be fighting to beat us, particularly in view of the recent publicity we have been getting but I feel the training we have done as professionals should help us to win the game.'

As the players left the dressing room Barrie Trippett told Tony that although he felt the timing of the announcement for changes was a bad one with regard to this game he realised it had to be done before the season started.

Owing to the Wednesday afternoon kick-off there were not many supporters standing around the touchlines. The ones that were, grumbled loudly about Davidson's managerial capabilities as he walked to the centre of the ground to a small corrugated tin hut which was used for the visiting teams.

However, unlike the previous friendly game at Beckham, Sharrington this time were attacking constantly, looking sharper than their opponents and playing the much better football of the two teams. The local junior team were finding it difficult to match the professional team and two minutes before half-time Simon Docker scored for Sharrington after good work by Poole, Chaddock and Hanby. At half-time Sharrington led 1-0.

In the second half Anstar Heath scored an equaliser straight from the kick-off, and, from then until ten minutes before time, the game went from end to end. However, with only ten minutes remaining of the match, Hanby, who was obviously trying to impress his future club's officials, scored with a powerful header from ten yards. Sharrington then pressed home this advantage and Graham Poole rounded off a four-man move to make the final score 3-1 in Sharrington's favour.

At the end of the game most of the players seemed happy with their performance and Tony Davidson suggested a final training session on

Thursday afternoon, leaving the players a rest day on Friday before their home friendly game against Swansbeck United of the Second Division on Saturday.

Sharrington had won their first game under Tony Davidson but although they were to rest on Friday he knew he would have to spend the day working to sort the club out by planning the immediate future.

Chapter 11

The following day, after the victory at Anstar Heath, was Tony's busiest at the club since his arrival. As the players had not used the facilities since Tuesday afternoon, the dressing room decorations had begun. Steve King's men had worked a 24-hour rota between them since Tuesday evening so the work could be completed and dry, before the game on Saturday. The work was progressing extremely well and the red, white and black colour scheme certainly gave the dressing rooms the much needed uplift both inside and outside.

Tony was too busy to inspect the painting as Thursday morning had been spent in his office, mainly speaking on the telephone. He never realised such a lowly considered club from the Fourth Division could attract so much press. Whilst accepting that his changes within the club were drastic he did not anticipate that so many people from outside of Sharrington would show an interest in the club's affairs.

The morning started with an enquiry from Verrington's manager, Albert Fisher, about the sale of either Basil Sanders or Tony Braddock owing to the fact that they had been recently transfer listed.

'Now look squire,' said the old and canny Albert Fisher. 'I need a decent winger and first team goalkeeper for my squad this season. Our club's not too far from Sharrington, therefore the lads won't have to move houses if they come here. I realise you'll want them off your hands pretty quick owing to the recent revolutions in Sharrington, so I'll give you £5,000 for the pair of 'em. What do you say young man?'

'I'd say it was a bargain if you rephrased your offer to £5,000 for each of them and that one or both accepted the terms, Mr. Fisher,' replied Tony who felt that possibly Verrington's offer was about right but after all they expected him to be a bit green, so why shouldn't he stick out for a little above the odds.

'Now then, son; that puts me in a spot, you see,' replied Fisher, quite slowly and deliberately. 'Like your club, our bank account's the same colour as your shirts and I have to be careful. But I certainly need another goalkeeper so…' after a brief pause, '…I'll agree on £5,000 for Braddock and I'll give you £2,500 for Sanders.

'It's a deal Mr. Fisher,' stormed Tony before the offer was retracted. 'I don't think the players will object. I'll get them to call over to see you this afternoon.'

Tony arranged for both players to be taken to Verrington by Jack

Elliott in the afternoon.

Immediately after the deal of Sanders and Braddock was concluded, Tony telephoned the manager of Ringstone United of the Second Division to enquire into the possibilities of signing Alf Henning, their club centre-forward. Jack Farnsworth, Ringstone's new manager, was an old colleague of Tony's and both men had discussed the transfer of Henning at an earlier time, but strictly off the record.

'It may be a bit tricky, Tony, to agree to the transfer of Henning at this stage, simply due to the fact that we haven't a fit replacement centre-forward,' answered Jack Farnsworth.

'I appreciate your difficulties, Jack, but this player is vital to my plans this season and I need him as quickly as possible. Can I leave it with you for now, Jack, and if you get your Board's O.K. to the deal let me know straight away, please,' said Tony, quite businesslike.

'I'm not promising anything, Tony, and I feel that if the board and player agrees to the move they will want more like £15,000.'

'Look, Jack, I've got to go now but remind your board that Alf's not likely to get a first team game once McStewart's fit again; however, I'll go up to £12,000. See what you can do. See you.' Tony hung up the receiver and simultaneously called in Sid and Peggy to make the final arrangements for Saturday's friendly home game against Swansbeck.

In the afternoon the last of the week's training sessions was completed much to the satisfaction of Tony and Barrie. The players who were retained, were showing a great deal of enthusiasm to the hard training sessions and as the six teenagers had joined the professionals for the first time the atmosphere was a noticeably good one. Even the players who had been transfer listed, with the exception of Braddock and Sanders, were making the most of the new training methods.

At about 4.00 p.m. Tony returned to the office with Barrie to pick the team for Saturday and complete the unanswered paperwork. Once again the phone calls flooded in.

'Davidson,' answered Tony, as he lifted the receiver.

'It's Jack Elliott here, Tony. I've been trying to get you earlier. Just to let you know Sanders and Braddock have agreed to join Verrington and what's more old Albert Fisher's given me a cheque and told me to cash it on the way back whilst the bank manager still looks in favour upon them.'

'That's good news, Jack – I think things are starting to go better than I'd expected,' replied Tony.

As soon as Tony had rung off he telephoned the Evercroft club to confirm the friendly away game for the Saturday, prior to the league getting underway.

Finally Tony and Barrie selected the team to play Swansbeck United, realising that they would be on a hiding to nothing if they played the six youngsters against the team that only last season had been relegated from Division One.

'I'm sorry to have to do this, Barrie, but I wish to play three of the six youngsters on Saturday,' said Tony quite sternly. 'I hope you agree because I want to start the team playing together as soon as possible.' They both discussed the team and finally agreed upon:

      1. Alan Hawkins
      2. Graham Bond (Captain)
      3. Allan Smith
      4. Steve Fisher
      5. Stephen Holland
      6. Mike Thomas
      7. Graham Hart
      8. Graham Poole
      9. Greg Hanby
      10. Simon Docker
      11. Sammy Chaddock
Substitutes:
      Tony White
      Paul Cracknell
      John Turner
      Collin Bird

'It will be a hard game for all of them but I think they will gain from it,' said Barrie, knowing just how difficult an experienced First Division team can be to play against.

'I agree, but hopefully the lads will come out of the game as a more collective unit,' said Tony quite convincingly. Both men finished off the extra paperwork and finally went home at 7.00 p.m.

During the evening, whilst Tony and his wife, Penny, were entertaining his ex-business colleagues from the Driving School he received a telephone call from Jack Farnsworth.

'Tony,' he shouted. 'It's a deal. The board and player have agreed to the transfer. I'm sending Alf Henning to discuss the terms with you tomorrow. The board insist on £15,000 though, Tony.'

'That's great news Jack. Thanks for everything. He's just the player I need and we'll pay £15,000 for him,' chirped Tony, enthusiastically.

Chapter 12

At 10.00 a.m. sharp Alf Henning arrived at Sharrington F.C. and was ushered into the manager's office by Sid Parkin.

'Come in Alf and sit down,' said Tony, as he walked towards the door to greet him. As both men sat down Tony said, 'Alf, I've been a long admirer of your ability to play centre-forward. I've seen you play for Hambridge, Steeple Bay and Ringstone, and more importantly, I once remember playing against you in a cup match over ten years ago. Without any doubt I have a tremendous task to achieve at Sharrington but with the plans I have in mind, I know the club can be successful. Point One – I have sorted the wheat from the chaff. Point Two – I have introduced six young lads with great ability to join the club on a part time basis. Point Three – I have the backing of the board and chairman and Point 4 – you are the key to giving the team valuable experience during the games and turning our chances into important goals as I know you can still do.' Tony continued without interruption: 'I know you will find it hard to get a game at Ringstone, and if you give this club the effort, determination and goals you have given the clubs in the past I will pay you, on approval with the board £65 per week plus £20 win bonus or £10 home draw, and £15 away draw, plus the usual appearance money of £5 per game. Alf, this is the standard bonuses but the weekly wage is the same as the club captain's rate. I think you will know now how important you are to Sharrington. How do you feel about it?' asked Tony.

Alf Henning didn't answer immediately. He was a 6'4' giant of a man, 33 years of age with a broad but athletic physique. His face was honest and there were signs of a few scars and bruises around his eyes and temples. Eventually he spoke quite calmly. 'I'll lay the cards on the table, Mr. Davidson. I haven't more than three seasons left in football. I'm flattered by your interest and feel that I would like to play for Sharrington under your management but – and I must stress "but" – I must ask for a signing on fee of 10% of the transfer and a regular wage of £75 per week, plus bonuses regardless of first team football or not. I have to match my old club's salary at least, and as I an unlikely to obtain an immediate job in football after my career has ended I need to earn as much as I can now.' Alf Henning stopped speaking and awaited Davidson's reply.

'I appreciate your needs, Alf, and whilst I cannot see Ringstone objecting to 10%, and not 5% of the transfer fee, it may be difficult for me to agree to £75, regardless. I know you are an honest man, Alf, and would not use the club unnecessarily for financial rewards but my board might. As I said before they give me their backing but by upping the standard rate to £75 from £65 they may object. However, leave it with me for the time being,' said Tony.

The two men discussed the possibility of the transfer for a while. Finally Tony promised to give him the club's answer on the following Wednesday, after discussing the transfer with Ringstone and his Board. The two men shook hands and Alf Henning left the office.

Tony was a little despondent at the thought of losing the centre-forward he considered was the only man to score the goals Sharrington would so badly need. In order to try and get the board to see his way he telephoned Alan Tomlinson, the manger of Ravenhead Athletic, to discuss the transfer fee of Greg Hanby.

'Mr. Tomlinson, this is Tony Davidson, manager of Sharrington, here.'

'Ah good, have you agreed our offer of £15,000 for young Hanby?' replied Tomlinson.

'Well not exactly, but I can inform you that we are prepared to negotiate a figure for the transfer.' said Tony optimistically.

'Mmm, what sort of figure have you in mind Davidson?' answered Tomlinson carefully.

'To be honest with you Tomlinson we need a player as gifted as Hanby but, and I'm sure you will appreciate, we also need the money too. He's a good young player and will do well in a higher division and although he is keen to join your club I cannot agree to your offer of £15,000. The board and I feel it is quite low but if you are still interested in signing him and, bearing in mind similar transfers of young hopefuls, we were looking for something in the region of ,' Tony paused trying to sense his listeners interest or mood ' £35,000.'

Tomlinson had the answer seemingly prepared, 'You can keep him. He's not worth that much to us and I'm surprised you have the nerve to try and clear your overdraft with him,' he retorted in quite an offhand manner.

'I'm sorry you have taken that attitude Tomlinson,' spouted Tony hoping to hang on to the only possible solution of him signing Henning. 'You know the value of young players are rising daily and the club only want their fair share of the cake.'

There was a brief pause after Tony had finished speaking then Tomlinson said 'Look he can do a job for us   not a £35,000 job at this stage but go back to your board and tell them we will give you £20,000 now and £5,000 in settlement as soon as he scores 30 goals for us.'

Tony was unsettled by this sly negotiating of Tomlinson's and in an effort to resolve it all said 'If he scores 30 goals for you in two seasons you know you are on to a winner. I can't wait for Hanby to score 30 goals for you for an extra £5,000 but if you give the £25,000 now I'll agree to that.'

Once again Tomlinson was ready with an answer 'I think my proposals are fairer but to save the messing around I'll give you £25,000. Quite amicable, don't you think Davidson?'

'Yes,' said Tony quite amicably 'I'll send Hanby over tomorrow to discuss the terms with you.'

About 10.30 a.m. in my office will be agreeable to me,' mumbled Tomlinson.

'I'll see that he's there,' said Tony as he replaced the receiver. He was only too glad that the wheelings and dealings were over for one day. He knew Tomlinson was an old hand at negotiations and that he had signed Hanby for lower than the going rate however, he thought that perhaps one day he would be able to sign young talented players on his terms only. He would just have to put it down to experience.

The following day Greg Hanby signed for Ravenhead Athletic of the Second Division for £25,000 and played and scored a goal in their 2-0 friendly against Rodd Bay F.C. from the Third Division.

Chapter 13

As Flannagan, Boothroyd, King, Elliott, Parkin and Davidson took their seats in the Directors' box in the Sharrington stand they could see the above average crowd gathering around the ground.

'Well, if we beat this lot today the papers will change their tune,' gruffed Flannagan as he lifted his trilby to scratch his bald head.

'Don't expect too much Mr. Flannagan,' said Jack Elliott butting in. 'We have a young and inexperienced team , but hopefully a side which shows more skill and determination.'

'Yes, it all begins today, gentlemen. At least in an hour and a half we will have seen the beginnings of change at this club for many a long time,' replied Steven King as he was reading through the programme.

'Look at the crowd building up,' said Boothroyd like a young excited schoolboy.

'Yes, the press has done us a favour at last,' said Flannagan.

Just as he finished speaking the Sharrington team ran out onto the pitch below to a loud and authentic cheer from the spectators. Tony Davidson remained quiet and hoped the young players would not lose their nerve and that all of them would remember his instructions to play hard, for each other and attack down the wings. His hopes were soon to be found out as the team from Swansbeck ran out onto the pitch. They were a big side compared to Sharrington and, as they had played in the First Division last season, three or four of the players were known to most footballing people. They had John Simmonds in goal, Andy Carr, Brian Fox and John Bellamy in attack. These four were particularly good players and the footballing world was expecting their transfer to other clubs in a short time owing to their new Second Division status. Swansbeck's captain won the toss and chose to kick towards the office end.

As John Turner, the replacement centre-forward for Greg Hanby kicked off, Swansbeck's new manager, Eddy Phillips, shouted over to the Sharrington Director's box, 'Anyone take a bet on 6-0 to Swansbeck – £1 a goal, eh.' There were no takers only a few smiles from tense faces.

From the start Sharrington looked uneasy as the Swansbeck team challenged hard and often unfairly for possession. They were depending upon putting the young Sharrington team off their game by fierce tackling. Surprisingly the Swansbeck team seemed content to rely upon a defensive approach to this friendly game. The young Sharrington team attempted to play attacking football but were frustrated too often by the

Swansbeck defence. At half-time the score remained 0-0.

As Eddy Phillips walked towards the dressing room at half-time, Flannagan was so distressed with Phillips' team tactics that he stood up, shook a fist in his face and shouted, 'Good grief man, get a grip on that team of yours. It's only a friendly you know. Save the aggression for Division Two. Your team are spoiling the game.' Flannagan brushed passed Phillips and disappeared to the tearoom. No more was said.

In the dressing room Tony Davidson complimented his team and told them to keep their concentration. He agreed that Swansbeck were treating the game more like an end of season relegation battle but asked them to try and slip behind their defence and get the ball in the penalty area as much as possible. Before the teams went out for the second half Mike Thomas complained of an ankle injury and was replaced with Collin Bird, the transfer-listed central defender.

The home team were urged on by the good crowd as they came out for the second half. Tony thought that at least the majority of the crowd were reasonably satisfied with the players' effort during the first half and he hoped the team could get the result to build their own confidence and also bring back the supporters.

In the second half Swansbeck's first half tactics appeared to have paid off. Sharrington were reluctant to keep possession of the ball. They could not get the ball into the penalty area and it was noticeable that the visitors were taking control of the game. Although Sharrington's young centre-half Stephen Holland was winning a great deal of high balls which were pumped forward into the defence, the experienced attackers of Carr, Fox and Bellamy were making more chances.

However, and quite unexpectedly, when Swansbeck were attacking feverishly one of their moves broke down and captain Graham Bond played the ball to young Graham Hart, who found himself for the first time in the game without an aggressive marker. He soon showed why Tony Davidson wanted to sign him as a professional. He moved straight and quickly down the right hand wing with the ball at no more than a yard in front of him. The break was on and there was a three against two situation: Hart, Turner and a supporting Chaddock against two Swansbeck defenders. Hart released the ball to the unmarked Chaddock perfectly, as soon as he was challenged by the centre-half. Without any delay Chaddock drove the ball with his left foot into the bottom right hand corner of the Swansbeck goal, leaving goalkeeper Simmonds stranded. Sharrington were 1-0 in front with nine minutes to go. The players, directors, supporters and even Tony Davidson jumped up and down in excitement. It was as though Chaddock had scored the winning goal in the Cup Final. The goal spurred Sharrington to combat the experience of Swansbeck and gave as much as they were given. With only three minutes to go, a three-man raid from the half way line by the visitors' attack caused many problems in the home defence. The ball went in and out of the penalty area but finally Allan Smith was adjudged by the referee to have tackled Brian Fox unfairly inside the six-yard area. The referee gave a penalty and although the home crowd jeered John Bellamy, as he ran up to take the kick, he managed to send goalkeeper Alan Hawkins the wrong way and the ball flashed into the opposite corner of the net.

The score ended 1-1 but the crowd's response to the players at the end of the game gave the players, Tony Davidson and the directors hope for the future. After the Sharrington players had bathed and dressed Tony Davidson congratulated their efforts enthusiastically. There were two or three injuries, a few stiff bodies and aching limbs but Tony Davidson knew that after witnessing his team's performance his ambitions for the club had finally got underway.

Chapter 14

On Sunday morning Tony Davidson arrived at the ground at 10.00 a.m. and started by reading the reports in the national newspapers. Although the game was a friendly it had attracted five or six reports. The general comment on the game was that Swansbeck had tried to spoil the friendly affair by their rough tackling and also that the Sharrington team had responded well to the challenge.

Tony Davidson was well pleased with his team's performance. Although he accepted the newspapers' comments he didn't need them to tell him how his team had performed. He knew he would have to get his team together more often and hoped he could start the ball rolling by getting the directors to agree to the signing of Holland, Hart and Thomas as full time professionals without any further delay. He mulled over the forthcoming week's training programme but couldn't get the thought out of his mind of trying to find some clubs who would take Turner, Henderson, French and Bird off the club's hands. Tony thought that this action was crucial to the club before any ill-feeling set in and in addition to this if he could transfer these four elsewhere the directors would not be so cautious in signing the three young lads and, of course, Henning.

Tony realised that the four players may have to be given free transfers but he knew the directors would expect him to bring some money in from the sales. As he was planning his next course of action, chairman Jack Elliott and trainer Barrie Trippett entered his office.

'Morning, Tony,' said both men simultaneously.

'I didn't get chance to congratulate you on the team's performance yesterday Tony,' said Jack Elliott. 'It was a good start for the club at home and I thought we were unlucky not to win too.'

'Yes, I was pleased with the way we stuck at the task and particularly with the youngsters,' added Tony.

'Yes, I agree entirely, I don't think they will be long before becoming professional players with this club,' stated a happy-looking Jack Elliott.

'I hope for the same, but I'm having a bit of a problem finding a home for our four misfits and unless someone comes forward to take them off our hands then I'm in lumber, or at least, the club getting off to a good start might be,' said Tony ruefully.

'Well, I think I have something of interest for you Tony,' said Jack Elliott. 'I was speaking to a colleague of mine from days gone by, who is now doing a bit of scouting for Warworth United, one of the newly promoted teams to our league. Anyway,' continued Jack, 'I know their manager, Bill Swift, wants an experienced centre-forward but, understandably he doesn't want to pay much, owing to their obvious financial difficulties, at this stage.'

'Turner would fit the bill, eh, Tony?' asked Barrie Trippett.

'He certainly would, Barrie, but without a replacement centre-forward I cannot afford to let him go just yet,' said Tony. Tony told both men of his plans to sign Alf Henning and also the player's demands. They all agreed to let the matter rest until the Tuesday meeting with their directors. Before they each carried on with their respective duties, they discussed the goal Greg Hanby had scored for his new club Ravenhead and that, according to reports, it was a well-timed overhead kick in the first five minutes of the game. Jack hoped that the directors wouldn't be too upset, but Tony reflected that he had no regrets at the transfer to Ravenhead, but felt they had signed him for much less than his worth owing to their bargaining power.

Chapter 15

Tuesday evening came around without any further transfer news. The town of Sharrington was buzzing with excitement. So much had happened in the first two weeks of Tony Davidson's reign at the helm of this unfashionable Fourth Division club. Not only was his appointment a sensation but the activities on the transfer market and his introduction of the six new youngsters in addition to the team's noticeable improvement had not only shocked but surprised everyone connected with the club.

The meeting commenced with all present in a light-hearted mood. Jack Elliott summarised the happenings over the last week and then introduced Tony Davidson to comment on the latest position on the transfer market. Tony rose to his feet with a serious expression on his face. He spoke clearly and slowly to his audience.

'My first experience with the transfer market, gentlemen, is that it is a cut-throat business and Sharrington are far from in a commanding bargaining position. Hanby went for possibly £10,000 less than his true value on the market, but I had no negotiating power. The reason behind this was due basically to my own limited knowledge on the transfer market and secondly Sharrington's obvious need for money.' Davidson continued in the same manner. 'In the meantime thanks to wheelings and dealings by our chairman we have also received £7,500 from the transfer of Sanders and Braddock to Verrington. Our total incomings are £32,500, a loss of three regular first team players, no financial outgoings at this stage, and the introduction of six part time professionals.'

Tony looked around his attentive committee as he mused. 'So far so good and after Saturday's performance against Swansbeck the club is looking much healthier. But gentlemen,' stressed Tony, 'I desperately need the signature of Alf Henning, the Ringstone United second team centre-forward. He will be an important player for my plans, the assistance of the other players and this club's future. I know, and value, the experience this player has had over the years and, for your information, I have spoken to this player and must now come to the crunch of this evening's meeting.'

Tony continued a little more sternly as he explained the detail behind the meeting with Alf Henning. After he had finished his speech Tony asked the committee to consider the importance of Henning's possible contribution to the early success of this club before finally deciding on whether to accept Henning's demands.

As the club spirit was high and there was no immediate challenge by the directors to Henning's demands Jack Elliott asked Tony to stay in the meeting. Surprisingly each director in turn gave Tony Davidson the support he had anticipated, on the condition that this exceptional wage demand did not cause a rift within the club. Steve King suggested that the club's captain, Graham Bond, ought to have his wage increased to £75.00 plus bonuses to bring the new signing's wage into perspective. The other directors agreed and the somewhat unusually relaxed Eddie Flannagan simply condoned everything with his blessing.

Jack Elliot was also amazed with the directors' final decision. He felt that they were confidently behind the wishes of Tony Davidson and that, as they had initially agreed to employ him, they would fall in line with any policy he attempted to adopt. He was pleased, not only for the club, but, for the first time in his 15 years service with Sharrington F.C, he felt that success would come to the club if Tony Davidson could be left to organise and control the whole affair. He was confident they had decided correctly and without any delay excused Tony from the meeting to confirm the transfer of Alf Henning from Ringstone United to Sharrington at £15,000 plus 10% of the fee and £75 per week plus normal bonuses.

Tony left the meeting only to return after twenty minutes to inform the directors that the deal had gone through successfully and that Henning would travel to Sharrington tomorrow to sign on the agreed terms. He also confirmed that Jack Farnsworth, the Ringstone manager, had permission from his directors to pay Henning 10% of the transfer fee.

Tony Davidson knew that the directors' decisions during the evening's meeting were so relevant for the success of the club. It had been a worthwhile meeting.

Chapter 16

On the Friday after the crucial directors' meeting Tony Davidson introduced Alf Henning to the other players and organised the training session. The training was strenuous even though Sharrington were playing a friendly on the following day at Evercroft, a Third Division club. The session commenced with two circuits of the pitch, followed by a number of sprints under the stand side of the ground. After this, Tony coached the team on a few tactical matters, which included some new moves from throw-ins, corner kicks and free kicks.

After an hour and a half the players were told to report to Barrie Trippett in the training area underneath the main stand to complete the final exercises of the day.

Once the morning session was over the players were asked to stay in the dressing room for a team talk. The players bathed, showered and changed. Tony entered the dressing room and waited for all the players to assemble before beginning what he had to say.

'Right lads, I know that over the last three weeks things at the club have been difficult for you,' commenced Tony, 'but whilst your efforts on the playing and training side have been better than I had first expected, as you all know the season starts a week tomorrow at Mannish and it's important we get off to a good start. That's why I've been pushing you in training. We must get a high level of fitness. It's important we have the staying power. Once we can maintain our fitness the playing side will develop. The team work, team spirit and confidence will grow as the season progresses.'

The players were sitting, relaxed, giving their complete attention as Tony continued. 'I assure you lads that once training stops feeling like hard work or that you are not learning or mastering anything new, your game, on a Saturday or whenever, will falter. After saying that I don't mean that training will not be enjoyable, but I think you will find that that will only come once you feel as though you are earning your money and not fooling yourselves, Barrie, or me.'

Tony sensed that two or three of the players wished to raise questions but before throwing the meeting open to a general discussion he advised all present that three part-timers, Hart, Holland and Thomas were signing professionally on the following Monday.

Graham Poole, the midfield player, asked if the signing of the three young players and Alf Henning meant that some of the existing

Sharrington players could expect to be transferred. Tony said he had no intention of transferring any more players, other than the four players still on the transfer list. Graham Bond, the club captain and full-back, asked Tony if each player would be picked on merit. Tony assured all the playing staff that if they proved their worth in the team then, even if they did have one or two poor matches they would not automatically be dropped. Tony informed then that he was certainly looking for a settled team but as there would obviously be injuries, a run of poor form and a lack of confidence at times a strong squad was his main priority.

Allan Smith delicately asked Tony if the club stayed in the top three positions in the league could they be guaranteed a bonus of some sort. Tony smiled, knowing Allan Smith to be a somewhat cheeky chap and said whilst he thought it was a nerve of Smithy to raise such a question he could see the point of offering incentives but concluded that he would reserve judgment but keep it in mind.

Before the meeting finished Tony announced the team to play at Evercroft in the friendly tomorrow. It was:

1. Alan Hawkins
2. Graham Bond (Captain)
3. Allan Smith
4. Steve Fisher
5. Stephen Holland
6. Mike Thomas
7. Graham Hart
8. Graham Poole
9. Alf Henning
10. Simon Docker
11. Sammy Chaddock

Substitutes:

Alan Bates
Tommy French
Tony White
Paul Cracknell

At that point both Collin Bird and Dick Henderson got up and stormed out of the dressing room. Nothing was said and there was an embarrassing silence until Tony finally asked the players to be at the ground for 9.30 tomorrow morning ready to travel to Evercroft. He then asked John Turner to stay behind for a few moments.

'John,' said Tony trying not to dwell upon the embarrassing exit of the other two transfer-listed players. 'I've had an offer from Warworth United of £5,000 for you.'

'Oh really,' commented Turner as though he had lost hope of ever being transferred to another league club. He didn't say anything more at that stage. He just stared into mid-air, seemingly reflecting the possibilities of a move some 75 miles away.

Tony judged the situation and slowly advised Turner that he was guaranteed 5% of the fee (£250) plus an identical wage to that of Sharrington's standard rate and bonuses. 'Do you want to go home and think it over, John. I understand there would be no problems on housing…'

Before Tony finished Turner asked inquisitively, 'Is that the only offer you've had for me?'

'Yes, so far,' replied Tony.

Without any further delay Turner said, 'I think I will accept the move. In fact I think I would prefer to start the season with a new club and perhaps I can help Warworth more than most clubs. If you can arrange for me and my wife to visit the club this weekend I promise I'll let you have my decision by Sunday evening.'

Tony was pleased with Turner's attitude and confidently wished him well. Turner left after Tony had contacted Jack Elliott to arrange for him to transport Turner and his wife to Warworth that weekend.

Tony and Barrie locked up the dressing rooms and offices as they discussed their anxieties over the problem of the two disgruntled players, Henderson and Bird. There was no immediate solution to the problem. No other club had enquired about either player, not to mention making Sharrington an offer of any sort. Barrie was concerned with the situation and informed Tony that the two players were constantly failing to meet his requirements during training and Henderson's timekeeping was getting worse. He was worried that if these two players were with the club much longer then it could affect the team spirit and confidence. Tony refrained from committing himself on a solution. Both men wished each other goodnight and drove to their respective homes with the major problem of dealing with Henderson and Bird uppermost on their minds.

Chapter 17

The team were expected at Evercroft at 2.00 p.m. and as the journey had progressed Tony Davidson had spoken to each player in turn to discuss general matters and tactics. As the coach arrived all the team were discussing methods of playing and raising viewpoints on particular aspects. The atmosphere was good and Tony could feel the blend of experienced players and youth beginning to take shape. The weather was poor, the rain had been falling constantly since departing from Sharrington and only a handful of supporters had bothered to make the trip for this pre-season friendly game.

The crowd was reasonable for Evercroft, approximately 7,000. Evercroft had been in the Third Division for the past ten seasons but had never been higher than fifth or lower than twelfth. They were an average Third Division side who had been managed by Tom Wilson for fourteen seasons. Tom had taken them from the Fourth Division, after the side had undergone a whole season without being beaten in the league. They were champions and the directors had given Tom Wilson a guarantee of a contract for as long as he felt he was achieving progress with the club. Whilst the club had maintained the average performances since promotion they had failed regularly towards the end of every season in defeating the teams above them in the league, and, although the directors stuck to their word, there was a group of supporters fighting to depose Wilson from the manager's seat. The club remained homely, but to pacify the action group Wilson had spent £75,000 during the close season on three new players. £35,000 on Ralph Bennett (centre-forward) from First Division Stanton Villa, £25,000 on Peter Jagan (centre-half) from Second Division Miltern Rovers and £15,000 on Paul Gardiner (midfield player) from Second Division Woodville. In the three other pre-season friendlies Evercroft had played the results were as follows:

Lost 0-1 (away) to First Division F.A. Cup holders Cotterton.
Lost 2-3 (away) to Second Division Billing Bridge.
Won 5-0 (home) to Fourth Division Aldway.

The scene was set for an important final pre-season game for both clubs. From the beginning Sharrington pressed forward down the wings and the ability of Alf Henning at winning the ball in the air on crosses was immediately noticeable. His skill with his feet was equally impressive as for the first twenty-five minutes he gave the home centre-half Peter Jagan, the run around. Ironically it was Evercroft who went into the lead.

Following a poor clearance by young centre-half Stephen Holland, Brian Turnbridge, the home team's veteran winger, attacked the visitors' goal before lobbing the ball over the advancing Alan Hawkins, into the net.

Whilst the Sharrington defence were making efforts to regain their confidence Turnbridge struck again. He advanced down the right wing beating young Steve Fisher and Allan Smith, then crossed the ball perfectly into the path of new signing Ralph Bennett, who thundered the ball into the roof of the net before the recovering defenders could make a challenge. Evercroft were 2-0 in the lead at half-time.

Tony Davidson was furious with his defence at half-time. This was the first time the players had seen him lose his self control. He was angry with Holland, Smith, Hawkins and particularly captain Bond, who had failed to steady the defence after giving away the first goal. He told them that they had thrown two or three good chances away before Evercroft scored. He was appalled at the work rate of the wing halves and inside forwards and clearly stressed his disappointment at the whole first half display. As the bell rang to call the players onto the field for the second half, Tony urged his players to be much more determined and positive in their tackles and distribution of the ball.

To conclude he told them he was far from satisfied by their first half performance and demanded more effort in the second half. The players were shell-shocked. They had seen the other side of their manager. He was not going to be a pushover and they realised that he wouldn't settle for a second rate performance. Alf Henning was urging his colleagues to give that bit more effort straight from the kick-off. Barrie Trippett was also lending words of encouragement as the players took the field.

Although the Sharrington players were extremely tired from the week's hard training the words of their manager had given them new-found strength to compete all through the second half. They pressed forward directly in attacks, challenged hard in every tackle, ran for each other and for the first time began to shout for possession of the ball. Tony Davidson smiled to himself. His team were tired from training, he knew that. He also knew they weren't used to playing together but had really played quite well during the first half. Now he saw the players much improved performance in the second half he realised his own managerial qualities were taking effect.

Steve Fisher scored a goal ten minutes from time but try as they may the more experienced Evercroft held out to win the game 2-1.

At the end of the game Tony congratulated each of his players in turn before leaving to join the directors in the Evercroft clubhouse.

There was no doubt that the Sharrington directors were pleased with the team's performance and the home club's officials commented quite refreshingly on Sharrington's endeavour and attacking qualities. Eddie Flannagan told Tony how pleased he was with the team's performance and expressed his delight in his usual alarming manner, with Alf Henning.

'Tony,' he shouted, 'that's a real good find for Sharrington. Credit where it's due, he's a very talented and experienced player. I like the look of him. He can do us nothing but good. Don't you agree Boothroyd?' asked Flannagan stuffing a pork pie into his already overfilled mouth.

'Yes, he can do nothing but good,' repeated Boothroyd.

Steven King was equally as enthusiastic as Eddie Flannagan. 'Great player, that Henning. I'm only pleased we gave you our full assurance for his transfer. He fitted in well and if he gets a bit more service as the season goes on he will score a lot of goals for us.'

At that stage, the steward of Evercroft was heard to be paging Tony Davidson to answer a telephone call. Tony took the call.

'Hello, Tony. It's Jack Elliott here. I thought I might catch you there. First things first, how have we gone on?'

'Lost 2-1, I'm afraid Mr. Elliott, but a good all-round performance and some definite signs of improvement from most of the lads,' replied Tony, only wishing he could report better news.

'Ah bad luck! But I'm pleased to hear we're on the right tracks. How did Alf Henning play?' enquired Jack Elliott.

'Oh, very well. He's still a very good player and will be an asset to the younger players around him and to this club,' enthused Tony.

'Tony, my second reason for calling is to inform you that John Turner has accepted Warworth's terms today and to complete the happy ending his wife just loved the place. He told me to tell you he would complete the transfer tomorrow, if it's all right with you.'

'Yes, that's fine with me and I'm pleased he's happy with the move,' said Tony. 'Can you tell him I'll meet him at the ground tomorrow at 10.30 a.m.'

'Yes, I'll do that Tony,' replied Jack Elliott. 'Have a safe journey back and I'll see you tomorrow about 11.00 a.m. Bye for now, Tony.'

'Bye, Mr. Elliott,' said Tony replacing the receiver.

The journey home was broken with a visit to a pub-cum-restaurant for an evening meal and a relaxing drink. The players were tired but pleased with the impromptu stop. The coach finally arrived in Sharrington at 11.30 p.m.

Chapter 18

On the following Monday, the week of the start of the season was upon the club. The town, newspapers, club officials, staff and players were eagerly awaiting the first game of the season at Mannish on Saturday. Tony Davidson had drawn up his weekly programme of events and posted it on the communal notice board outside the secretary's office. It read:

	A.M.	P.M.
8.8.77	Training	Team talk
9.8.77	Training (5 a side)	Afternoon off
10.8.77	Morning off	Practice game on pitch (weather permitting)
11.8.77	Training (cross country)	Training (skills)
12.8.77	Light training and team talk	Afternoon off
13.8.77	Travel to Mannish (10.00 a.m.)	- v - Mannish - 3.00 p.m.

There was also a notice attached to the bottom of the programme which stated "Henderson and Bird to report to manager's office after training on 8.8.77 at 12.15 p.m."

At the stipulated hour Collin Bird knocked on the manager's door.

'Come in,' shouted Tony. Collin Bird walked into his office and sat in a chair which was directly opposite to Tony Davidson's.

'You wanted to see me, I understand,' said Bird whilst chewing heavily on a piece of gum.

'Yes Collin, I did, but first of all where's Dick Henderson?'

'Oh, he's not turned in this morning,' reported Bird.

'Why?'

'Apparently his wife says he's got a bad cold or something,' said Bird without looking at Tony.

'Likely story, I bet; anyhow, I'll deal with that later,' said Tony somewhat off-hand.

'To get to the point, Collin, I am far from satisfied with your attitude in the training sessions, not to mention that embarrassing walk-out last Friday. I will accept that I've put you in a difficult position by placing you on the transfer list. However, I want you to apply a more sensible and adult approach to the other players and to the training periods.' Tony knew Bird wished to interrupt him but he continued in the same manner, 'and I've heard reports you've been trying to "stir up" the morale of the club. Well, I won't have it and insist it stops immediately.'

Bird finally spoke. 'To be honest Mr. Davidson I haven't enjoyed training or playing to your ideas. We are definitely not suited and whilst I'm sorry if certain people think I've been "upsetting the apple-cart" I must honestly say I can't wait to get away from this club,' stressed Bird most emphatically.

'I don't think any more needs to be said, Collin,' replied Tony, quite calmly. 'I will let you know as soon as an offer has been made for you, but in the meantime just make a go of it, eh?'

Bird stood up and with a persecuted expression shook his head slowly from side to side and walked out of the manager's office.

As soon as Collin Bird had left, Barrie Trippett came rushing into the manager's office. 'Tony,' he shouted, 'come quick, there's some trouble in the dressing rooms.'

'What's wrong?' enquired Tony looking bemused.

'It's Dick Henderson – he's finally turned up and is ranting and raving with the players,' said Barrie, quite breathlessly.

Both men rushed to the home team's dressing room, to find Henderson and young Sammy Chaddock lying on the floor in some pain. Graham Bond was attending to Steve Holland who was apparently cut above his left eye. Tony tried to sort out the confusion immediately by asking Graham Bond for his comments on what had happened. As he did so, Barrie Trippett attended to Sammy Chaddock who was clasping his stomach in agony. All the players were asked to stay, by Tony.

'Well Tony,' said Graham. 'It was all started by Henderson here,' as he pointed to him on the floor. 'He came in after we had finished training and started calling us one thing and another, then he had a go at the youngsters. It got a bit heated and he started to pick on Steve Holland. Steve tried not to take offence but Dick just went mad. He shouted at Steve and, as Steve pushed him away, Dick swung a punch at him and caught him on his left eye. At that stage, bedlam broke out and Sammy jumped on Dick to try and calm him down but Dick kneed him in the stomach. Then Alf moved over to Dick pushed him against the wall and threw him to the floor where he banged his head against the form. He's been out cold since,' concluded Graham Bond.

Tony knew he would have problems but he'd never imagined anything like this. It was like a schoolboys' scrap and he daren't think about the consequences. It quickly passed through his mind how he had woken that morning only thinking of the start of the season and before half the day was over he'd had a brief argument with Collin Bird and received a report of an outbreak of fighting amongst several of his players, not to say anything of witnessing the aftermath. He was mystified as to what his next course of action should be. The time between Graham Bond speaking and Tony breaking the silence seemed an eternity.

'Well lads, I'm honestly dumbfounded,' said Tony finally. 'What an unbelievable start to the season. Barrie, call an ambulance immediately for Henderson and ask the club doctor to look at Holland and Chaddock and report to me. The rest of you finish changing and go home, but not a word of this to anyone. Report for training tomorrow morning at the usual time. I will deal with the rest. By the way, I'd better see you Graham, Alf and Barrie in my office before you go.' Tony still couldn't believe the bedlam of the dressing room and he wondered how serious Henderson's injuries were, whether to call the directors immediately or what he could say once the news got out to the press, which he was certain it would, given a matter of time.

After the ambulance had taken Henderson to hospital and Dr. Ericson had promised to call to examine Holland and Chaddock as soon as possible, Tony returned to his office with Graham Bond and Alf Henning. Barrie Trippett had accompanied Henderson to hospital and been told to report on developments. He had also been told to say Henderson had fallen in the changing room and become unconscious after banging his head, which was technically correct but slightly incorrect in detail.

Whilst Tony was waiting for the medical reports he decided to call an emergency board meeting that afternoon, in view of the seriousness of the situation. He personally made all the telephone calls without stating anything other than an emergency meeting was warranted. The meeting was planned for 3.30 p.m. At 2.45 p.m. Barrie Trippett phoned Tony to say Henderson had recovered consciousness and was as well as could be expected. The hospital officials had insisted in keeping Henderson overnight. Tony Davidson phoned Mrs. Henderson to explain briefly what had happened. He knew from her reaction that she had expected some sort of trouble by the way her husband had stormed out of the house. She didn't appear vindictive towards the club. She was quietly spoken and didn't make a fuss of the sensational news. She said she would visit her husband and calmly replaced the receiver. Tony felt some sort of relief by her reassuring attitude but knew there would be other hurdles to overcome before the matter was allowed to rest.

The board meeting was on time. The whole incident was explained, with independent witnesses allowed to comment, and after three hours discussion it was agreed to:

(a) Sack Henderson for his unruly conduct.

(b) Make no approach to the press until forced to do so – the statement would be made by the club chairman.

(c) Take no action against Holland, Chaddock or Henning.

The meeting adjourned with all present feeling unhappy at the unpleasant incident. Tony Davidson didn't sleep that night and visited Henderson at the hospital at 8.00 a.m. the following morning, but found that the troublemaker had discharged himself earlier. He then called at Henderson's home to carry out his official duty. Henderson refused to speak to Tony but his wife said she knew her husband was all right now and apologised on his behalf. Mrs. Henderson also accepted the club's letter, which set out in detail the reasons for curtailing his services. Tony left wishing the Hendersons well and promised to be of service if they thought necessary. The last twenty-four hours had not been easy and he still feared that Henderson would cause trouble through the media.

Chapter 19

When Tony Davidson arrived at his office he was met at his office door by Jack Elliott, Barrie Trippett and Sid Parkin. He was informed that Dr. Ericson had given an all clear to the two injured players following the previous day's fracas. Apparently Sammy Chaddock had only been winded and was now O.K. and the cut above Steve Holland's left eye was not as serious as first thought and required two stitches. The doctor's report had concluded that whilst Sammy Chaddock would be fit for next Saturday, Steven Holland should be kept out of the team for two weeks at least until the cut had healed satisfactorily.

Tony Davidson scratched his head and, looking somewhat tired and bewildered, said, 'Poor old Steve. Can you imagine? He has waited many years to become a full time professional and on the day he signs, a crazy old pro beats him over the head and keeps him out of the team for two weeks. I just cannot understand why Henderson should have acted that way.'

'Rumour has it that he's been drinking quite a bit recently,' interrupted Sid Parkin.

'Yes, I'd heard that too,' said Barrie Trippett.

'Be that as it may, I feel his actions were irresponsible and seemingly pre-conceived,' uttered Jack Elliott.

'I agree with you, Mr. Elliott, and I only hope he will consider that, before reporting the reason for his dismissal to the press,' said Tony.

'By the way, before I forget, would you phone Mr. Bryant, the manager of Crookaby the newly promoted club to Division Four, please, Tony,' said Sid Parkin. 'He didn't say why he wanted you, only that he would prefer you to phone him before lunchtime today.'

'Yes, O.K, will do, thanks, Sid,' answered Tony as though his mind was on something else.

'I'll put the players through their paces if that's all right with you Tony,' enquired Barrie Trippett.

'Yes, that's fine. In fact I'll join you in an hour or so to take my mind off this latest problem. Before you go, Barrie: if the players ask about the outcome of yesterday's commotion give them the truth. I'll see you soon,' said Tony as he finally sat down in his chair. Barrie Trippett left the office, Sid Parkin and Jack Elliott also took their leave of Tony as he made a telephone call to Crookaby.

'Crookaby Town Football Club, good morning,' said a light voice.

'Oh, good morning. Mr. Bryant please… this is Davidson of

Sharrington F.C,' replied Tony.

'Just one moment please, Mr. Davidson. I'll get him for you,' came the light voice.

After a few moments a rather hurried voice spoke in a deep tone: 'Bryant here, good morning, Davidson, thanks for phoning.' Tony acknowledged, as the voice briefly paused. 'I'll come straight to the point, Davidson. We are both new to this game of league soccer management and I was hoping you would help me out first.' Tony wondered what was to be demanded from him, as the voice continued.

'I've got my centre-half, Maxwell, down with a broken bone in his foot and he's likely to be out for a couple of months; therefore, as I know you have Collin Bird on the transfer list, I was hoping you'd agree to his transfer…' Bryant paused again briefly before completing his speech, '… free.'

Tony knew that Bryant was a newcomer to the league and for one moment he reflected on the negotiations he'd had with Tomlinson of Ravenhead and whilst he didn't share the bargaining power of the Second Division team manager he felt tempted to push a four-figure fee on Bird in this deal.

'Oh, that's caught me a bit by surprise, Mr. Bryant,' said Tony slowly. Bryant did not reply.

Tony continued after a few moments thought. 'Actually, Bird is only twenty-seven years of age, and, although he doesn't fit into my immediate plans, I would think he would give a club similar to Crookaby a good few years' service.' Bryant still did not commit himself.

There was another brief pause before Tony asked, 'Can your club agree to… say… £1,000 now, plus £1,000 after Bird has played 20 games for Crookaby, on the assumption he agrees to the terms?'

There was another pause.

Finally Bryant spoke, again rather hurriedly. 'That's rather more than I value the player, actually, Davidson. In fact I was rather hoping you would agree to a free transfer. I saw him at the end of last season and again in your friendly against Beckham and I assure you he will only be a stepping-stone for us until Maxwell is fit again. I don't want to spend anything on the transfer if I can avoid it, Davidson,' commented Bryant.

Tony knew deep down that he had to transfer Bird to save any further ill-feeling in the club and felt once again that he was over a barrel in negotiations.

'I accept your needs, Bryant, but I'm sure you will appreciate mine,' said Tony trying one last ditched attempt to salvage something from the deal. 'Tell me, would you agree to £500 down now, and £500 after Bird has played ten first team games for Crookaby?'

This time there was no pause Bryant quickly snapped back: 'O.K. Davidson, as we're both in at the deep end with this negotiation lark, if Bird agrees to our terms, I will pay you £500 now and another £500 after his tenth league match.'

'Done,' said Tony feeling part of the load from his shoulders lifting already. 'I'll send him over to your ground tomorrow, Bryant, for a 12.00 appointment.

'That's fine Davidson, I'll let you know the outcome. Best of luck for the season,' said Bryant.

'You too Bryant, and thanks for your offer,' replied Tony, looking much more pleased with life.

Chapter 20

By Friday evening there had been an anxious but constructive board meeting, the players had trained hard, there was no report in the press about the Dick Henderson situation and the most pleasing news to Tony was that Collin Bird had agreed terms with Crookaby and signed for them in time to play in their home league match against Harloft on Saturday. Tony was only thankful that Sharrington did not meet Crookaby until later in the season when Bird would almost likely be on the sidelines.

The morning training session and "talk-in" had gone well and after serious consultation with Barrie Trippett during the week it was agreed to abide by Dr. Ericson's decision of Steven Holland and play Tommy French in his place. The team for the first away league game was announced as:

        1. Alan Hawkins
        2. Graham Bond (Captain)
        3. Allan Smith
        4. Steve Fisher
        5. Tommy French
        6. Mike Thomas
        7. Graham Hart
        8. Graham Poole
        9. Alf Henning
        10. Simon Docker
        11. Sammy Chaddock
        Substitute: Tony White
        Travelling reserves: Alan Bates and Paul Cracknell

As Tony was sitting in his office reflecting on the week he decided to look at the team and knew that, with the exception of Steven Holland, this was his full squad. Twelve full-time professionals and three part-timers. It was not a strong squad but one which was showing signs of blending well in training sessions. It was also pleasing to see the team spirit building amongst the new and more established players. The atmosphere was more relaxed, particularly now that Henderson and Bird had left the club. Tony also noticed how Tommy French had buckled down to some hard work now that the bad blood had departed. His game was showing signs of improvement and Alf Henning had trained hard with him on heading skills. The three newly signed youngsters had settled in well considering their disastrous first day and each one had listened to their more experienced club mates and worked hard in all aspects of training. Graham Hart had impressed everyone with his skill and excellent close control and accurate crosses. Mike Thomas had tackled ferociously and defended well and Steven Holland was improving his ground control work owing to his injured forehead. The three part-timers were obviously finding it harder to settle in but the other professional players accepted their presence openly and, in fact, comedian Allan Smith shared a sense of humour with young Tony White. Barrie Trippett had commented how Graham Bond's game and captaincy had improved over the last two or three weeks. He was apparently more confident and wanted to do well for the club. Steve Fisher, Simon Docker and Sammy Chaddock were the quiet members of the team but after the latter's heroic actions in defending Steve Holland from Dick Henderson the others had nicknamed him "action man" and tormented him about his bravery. The players had said he'd come out of his shell a bit since last Monday. Alf Henning was a good influence on all the other players and a respected one. He looked to be enjoying his game and relished helping the youngsters during training sessions. Alan Hawkins was improving with his goalkeeping, particularly as he knew he would have to play well to stop young Alan Bates from getting a chance to take his place. Graham Poole was the club loner who had been transferred from one club to another, and had never settled anywhere.

Tony was pleased with the progress of the club in such a short time but was aware that certain positions may have to be strengthened in the near future, depending, of course, on the performances of his players over the first part of the season. He must keep an eye out for one or two possible immediate replacements.

As he mulled over this problem he became aware that it was 6.30 p.m; therefore, decided to call it a day and go home. After his evening meal he discussed the state of affairs of the club with his wife, Penny, and explained to her how difficult he was finding the assortment of problems which had arisen, but how he was honestly enjoying every minute. Penny listened intently as she knew how dearly Tony had set his mind on making a success of professional football management. She hoped the early results would favour Sharrington because she knew Tony could make the club successful if he wasn't put under too much pressure from the start. Whilst she had told Tony she would prefer to stay at home rather than watch the game from the Directors' box, she assured him that she would follow the state of the game on the local radio station.

Tomorrow was in important day for Tony and the club. The adrenalin was flowing and Tony had to have a nightcap before retiring to bed.

Chapter 21

Saturday dawned, bright, dry and humid. The football season was underway. The excitement was apparent from the local radio station, newspapers, telegrams and phone calls from well-wishers. There was still no news on the Dick Henderson affair or any reasons put forward for Steven Holland standing down for Tommy French. The magic of the opening day had superseded all probing questions from reporters.

The hired coach from L. A. Allenby's arrived at the ground promptly at 10.30 a.m. Mannish was 83 miles from Sharrington. The journey would take two hours with a one-hour stop for lunch, making three hours in all. This would give the team plenty of time to relax after lunch and before the kick-off. All the players had arrived and appeared to be in good spirits; although, there was a look of apprehension on the younger players' faces. The board of directors and their respective wives, Barrie Trippett, Grant Evans, Tony Davidson and the players boarded the coach and they were on their way to Mannish.

Mannish had been in the Fourth Division longer than Sharrington, and, in fact, had only been in the Third Division for one successful season. They were usually a bogey club to Sharrington and for the six games played between the clubs over the last three seasons Mannish had won four, one game had been drawn and Sharrington won the other. In last season's games the result was 1-1 at Sharrington and Mannish had won at home 4-1. Mannish had finished in eighth position last season and had only lost two of their home games. Sharrington had finished thirteenth and had lost an overall total of seventeen games, six at home. Mannish had signed two new players in the close season, Chatterton from Crest United for £17,000 and Toddy from Blackway for £25,000 with a view of strengthening their push for promotion. This was to be a hard opening game for Sharrington.

Some of the players read newspapers and books and some preferred to play cards, during the journey. Allan Smith usually kept spirits high with his infectious humour but, today, even he seemed tense. Apart from the jingling of money changing hands in the card games and discussions between the two goalkeepers, Mike Thomas and Graham Bond, the overall silence was only too noticeable. The regular driver of the coach, Sam Johnstone, sensed the nervousness and opted to select a radio station to ease the tension.

The journey had been underway for an hour and a quarter when the coach pulled into a roadside cafe-cum-restaurant. After lunch of steak and toast followed by a cordial drink, the party returned to the coach for the last 30 miles of the journey to Mannish. Tony was sitting next to Barrie Trippett when suddenly during the lunchtime radio sports programme the presenter was heard to say, '... *and a sensational start to the season for Tony Davidson, the inexperienced manager of Fourth Division club Sharrington, when, according to reports received today their veteran centre-half, Dick Henderson, was involved in a dressing room brawl, with three other team mates this week which resulted in Henderson being sacked from the club, immediately. Apparently Henderson was knocked unconscious and it is understood the club held a board meeting and decided to dismiss Henderson without listening to his side of the story. Henderson is claiming unfair dismissal. There has been no official report from the club... well quite a dramatic affair for Sharrington to cope with on their opening day... hopefully, we will try to get Tony Davidson's comments on arrival at Mannish Town, where they play their game today.'* The presenter moved onto another subject.

The members on the coach were speechless. Tony Davidson stood up from his seat and went to discuss this unexpected news with Jack Elliott and the three directors. However, no one was more surprised than Grant Evans, the local sportswriter from the *Sharrington Echo*. All the others were, at least, aware of the stormy incident.

Grant Evan pulled his notebook from his pocket and rushed towards the front of the coach where the impromptu board meeting was being held.

Tony Davidson was the first to speak to him. 'I'm sorry, Grant, but all we can give you is a prepared statement by Mr. Elliott. Whilst we were aware of the incident which has just been referred to, we did not wish to announce it publicly unless it was forced upon us, which now certainly appears to be the case. Henderson has obviously spilt the beans and, as pre-conceived as the dressing room incident was, he has calculated his announcement of the whole affair to affect me and the team's performance today.' Tony was becoming more annoyed at the situation, but, as he hit his fist against the front chair's armrest, everyone heard him say, 'Well no man will upset this club, me or my players. The Henderson affair has gone now and is finished as far as I am concerned. Let the tribunal decide the outcome on presentation of all the facts. I'm totally committed to the players who represent Sharrington today. If he thinks we will stumble by the wayside then he's picked the wrong club. We know what's expected of us today. We're here for a result and a good start to the season.' Tony now turned to Grant Evans and said, quite simply, in a normal voice, 'and don't quote me, O.K?'

'But why didn't you mention the incident to me, at least?' asked Grant Evans.

'We considered it was an internal affair and didn't think, in view of the circumstances, that Henderson would make an official complaint,' replied Jack Elliott.

'But gentlemen, you could have at least prepared me for the worst. Fancy, I'll be the laughing stock when I get back to the office,' stammered Grant Evans.

'Oh, stop worrying about yourself, man. It was a delicate matter to the club and one which we thought would blow over,' shouted Eddie Flannagan, trying not to unduly upset the ladies on the coach. 'Just say you were keeping it under your hat and publish the official club quote on the incident in tonight's paper.'

'But I'm supposed to be the official club reporter and if you can't trust me who can you trust?' enquired Grant Evans.

'Look, Grant, we are all as one on this matter, so don't push us any more. If it goes to a tribunal we don't want quotes from club officials being misinterpreted in the press. Just take the official statement,' said Jack Elliot quite forcibly. Grant Evans took a copy of the statement and returned to his seat.

The players had heard all that was discussed and if they had felt nervous beforehand they knew that there would be extra pressure upon them once they arrived at Mannish. The journey continued without any further reference to the Henderson incident, both from the radio or amongst the club officials or players.

The arrival at the Mannish ground was 1.45 p.m. and as expected the presence of the Sharrington coach created special attention. Reporters from national and local newspapers, radio and a small crew of T.V. personnel rushed to ask Tony Davidson questions on the sensational sacking of Henderson. All he would say was 'No comment.' He referred everyone to the club chairman's report and was quickly ushered with his players into the visitors' entrance by Mannish Town officials and towards the dressing rooms. This was not the press coverage Tony wanted for Sharrington, but once all the team were in the dressing room he told Barrie Trippett to stop anyone entering for quarter of an hour or so until he had had a chance to speak to the players.

The dressing room was small; therefore, some of the players had to stand. Tony asked for everyone's attention, although he knew it would be difficult, as clearly the men from the media had gathered outside the dressing rooms.

'Now, listen lads. If you want to comment, or discuss the Henderson affair, I want it to wait until after this game. There's a two-hour journey home and this will be ample time for each of us to think about what is likely to happen and discuss all foreseeable problems.' Tony kept a serious expression on his face as he continued, 'My main concern is what happens on the pitch this afternoon. Let's get back to basics. This is a Fourth Division game and a hard one for us. What with our problems since I took over, let's not forget this afternoon is just the start of a difficult season for each and every one of us, and although I know we have not played together often or got used to each other's style of play, there are definite signs already of this squad of players doing well this season. This is our bread and butter. Obviously the club will attract attention but let's show people we intend to seek further attention of a club which is planning to be successful.' The noise and disturbance outside the dressing rooms was causing Tony to raise his voice. He looked around the players and counted on his fingers as he stressed certain points.

'Now, with regard to today's game I want: (a) total concentration on the game, (b) hard work, (c) running for each other, (d) shouting for possession, (e) helping one another, (f) strong and definite challenges, (g) working the ball to the wings and for high accurate crosses into the box, and, finally lads, above all, never let your heads drop, regardless of what happens out there. Right get changed, lads. Listen to Graham for instructions, forget the news this morning and let's bag our first couple of points. Best of luck. Try and get changed quickly and have a work out on the pitch for ten minutes before the majority of the crowd get here.' At that point Tony left and pushed his way through the pressmen before joining the Sharrington directors and Mannish Town officials.

At five minutes to three the two teams took to the pitch. Mannish Town were first out to a tremendous crowd reception. About 8,000 supporters had turned up for the game; this, 2,000 up on Mannish Town's average crowd last season. No doubt the unorthodox happenings at Sharrington had intrigued the extra number of supporters. Mannish Town wore white shirts and red shorts and Sharrington were kitted in their normal strip of red shirts and black shorts. The referee had called the two captains together and the teams changed ends with Mannish starting the game. Both managers were sitting in their respective dugouts on the touchline. Tony, Barrie and sub Tony White in the visitors', Greg Hellenby, the manager, Steve Ploys, the trainer, and sub Heddon in the home team shelter.

Barrie said to Tony just before the kick-off, 'Here we go then. I don't think for one minute the players will be unaffected by the Henderson news this morning and I'll be more than surprised if we can manage a point today. The lads seemed worried and extremely nervous.'

'I'll be annoyed if we throw it away due to this stupid affair. They are professionals, albeit some of them are new to the game, they're going to have to get used to it. They're off, Barrie,' said Tony, nudging Barrie.

In the first twenty minutes the home team had been sharper to the ball and taken up some good attacking positions. Their new forward, Toddy, had headed just wide, centre-forward Bennison's shot was turned over the bar by Alan Hawkins and an appeal for hand ball by Steve Fisher was judged by the referee to have been outside the penalty area. Mannish Town wasted the free kick.

Sharrington had challenged hard and given little away in defence but the passing through midfield to the attack was poor. In the latter half Passon had headed a corner by left-winger Staff against the Sharrington crossbar, then No. 10 Shilton's shot was blocked on the line by Allan Smith before Tommy French cleared the danger. Just before half-time, with the home crowd chanting for a goal, on a rare break by Sammy Chaddock, his cross was brilliantly headed by Alf Henning against the post only to bounce out of play. At half-time the score was 0-0.

During the interval Tony urged his inside-forwards to push further forward as they were failing to support the attack. He stressed that they should bring Graham Hart and Sammy Chaddock more into the game as he thought Mannish Town's full-backs were weak. The players seemed more satisfied with their performance; although, they knew they would have to take the game to Mannish rather than soaking up pressure all the time.

At the start of the second half, Mannish's No. 8, Toddy, was injured in a tackle with Mike Thomas and after limping for some ten minutes he was replaced with sub, Heddon, who failed to make the same effect upon the Sharrington defence. Although the tackle appeared fair the home supporters booed Thomas every time he touched the ball. In the last fifteen minutes of the game Sharrington played some good football and went close to scoring through Simon Docker and Graham Poole. As far as a spectacle was concerned this game had not lived up to its early first half excitement. The game ended on a drab note with both teams involving their goalkeeper with long back-passes, as each had seemingly settled for a goalless draw. The game ended 0-0.

The Sharrington directors were pleased, the wives looked pleased, the few supporters who had made the journey acted as though they were pleased, but most of all Tony Davidson was delighted. He had witnessed his team take pressure and soak it up, sort out their own game, create good chances and end up in control of the match. He also saw signs of improvement in individuals and the team as a whole. He was happy with a point and told his team so in the dressing room; in fact his pleasure radiated to the team, who although they seemed to be satisfied with the result, expressed their delight once they knew their manager had confirmed what they had individually thought. The atmosphere was better in the camp already and both Tony and Barrie knew the players could overcome the torment of the Henderson affair which had dominated the day's news and which would be likely to be the centre of attention in the weeks to come.

The coach party returned to Sharrington more relieved of tension than it had been during the journey to Mannish, but the black cloud of the Henderson affair hovered in everyone's mind.

Chapter 22

On Sunday afternoon, as Sharrington were due to play at home against Aldway on Tuesday evening, all the players had been requested to attend the ground for training. At 2.00 p.m. everyone had arrived and congregated in the dressing room, reading an assortment of Sunday newspapers. The overall opinion of reports on the goalless draw at Mannish were reasonably complimentary of the Sharrington performance, but the Dick Henderson affair featured more prominently in all papers.

Tony and Barrie discussed the previous day's game with the players and pointed out noticeable weaknesses and errors as well as remarking on the good things that happened. Tony suggested that the players "loosened off" by doing two or three laps of the playing area, sprints and exercises before finishing off with a massage and hot bath.

The training session was relaxed and enjoyable and as there were no injuries from the game at Mannish the players had all left the ground by 3.30 p.m. Tony had informed them that on Monday they would concentrate on shooting, set moves and covering in defence, with light training on Tuesday morning. The team for Tuesday night was announced as the same as it had been on the previous Saturday.

After the players had all left, Tony turned to Barrie and said, 'I've been hounded all last night and this morning by the press on this Dick Henderson business. In fact I'm absolutely fed up of saying "no comment." The sooner the true story is out the better.'

As Tony walked towards the notice board to pin up the team sheet for the Tuesday game Barrie said, 'The press have been on my back about the dressing room incident, as well. I just can't understand Henderson at all.'

'Yes, it's beyond me why he should make a false declaration of the facts to the press,' said Tony.

'It must surely put an end to his professional playing career once the truth comes out,' replied Barrie.

'The sooner it does, the better. We will be able to concentrate on the playing side,' mused Tony as he inspected Sharrington's fixture list. 'Enough of Henderson, Barrie. I want us to travel to Low Grove tomorrow night to watch their game against Holydice-on-Sea, who are our opponents next Saturday. It will also give us some indication of Aldway who drew against Low Grove 1-1 yesterday.'

'Yes, that's fine with me, Tony,' said Barrie looking over Tony's shoulder at the fixture list.

'Good, we'll leave about 4.30 p.m. tomorrow night. I've got a bit of paperwork to clear up before I go home tonight. I'll see you in the morning Barrie,' said Tony.

Tony heard Barrie drive his car from the car park in front of the offices and suddenly realised he was not alone as he had first thought when he heard footsteps walking towards his office. The footsteps stopped right outside his door and there remained silence. Tony waited wondering who it could be. The silence remained for almost thirty seconds when it was finally broken by a gentle knock.

'Come in,' shouted Tony rather forcefully. Again there was a silence for some ten seconds before the door handle was moved, the door slowly opened and cautiously the figure of Mrs. Henderson shuffled in, letting the door close behind her as she confronted Tony Davidson. She was the first to speak.

'Mr. Davidson, I'm sorry to trouble you while you are at work but I just had to come and see you about my husband.'

'That's all right, Mrs. Henderson. Please sit down,' said Tony.

Mrs. Henderson was of average height, slim, attractive with long dark hair. She was very fashionable and had exceptionally striking, blue eyes, she paused and continued, 'Thank you sir, may I come straight to the point,' said Mrs. Henderson, as she sat upon the edge of a high backed chair.

'Please do,' said Tony, as he made himself comfortable in his own leather chair.

'Well, it's Dick. He really knows he's done wrong and I know he's no intention of letting this matter go to a tribunal,' stammered Mrs. Henderson.

Those words pleased Tony to such an extent he felt the relief of pestering pressmen immediately, but, as he sensed Mrs. Henderson had more to say on the subject, he remained straight-faced.

Mrs. Henderson continued, 'He's such a blockhead at times and it's only because he doesn't get his own way. I know, I've lived with him now for eight years. Anyway, sir, I digress – you see the thing is, Dick has had this drinking problem since the end of last season and just recently it's got steadily worse.

'It was during last Friday night when he got drunk and telephoned the national press about being sacked from the club. Since then he's been hounded by all different types of journalists wanting to make the whole affair into something sensational. Really I think it's this that has brought him to his senses and he realises he couldn't substantiate his claim for unfair dismissal.' Mrs. Henderson paused carefully stroked her long dark wavy hair away from her face and said quite clearly, 'To be absolutely honest with you he is not man enough to come and see you himself but wants you to know he is prepared to end this nonsense and would appreciate it if you would accept his apologies.' Mrs. Henderson finished speaking and calmly relaxed in the chair.

Tony sighed quite obviously though he was in deep thought and said, 'I am sorry to hear of Dick's problems and sympathise with you Mrs. Henderson. Obviously I would have much preferred for Dick to have called to see me but I must say, in all honesty, I am delighted he has decided not to proceed to tribunal.' Tony did not feel it was necessary to say any more but asked, 'Tell me, what will Dick do now, Mrs. Henderson?'

She crossed her legs, picked up her handbag searched inside it frantically and gave Tony a white card. On the card was printed in black letters:

DR. LEE STRIDE
6-week course in curing alcoholic problems
Phone SHEFFORD 27735
or write to THE IVY WELLS, BRICOMBE, SHEFFORD
for further details.

'We wrote for details weeks ago and finally Dick has agreed to go to Dr. Stride's and take the treatment. We have enough money and if he can be cured I'm sure he can pick himself up and settle down again, even though he appreciates that his playing days in football are over,' said Mrs. Henderson.

'I am delighted he is sorting himself out and if there is anything the club can do to help, please don't hesitate to get in touch,' said Tony standing up from his chair and offering his hand to Mrs. Henderson.

'Thank you, Mr. Davidson. Dick has said he would make a statement to retract his earlier allegations and I think this is the last you will hear on this unfortunate case,' remarked Mrs. Henderson as she lightly shook Tony's hand. Mrs. Henderson left as calmly as she had arrived.

The news Mrs. Henderson had given him was so pleasing, Tony phoned each director, Barrie and Jack Elliott to inform them accordingly. The black cloud had blown over quicker than he had hoped. Tony could now get on with managing the team and preparing for the visit of Aldway on Tuesday evening without any distractions.

Chapter 23

By Tuesday evening a statement by Dick Henderson had appeared in the national and local press retracting all that he had said beforehand. Also, albeit brief, was a sentence from Mrs. Henderson to say that her husband had succumbed to the evil of alcohol but that he was now seeking advice on a permanent cure. Dick Henderson had suffered great shame, but in some ways his apologetic statement had won him sympathy. The club had issued a statement to the effect that while they wished Henderson every success with the cure and the future they considered the matter amicably closed.

Tony and Barrie had also driven to Low Grove on the Monday evening and witnessed an impressive home team beat Holydice-on-Sea 2-0. Both men were surprised with the Low Grove team who were extremely sharp and difficult to dispossess. That was the second defeat for Holydice-on-Sea and Tony only hoped his team could make it three defeats on the following Saturday. He did not feel that Holydice-on-Sea were as good as Sharrington but he knew the outcome of next Saturday could well depend upon the confidence of his team's performance against Aldway on Tuesday evening.

Aldway had drawn 1-1 at home to Low Grove on Saturday, finished ninth in the league and beaten Sharrington 1-0 in the same fixture last season. As this was Sharrington's first home league game of the season there was a crowd of 7,500 waiting to witness their new-styled team; this was a good gate for Sharrington. Aldway was almost 100 miles away from Sharrington and therefore only a couple of coachloads of supporters had made the trip for this 7.00 p.m. kick-off.

Tony had raised his team's spirit for the game. He impressed upon them how important it was for them to do well in their first home game. He pointed out the set moves and refreshed their memories on their basic style of play. He also remembered that Aldway had been beaten 5-0 by Evercroft in a friendly earlier in the season. Sharrington took to the field to a good reception from the supporters. Aldway were the second team to run out and kitted in blue shirts and yellow shorts. It was a pleasantly dry and calm evening.

Both teams started with trepidation as passes were hurried and inaccurate. The visitors settled first and quickly found some confidence to attack the Sharrington defence from all angles. Sharrington seemed to be playing the ball up to Alf Henning but failing to give him any support.

They did not seem to attempt to use either Graham Hart or Sammy Chaddock on the wings. Graham Bond rallied his team during the first half but when they did use their own wingmen the opposition seemed to anticipate the move and make timely interceptions. With five minutes to half-time remaining Aldway scored. Young Mike Thomas was dispossessed in midfield and the Aldway attack was crisp and positive. Gregory, the visitor's captain played a one two with Jacques before squaring the ball to centre-forward Allison whose shot was blocked by Alan Hawkins only for Palmer to smash in the rebound. Sharrington trailed 1-0 at half-time. The crowd were not impressed and neither was Tony Davidson.

'What's the matter, lads?' enquired Tony, quite firmly. 'We have not started to play yet. They are not a good side but they are organising themselves better than we are.' Tony looked at his players and then pointed to Poole and Thomas and said, 'You are both not challenging for the ball, lads, and you are not playing positively. All of you are banging the ball up to Alf and then failing to support him.' He paused again, 'I know you are nervous but come on, men: where's all the ideas and plans from training gone to? We must start looking for the ball – giving and going for the return, playing balls wide and helping each other. Now get out there and just put it into practice. We can win this game yet.' The players stormed out onto the field looking more confident. Tony followed with Barrie, to sit in the trainer's box.

Straight from the start of the second half Aldway kept possession and a high, first time cross from right winger, Hasson, was won by the ever-busy and dogged Allison to head a good goal past Alan Hawkins. Sharrington were trailing 2-0. Tony stood up and shook his fists in anger at his players. They had been caught while still cold. Sharrington players, now with their backs to the wall, fought harder and gradually began to take control of the game. Possibly this was as much the fault of an indisciplined Aldway side who quite obviously were relaxing as they were 2-0 in front.

The home crowd also became more involved as Sharrington were fighting against all the odds. The attacks were more positive and the style of play was taking shape. Tony and Barrie urged their players. Aldway were becoming sluggish at the back and Alf Henning was constantly a threat on high, crossed balls. In fact with twelve minutes remaining Graham Hart beat the Aldway left-back, Boon, and crossed to the far post. Henning headed the ball into the path of Graham Poole whose shot was fiercely struck through the crowded goalmouth and into the net. The players and crowd went wild. Tony again urged his players to press forward into attack. There was a buzz of excitement as, quickly, Sharrington stormed for possession and built another fast break into attack. Aldway were rattled. They now fouled deliberately as they tried to hold on to the 2-1 lead. They were booed by the crowd who were now totally involved in their team's efforts. The fouls continued and two of the visiting team were booked by the referee. The Sharrington attacks were now constant. Shipp, the Aldway keeper, had made two super saves from Thomas and Henning and the action was thoroughly entertaining.

With four minutes to go a long, accurate clearance by Tommy French sent Sammy Chaddock down the left wing. He beat the full-back, Manners, at the goal line and crossed the ball back towards the penalty spot. As Alf Henning rushed in with the Aldway centre-half, Ballantyne, he appeared to be pushed away from the ball. The crowd and Sharrington players roared penalty but the referee waved all appeals away. The ball spun to the edge of the area and Steve Fisher raced ten yards to beat an Aldway defender to shoot the ball high and hard under the crossbar and into the roof of the net. The crowd roared, the players were ecstatic and the score was 2-2. Although Sharrington launched two more attacks before the final whistle they couldn't manage to score a third goal. Sharrington had fought back marvellously and had earned another valuable point. The crowd were impressed and cheered the team off the pitch. It had been another game where Tony Davidson's squad had proved to him that they were capable of promotion. If only he could get them to work harder at the start of the game, and get three or four wins under their belts, he knew he wouldn't have to look for too many extra players.

'What a team, eh, Bob?' asked a jubilant Eddie Fisher.

'Ahhh, it was an incredible fight back,' blurted Bob Bennett with great excitement in his voice.

'A real good game to watch. I never thought they would get that equaliser,' cried Frank Sneddon, drawing heavily on his freshly-lit cigarette.

The three men arrived at Frank's car and quickly drove off to their local public house, The Village Arms to discuss, analyse and examine their favourite football team, Sharrington F.C. They had been partisan supporters of Sharrington F.C. for many, many years and while they had never witnessed a truly successful team they all felt things at the club were making a turn for the better. Frank, Eddie and Bob travelled to all home and away games together, and, although they had been quick to criticise the directors in their selection of the inexperienced Tony

Davidson and the early drastic changes within the club, as they settled down to drink their pints of beer, they were becoming more complimentary of the club's developments.

Bob was a chubbily-built man of some 40 years of age. He had supported Sharrington since a boy and was at one time secretary of the Supporters' Club before standing down due to ill health. Eddie was a true supporter of Sharrington and refused to hear a bad word against the club. In fact he'd been involved in dozens of heated arguments over the years. He was the same age as Bob, slimly built with tousled hair and beard. Frank was an astute spectator who always made unbiased statements on the state of the club and visiting teams. He was slightly older than Bob and Eddie and an ex-professional footballer with Rondale many years ago. He was an amiable character and the only married man of the three.

'I tell you this, chaps, we were wrong to criticise Davidson. He looks as though he's getting the players to believe in themselves for once, and I like the way the youngsters have settled down,' said Bob Bennett after drinking approximately half of his pint in one movement.

'Yes, I tend to agree with you, Bob, but I would prefer to reserve judgment for a few months until the newness of a new manager has worn off and the team have played some of the better teams from the division,' remarked the thoughtful Frank Sneddon.

Eddie Fisher still appeared to be on cloud nine as he shook his head in disbelief and repeated, for the tenth time, 'What a team.'

'Look Eddie,' shouted Frank 'the team have only played two league games and to be honest, judging the games as a whole, we didn't deserve to win either of them. In fact I'm not too happy about our defence yet and I hope Davidson can strengthen it before we meet some better teams.'

'What's wrong with the defence, Frank?' cried Eddie.

'I just don't think two or three of them are up to top of the table form,' replied Frank, quite relaxed.

'Which players?' asked Bob Bennett after finally finishing his pint with only his third drink.

'Well, for a start, I don't rate Hawkins too highly. He's not commanding enough in his area and always gives me the jitters when the opposition are attacking around the eighteen-yard line. I also feel Bondie is a little too slow, but, after saying that, there is certainly a marked improvement in his approach to the game this season.' Frank didn't pause in his analysis of the defence and quickly moved on to say 'and as for Tommy French, I think his days are numbered.'

'What about young Steve Holland? As soon as he's fit again he will surely get back in the team as centre-half. I like what I saw of him in the few pre-season friendlies,' stated Bob Bennett.

'Yes. I agree. Bob. He will make a good lad with a few more games under his belt,' commented Frank.

Eddie Fisher returned from the bar with three more pints of beer and said, 'You might not be happy with the defence, Frank, but I think Davidson's main priority is to find a player to play off big Alf Henning. He is certainly making the chances, but Poole and Docker don't appear to be able to read his style of play.'

'Maybe not, Eddie, but I think they showed signs of understanding his game as the game progressed tonight. The forwards all played well in the second half and I think if Hart and Chaddock can get the ball over much quicker than they are doing the goals will certainly come,' remarked Frank astutely.

'I just hope they get a hatful on Saturday against Holydice-on-Sea. They have lost both their games so far and we need two points to build up the confidence a bit,' said Bob.

'If tonight's performance is anything to judge by I can't see Holydice holding our forward line,' replied Eddie. 'Football's a funny game,' said Frank as he lit up another cigarette. 'Maybe Holydice are struggling a bit but they usually do well at Sharrington and they will make it hard for us, make no mistake of that.'

The three men continued to discuss the club, as a whole, for the remainder of the pub's opening time before returning home. They had made the necessary arrangements to meet in the Village Arms on Saturday lunchtime for a drink or two before going to the home game against Holydice-on-Sea.

Chapter 24

On the Wednesday evening after the home game against Aldway, there was the re-arranged board meeting. Barrie Trippett was the only absentee as Tony had asked him to go and watch the Second Division game between Hambridge and Storr Town. The purpose of the journey was to look at Neil Baynes, the Storr Town 29-year-old inside-forward and Dennis Butler the 34-year-old Hambridge back four central defender. This spying mission had not been released to the members of the board or the local press.

The board meeting opened in high spirits. The 'Dick Henderson' affair was briefly discussed, recorded and dismissed within five minutes. The second item on the agenda was the manager's report. Tony, as usual, stood up to give his report. The three directors and chairman Jack Elliott awaited Tony's official comments on the club's start to the season with great interest. Tony spoke calmly. 'Gentlemen, our first two results have been pleasing to me. Not only have the players responded to hard training sessions, new tactics, problems within the club and an inexperienced manager but they have shown me they have the right calibre to take this club out of Division Four. The signs are clearly there and, without a doubt, the team spirit both on and off the pitch is developing satisfactorily. I personally felt it would be a harder task and take a longer period of time for these signs to show. I am, at this stage, therefore delighted with the current state of affairs and do hope you gentlemen also feel the same.' Tony paused as Eddie Flannagan muttered, 'Here here,' and Bill Boothroyd and Steve King nodded their heads in agreement. Jack Elliott remained perfectly calm but with an extremely self-satisfied smile across his face.

Tony continued, as he referred to notes in front of him, 'Taking the away game at Mannish Town, without dwelling on the depression of the Henderson news, I felt the players improved as the game progressed. Performances of special note were Allan Smith, Tommy French and young Mike Thomas. They are defending exceptionally well and once we get Graham Bond into tip-top fitness I feel he will also put more aggression and sharpness into his play. Mannish Town started the game well but were soon put out of their stride by our lads' more positive approach to the game in the second half.

'Turning now to our home game last night against Aldway, once again after a very disappointing first half the lads certainly buckled down to their game in the latter part of the second half and were possibly unlucky not to win the game at the end.'

Tony rested his papers on the table and looked around the members of the Board. He continued in the same tone as before. 'The ability and strength of Alf Henning was apparent to everyone in the ground and I'm only pleased he's enjoying his game of football again. He will be a big asset to the club this season. Finally the only thing on the playing side which has annoyed me is the way we got caught cold after the restart of the second half but I can assure you gentlemen the emphasis of positive defending will be stressed and stressed until we are so solid at the back Alan Hawkins doesn't have any opponents' shots to deal with,' Tony smiled and sat down.

Steve King was the first to ask Tony a question, 'Tell me, Tony, do you propose to strengthen any position with a new signing in the near future or can you honestly say you feel the squad we have now will carry the club into serious promotion contenders?'

Tony answered immediately, 'Basically, Mr. King, the present squad is good enough but I am forever looking for a more suitable player if I feel he can do a better job for the club than a player we have at the moment, and, in fact, I have sent Barrie Trippett to Hambridge this evening to check on the form of Butler of Hambridge and Baynes of Storr Town.'

'Would you anticipate a signing of one or both of these players?' asked Bill Boothroyd, quite independently.

'I really cannot say at this stage, Mr. Boothroyd, but depending on reports and fees etc. I promise you that I will consult the board before making a final decision,' said Tony, positively.

'Tell me do you plan to bring young Steve Holland in for Saturday if he's fit, Tony?' asked Eddie Flannagan in his blunt tone.

'Well, young Steve is having the stitches out tomorrow but quite honestly if he is considered fully fit by the doctor for Saturday's game I cannot see how I could drop Tommy French on his two performances so far,' said Tony.

'Yes, I think he has played very well, particularly when he's on the transfer list,' said Eddie Flannagan.

'I agree,' muttered Bill Boothroyd.

'He's buckled down well and if he continues with the correct attitude it may be necessary to take him off the list to reward him for his efforts,' replied Tony.

'Aye, now that the bad influence, Henderson, has left us it looks as though French will become a club man again,' said Flannagan.

'What about Saturday's game against Holydice-on-Sea, Tony? What are your plans?' asked Jack Elliott, changing the conversation.

'I am confident we can win the game, Mr. Chairman. I travelled with Barrie to Low Grove on Monday evening to watch Holydice-on-Sea and although I must confess the home team were particularly effective I didn't rate the visitors' performance too highly. They were hard in defence but their attack and midfield play was weak. I appreciate Holydice only missed promotion by four points last season but we must remember they had three of their young starlets transferred to First Division clubs in the close season and this must have put them out of their stride. I do hope so,' concluded Tony smugly.

'I only hope we bag our first two points. It seems a long, long time since we won at home,' mumbled Eddie Flannagan.

'Mmm, last February against Dabrook, 2-0, if my memory serves me correctly,' reflected Steve King.

The men continued to discuss other club matters for a further hour before concluding the meeting at 9.00 p.m. and retiring home.

After Thursday morning's tiring training session the players were joined in the changing room by Barrie, Tony and Jack Elliott to listen to the draw for the first round of the League Cup. All the teams from the Third and Fourth Division were entered in this round and each round was to be played on a two-leg basis. Since the competition was started some five seasons ago, Sharrington had never qualified to the second round. This season they hoped for a favourable draw, a few good results and most of all the chance to play against a First Division club. Tony believed the opportunity to play against a top team would be good experience for the team and the intrigue and interest would whet the appetite of the supporters.

Jack Elliot carried the small portable transistor radio into the changing room and placed it on the treatment table with the volume up to its highest for all to hear. Everyone gathered around listening to the introduction of the club draw from the League Headquarters. The players suggested different teams to meet in the first round but the talking soon stopped when a voice of a league official called out Number 17. Another voice shouted Treecliffe. The original voice then said Number 27. The team caller voice said *'will play Sharrington F.C.'*

There was an uproar in the dressing room. Some of the players shouted: "fix!" others: "oh no!" and Tony, Barrie and Jack just stood motionless. Sharrington had been drawn out to their local neighbours Treecliffe, also of the Fourth Division. It was not the draw they had anticipated and they all knew the local derby would be a fiercely contested game. In fact, both games would be hard and competitive. The only bonus from Sharrington's point of view was that the games would attract a bumper crowd.

The disappointment of being drawn against Treecliffe was that they were Sharrington's number one bogey club. At no time had Sharrington ever beaten Treecliffe in a league game although for many seasons they had been in the Third Division. They had been relegated to the Fourth Division only three seasons ago, much to the delight of the town of Sharrington. Not only was there a love-hate relationship between the football clubs but the towns as well; Treecliffe was only five miles from Sharrington and had always had the upper hand when it came to football.

As the first game at Treecliffe was some two weeks away, the whole area would be buzzing with excitement at the thought of the game and the local media would relish the thought of displaying propaganda arguments from now until after the games had been played. The scene for two tremendous cup-ties had been set by the distant voices of the league officials.

The rest of the draw continued but no one appeared to be listening to it now that Sharrington's name had been called out.

'Not a good draw for us, eh Boss?' asked captain, Graham Bond.

'No, it certainly won't be an easy opening round for us,' replied Tony, rather miserably.

'As if two league games a season isn't enough without having to face each other a further two times in the cup,' remarked Jack Elliott rather solemnly.

After debates on the draw of one sort or another the players finally finished changing and left the ground knowing they had to return on Friday morning for light training. Tony, Barrie, Jack and the busy Eddie Connelly remained in the dressing room.

'How was the match last night, Barrie?' asked Tony.

'Very poor, actually, Tony. I didn't enjoy it at all and Hambridge stole the game in the dying seconds with the only goal,' replied Barrie.

'What about Butler and Baynes performances?' asked Tony as he sidestepped Eddie and the wielding sweeping brush.

'Can't honestly say they had good games but Baynes must be the hardest worker I've ever seen. He never stops chasing and is keen to help in defence as well as in attack. Butler was demanding in the air but some of his distribution was bad. Personally, on last night's performance, neither of them seemed too interested in their respective games. Although Baynes tried desperately hard he appeared to lack an interest in his game, if you know what I mean,' reported Barrie.

'Yes, I think I do, Barrie,' said Tony nodding his head slowly. 'I'll check up on them next before deciding whether or not to pursue our interest.'

The telephone rang in the referees' room and Jack Elliott answered it. 'It's for you, Tony. Grant Evans wants to have your comments on the draw,' shouted Jack.

Tony went to talk to Grant Evans, mumbling loudly above the singing voice of Eddie Connelly. 'Here we go already, verbal warfare begins now – Round One – Ding Ding.'

Chapter 25

The Sharrington dressing room was a hive of activity prior to the game against Holydice. Well-wishers, reporters, local businessmen, visiting officials and faces Tony Davidson didn't recognise popped in and out in a constant stream from 2.00 p.m. until 2.35 p.m. when finally Tony asked a club official to stand at the outer door and prevent anyone else from entering.

'Right lads, let's have some concentration on today's game. I've seen Holydice play this season and witnessed an extremely hard defence. They are quick to cover and sharp in the tackle. Good in the air and well disciplined. Their midfield was slow and deliberate and the forwards were starved of the ball. Mind you their left-winger, Dearne, is a bit nippy and good on crosses.' Tony carried on as he continued to pace up and down the dressing room floor. 'I know we can win this one today, lads. I want to see you start where you left off on Tuesday night. Let's see the ball being pushed wide to Graham and Sammy. Graham and Simon give them support, and Alf make yourself busy and keep those challenges going in on crosses. Steve, be looking for that one-two and creating the extra man upfront.' Tony turned to his defenders. 'Defence, I can't see you having too many problems today. Keep it tight and make the early tackles positive. Graham, you'll have to check young Dearne early-doors because he could be a problem for us. Alan, marshal your defence and make a clear call for balls in the area.'

The players were tapping their feet, exercising muscles and generally trying to keep the nerves away. Ten minutes from kick-off time, Tony sent them out onto the pitch.

Holydice-on-Sea came out onto the pitch five minutes after the Sharrington players. As Holydice-on-Sea was some 260 miles from Sharrington they had travelled early in the morning and spent half an hour limbering up at about 2.00 p.m. They were in all yellow kit. The attendance was slightly higher than Tuesday night's game, 7,890.

As Tony had hoped, Sharrington attacked from the kick-off, but, as he had feared, the quick challenging and covering of the Holydice team were thwarting all the home team's moves. It was clear that Holydice were struggling to find form in midfield and in attack. Although a new youngster had been brought into the visitor's midfield, his performance was as aimless as the player he had replaced. There was no danger to the Sharrington defence at all. The first half progressed in the same vein with Sharrington attacking constantly down both wings and through the centre of the pitch. At half-time they had not found a way through or gone close, and the two central defenders for Holydice, Hyton and Rushton, were a tower of strength to their team.

During half-time, Tony told his team to start shooting from outside the penalty area. He said, 'I cannot fault your play at all but their defence is so strong we've just got to change our style for the second half. As they are cutting out our crosses and getting enough men back to block our direct attacks, we will just have to try and beat their defence and goalkeeper by shooting from outside the area.' The players discussed some moves with Tony before trudging out for the second half.

Rain began to fall quite heavily as Holydice kicked off for the second half. The thick grass soaked up the moisture but the ball began to skid off the surface quite sharply. The spectators made a dash for the cover under the stand but those who couldn't make it huddled closely together. Sharrington pressed forward again but shots were difficult to attempt. Holydice defended in numbers and were clearly playing for a point, like the same fixture of the previous season.

With twenty minutes to play, some skilful play by Graham Hart had won a corner on the right hand side of the field. This was only Sharrington's fourth corner of the game. Hart took the corner, the ball hit the Holydice full-back Cross and deflected to the visitors' far post, as it looped into the air. Most players had lost sight of the ball but Alf Henning ran in from the blind side of his marker and soared to meet the greasy ball with his head and crash it firmly back across the face of the goal into the far corner of the net. Sharrington were leading 1-0. The drenched crowd cheered and even three young schoolboys ran onto the pitch to celebrate the goal. Tony and Barrie urged their players to continue to push forward to stop Holydice pressing into attack. However, much to the surprise of everyone Holydice simply stayed on the defensive. They didn't seem to have much idea of how to build an attack. Sharrington couldn't break the visitors' defence again but they settled for a 1-0 win and their first two points of the season. The Sharrington players were cock-a-hoop in the dressing room but Tony was quick to bring them down to earth by saying 1-0 was not a conclusive result against a poor team like Holydice and that they would have harder teams in the league. At least Sharrington were undefeated in the first three games but Tony knew the more skilful teams of the division were yet to come; but so far so good.

Chapter 26

The following week brought headlines on the forthcoming local cup derby, an in-depth article on the man behind Sharrington F.C, a review of the happenings at the club since the appointment of Tony Davidson and an analysis of the Fourth Division results. Sharrington were midway in the table after the first three games but, surprisingly, with the exception of one of last year's relegated teams from Division Three, Seamingway, who had convincingly won all their games, the majority of teams were drawing their games. There had been 13 drawn games from the opening 24 fixtures. The top teams were Seamingway on six points, who were followed by seven teams on four points, one of which was Sharrington. The only team not to register a point, at this stage, were Holydice-on-Sea, Sharrington's last opponents.

By Wednesday afternoon Tony had called the players in for training on Sunday afternoon, Monday morning and afternoon, Tuesday afternoon and Wednesday morning. The players were noticeably sharper to him, more positive in their attitude and developing on all skills. After the Wednesday training session the team had a meal at a local hotel before travelling the 65 miles to Dabrook for the evening league match. Tony had to make one change to the team which beat Holydice. Unfortunately, Graham Hart suffered an ankle injury in the game and was replaced by Paul Cracknell the young, part-time player. He had been chosen in preference to substituted Tony White, basically because he was essentially a stronger right-footed player. Paul was more familiar in an inside-forward position but Tony was confident that would not let the other players down.

Dabrook had been in Division Four since entering the league 15 years ago and never finished higher than half way. During the seasons 1971 to 1975 they changed the club's manager no less than six times. However, Bill Hemmingway had been manager for the last two seasons and brought some respectability to Dabrook. In his first season he had strengthened the team with three new signings: Thickett, Bridge and French, and transferred some of the dead wood from the club.

In both seasons since he had taken over the manager's position, Dabrook had been placed 12th and last year this put them one slot higher than Sharrington. The same fixture last season ended 2-1 to Dabrook but Sharrington had won there three times over the years. Dabrook's opening game was at home to Prent Park and ended 1-1. The other two games were away to Seamingway and Low Grove where they lost 3-1 and drew 2-2 respectively.

The Sharrington team arrived at Dabrook at 6.30 p.m. in time for the 7.30 p.m. kick-off. The players inspected the pitch to decide on the correct boots to wear. The playing area was well-grassed but extremely wet owing to the heavy rain in and around the district over the past week. The ground was small and secluded with cover on all sides. The floodlights were of a rickety appearance and the seats in the stand likewise. The terracing was made of old and rotten railway sleepers. There were three large oak trees towering over the stand, which gave the ground a pleasant and rustic setting.

The Sharrington players changed into their second strip of white shirts, black shorts and black socks, as Dabrook's kit was red and white-hooped shirts, white shorts and stockings. Tony had not taken the opportunity to have Dabrook watched in their first three games but if the result at Low Grove was anything to go by he knew they must have played very well to get a draw. Tony gave his usual team-talk before the game started and whilst stressing the importance of settling down in defence and constructively building attacking moves, he purposefully stimulated his players' egos with encouraging and complimentary words. He realised it was important to keep the team on the right course. The players left the dressing room with confidence. Tony walked unaccompanied to the visitors' directors' box to join Jack Elliott, Steve King and Eddie Flannagan. Bill Boothroyd was absent from the game owing to business commitments.

'Confident Tony?' asked Jack Elliott.

'Regrettably, I'm not,' answered Tony. 'The attitude of the lads doesn't seem right and funnily enough I don't think we are going to take the next step forward until we get a good thrashing.'

'Strange talk, Tony. Very strange indeed,' muttered Eddie Flannagan.

'Yes, it probably does seem that way but I just have a feeling we will suffer a painful defeat before much longer,' replied Tony with a half smile on his face.

'Hope it's not tonight that's all. We usually do well here,' shouted Eddie Flannagan as the game started.

Steve King leaned over to Tony and whispered, 'I know what you mean. I have an uncanny feeling Treecliffe will give us that lesson in the cup.'

Tony replied, 'I'd rather it was here tonight. It would be unbearable at Treecliffe.' Both men looked pensive and concentrated on the game.

There was a poor crowd scattered around the ground; the main blocks of supporters clustered behind the two goals. The stand which held only 1,000, was sparse of spectators, in fact every word uttered echoed from one end to the other. The game got off to a slow start with the early play in the centre of the pitch. Neither team were controlling the state of play and no chances were created during the whole of the first half. As both teams left the field the local crowd, on the terracing, slow handclapped them off. The game was uninteresting and Sharrington, although defending well in depth, failed to make adventurous forward moves, which consequently spoiled the game, as a spectacle.

In the second half Sharrington were under severe pressure from the busy Dabrook forwards. In the third minute of the restart the home team centre-forward French shot quite unexpectedly and the ball rocketed past the surprised Alan Hawkins, but fortunately for him it hit the post, ran across the goal line and was cleared for a corner by Alan Smith. Following that action, Potter, Heaton and French again almost scored within the space of ten minutes. Sharrington's attacks were now non-existent. Two free kicks on the edge of the Sharrington penalty area were cannoned accurately by the home team captain, Bridge, only for Alan Hawkins to match his efforts with superb saves. So much were Sharrington under pressure that the defenders were simply kicking the ball aimlessly up the field. These desperate measures showed Tony Davidson another weakness, which he would have to work on with his team. Fortunately for Sharrington, Dabrook seemed to become so frustrated with their bad luck that they lost their way when attacking. The referee blew the final whistle much to the relief of the Sharrington camp. They had managed another goalless draw away from home and while the point from the game was welcomed it was a disappointing performance, with Sharrington failing to play to the same level as they had done in their two home games during the previous week. The only consolation from this game was the excellent goalkeeping of Alan Hawkins. His position, agility and judgment had been faultless. Tony had noticed an improvement in Alan Hawkins' game over the weeks and without a doubt his performance tonight had confirmed to him that he was a definite first team choice for the position of goalkeeper.

On the return journey to Sharrington, Tony went round all his players to discuss the evening's game. He still sensed the majority of his players were gloating over the fact that they were undefeated in the first four games. He stressed to them that they were lucky to escape with a point from tonight's game and that they had shown no signs of scoring. By the time the coach pulled up in Sharrington at midnight everyone had had their say on the reasons for the poor performance at Dabrook. Tony finally announced to his players to have the day off tomorrow but report for light training on Friday morning. It had been a far from satisfactory day.

Chapter 27

After the players had gone home after training on Friday morning Barrie Trippett went to the manager's office to help select the team for the game at Prent Park.

'How's training gone today, Barrie?' asked Tony as he sipped from a cup of coffee.

'Not bad, really. Although the lads have been buckling down very well, I still sense some of them are on cloud nine,' replied Barrie sitting opposite to Tony.

'Yes, and although we've talked about this attitude business over and over again I think the likes of Smithy, Fisher, Thomas, Poole and Chaddock are in for a big surprise before much longer. I hate to say it but the only way they will learn will be from a playing experience. An embarrassment in front of thousands of people. That will knock it out of them I'm certain of that,' stressed Tony as he rang for Peggy to make Barrie a coffee and sandwich.

'I can't agree more,' said Barrie.

'Attitudes are always vitally important in this game, Barrie, as you know, but I'll try not to make too much of an issue of it as I'm sure it will run its course in the next few weeks,' remarked Tony with a wry smile.

Peggy entered the office to bring Barrie his snack, and left to the pleasing news from Tony that Sid and her could take the afternoon off.

'Now then, Barrie,' said Tony in a more serious tone, 'let's select a team for tomorrow and make our plans for the midweek game at Treecliffe.'

The two men selected the team to play at Prent Park. There were two surprise changes in the line up. The team was:

1. Alan Hawkins
2. Graham Bond
3. Allan Smith
4. Steve Fisher
5. Tommy French
6. Stephen Holland
7. Graham Hart
8. Paul Cracknell
9. Alf Henning
10. Simon Docker

11. Sammy Chaddock
Sub: Graham Poole
Travelling Res: Tony White, Mike Thomas, Alan Bates

Both men decided to rest Mike Thomas and Graham Poole, basically because their attitudes were wrong, and Thomas had become a little too cocky since turning professional. Graham Hart had recovered from his ankle injury and the decision to play Paul Cracknell was made on the basis that he had tried particularly hard at Dabrook and Tony wanted to see how he faired in his normal position. Stephen Holland was now fit again was brought back to play alongside Tommy French.

'I will explain the reasons for the changes with the lads tomorrow lunch time, so don't notify anyone of our choice beforehand,' stated Tony.

The training sessions were discussed and written down in detail. Before leaving to go, Tony said, 'I'm going to travel to Storr Town this afternoon to watch their game tonight against Woodville. I'm keen to watch Neil Baynes play again and generally see how the land lies on the transfer market. Therefore, as I'm staying overnight in Storr and travelling on to Prent Park in the morning, can you organise things at this end and I'll see you there tomorrow lunchtime. I've already told Mr. Elliott and arranged for our lads to have lunch at the Vosborough Hotel, which is only five miles outside Storr and fifteen miles from Prent. Lunch is planned for 1.00 p.m.'

'O.K, that's fine, Tony. Have a good scouting mission and I'll see you at the hotel tomorrow lunch,' replied Barrie. Barrie left the office with the details of the journey to Prent Park for pinning onto the official notice board in the reception area.

Tony eventually left his office at 4.30 p.m. and travelled, on his own, to Storr. During the journey he was thinking constantly of the best ways of strengthening his squad. He was basically happy with the fifteen players at the club but knew deep down inside how he desperately needed replacements for three positions. The first and, in his considered opinion, the most vital position to strengthen was the inside-forward spot. Tony felt that Graham Poole was lacking in this role and he hoped his journey to Storr would prove worthwhile with the eventual signing of Neil Baynes. However, he knew it would not be a straightforward deal as there were obvious loopholes such as, would Baynes still play the same type of game as he remembered him, what would be Storr Town's asking price, would Baynes want to move to a club two divisions lower and would Sharrington have a competitor for Baynes' signature? Tony only hoped there would be no complications.

As Tony's journey neared its end he considered the other positions which would have to be strengthened in the near future. He had in mind the right full-back spot which was currently occupied by captain Graham Bond, and the outside-left position held by Sammy Chaddock. Tony had known for some time that these three positions would have to be strengthened in the future but the recent performances by Poole, Bond and Chaddock indicated to him how important these changes were for the progress of Sharrington Football Club. Once again he realised the potential public outcry if a replacement was bought for club captain Graham Bond but knew he would have to follow what he felt would be best for the club. However, at this stage, he did not have any players in mind to take over the positions of Bond or Chaddock. Finally, Tony gave a little thought to tomorrow's match at Prent Park. He was aware that they had also drawn three of their first four games and scored only two goals with eight conceded, six of which came from the current leaders Seamingway. They had redeemed themselves after that 6-0 defeat by drawing 0-0 at home in their last game to Low Grove, who were a team Tony rated highly. He knew his team would have to take the game to Prent Park from the kick-off and try to get an early goal or two because it was evident Prent were struggling to score this season. Tony eventually arrived at his destination and quickly had a snack in a local cafe before rushing to the Storr Town ground to find a seat in the main stand before the game started.

Storr Town had only taken three points from their opening four games and Woodville, the visitors, were undefeated with seven points. Tony noticed immediately the fluency of the game to those in the Fourth Division. The quickness of players reading the game, the individual skills and passing ability was far superior to anything Tony had seen all season. Woodville were 1-0 in the lead after ten minutes but Storr equalised shortly before half-time. In the second half Woodville seemed to step up a gear and showed up weaknesses in the Storr Town defence. Two excellent moves by the Woodville outfit reaped two equally superb goals and nine minutes from time the visitors increased their lead to 4-1 and gave Storr Town a lesson in possession football for the remainder of the game. Neil Baynes had worked hard but to no avail. He certainly showed signs of frustration with his colleagues' play and Tony thought there may be more behind the scene problems, particularly as Storr Town were having a bad start to the season. Tony knew Baynes was the type of player he was looking for; therefore, decided to stay behind and made arrangements to have words with John Briggs, the Storr Town manager.

Eventually, after a long wait, John Briggs invited Tony into his office.

'Pleased to meet you, Mr. Briggs, and I'm sorry to trouble you at this moment in time,' said Tony, as he entered the plush, manager's office. The two men shook hands.

'That's all right, Mr. Davidson, what can I do for you?' replied John Briggs, the veteran Storr Town manager.

'I'll come straight to the point. I am very interested to know whether Storr Town would be prepared to transfer Neil Baynes and, if so, on what terms,' said Tony as he unbuttoned his heavy overcoat.

'Neil Baynes, eh?' pondered John Briggs as he leant back in his comfortable-looking, high backed chair.

'Yes, I know this lad's ability and want him to do a job for me at Sharrington,' answered Tony almost immediately. There was a brief pause.

'Well, Mr. Davidson, I can't hold out much hope for you. Baynes is a good player and is still important to the future of this club. I will admit however that he is not putting everything into his game, but even an 80% effort from him is as good as some players' 100%,' said John Briggs, scratching his bald head. Tony smiled and nodded.

'That's fair comment, but what would be your asking price?' remarked Tony quite directly.

'Mmm, persistent aren't you, Davidson,' murmured John Briggs. 'I'll put you out of your misery young man. He's not for sale.'

Tony felt exactly the same as he did when Alan Tomlinson of Ravenhead spoke to him in that tone during the negotiations of the transfer of Greg Hanby. It was the awkwardness of the situation and his poor bargaining position. He decided to be more positive in his approach. He snapped back. 'Right I'll make my offer in writing and you can put it before your board of directors. I think you may be surprised at our offer, Mr. Briggs.' Tony hadn't any idea of an offer but thought a bit of bluff would spark John Briggs into giving him some indication of a figure. Tony knew Sharrington had made over £50,000 since he came to the club, albeit the board had agreed to pay back to the bank £35,000 to reduce the club's deficit. He waited for John Briggs' reaction.

'As I said, you are persistent, but I really can't envisage the board agreeing to the sale of Baynes, nor for that matter can I see him wanting to go to a Fourth Division club. He's still only 29 and, knowing him, he will want to stay at this level for a good few years yet,' said John Briggs patiently.

Tony sensed his counterpart was speaking honestly and was just about to reiterate that he would put an offer in writing when to his surprise John Briggs added a lifeline to the deal when he said, 'Even though there have been rumours of Baynes being unsettled here, if everyone O.K.'d the deal, I'm afraid our board would demand an amount well in excess of Sharrington's capabilities.'

Tony smiled broadly, shook hands with John Briggs and left the office as he said, confidently, 'You'll be hearing from me. Goodnight.'

Chapter 28

Tony greeted the Sharrington team coach as it arrived at the Vosborough Hotel at 12.45 p.m. He had stayed overnight in the hotel and had got to bed rather late after joining the Woodville party who were also registered overnight following their game at Storr. He immediately ushered the players into the restaurant for lunch and after that took the players into a private room to read out the team news.

'I've made one or two changes today, lads, after our disappointing performance at Dabrook in midweek. I think it is an ideal time to experiment with certain positional changes. I don't want any secrets in the club; therefore, I'll be perfectly honest with my reasons for the team I have chosen today.' Tony knew his players were giving him their total concentration as he continued. 'The number six shirt will go to Stephen Holland. Mike,' continued Tony as he purposely pointed to young Mike Thomas sitting in the corner of the room, 'you've let this newly found status affect your attitude to the game. I'm not too happy with your performances and I've decided to drop you for today's game to let you know that I'm not prepared to pick players on their name only. Each performance is vital and unless 100% goes into every game you're out and that applies to all of you.' Tony paused briefly as he sensed that Mike Thomas had got the message. He continued as he turned to Graham Poole. 'Basically Graham the same goes for you as I've just pointed out to Mike. You've been losing your way recently and clearly not working hard enough at your game. You will be sub today.' Graham Poole nodded, looking rather disappointed. 'I'm giving your position to Paul today. I was pleased with his efforts on Wednesday and want to see how he performs in his correct position.' Paul Cracknell smiled at Tony's announcement.

'Graham,' said Tony pointing at Graham Hart, 'now you're fit again I'm bringing you back onto the right wing. You've played alongside Paul before, so I'm expecting a good right wing display from you two this afternoon.' Once again, Tony paused to sense the players' attitude. Everyone was quiet and there were no problems or signs of dissent evident to him. 'Right lads,' he said sternly, 'the league's wide open and two points will be handy for us today. Prent Park have struggled to find the net this season and that 6-0 thrashing they got at Seamingway the other week clearly shows their defence is suspect. Keep it tight at the back, lads, let's have an understanding Tommy and Steve, early doors, and let's mount the attacks like we did against Aldway and Holydice. I want to see plenty of aggression and some good team play. Graham, make them talk and want the ball. Alf, make a nuisance of yourself and cause a bit of havoc in the box. Steve, look for the shot at goal, and Simon, I want to see you mixing it a bit more and linking up with Sammy down the left hand side.' Tony stopped talking as he looked around his team before him. He knew his approach had stunned some of them and, whilst he had sounded ruthless, felt it was the only way to get his ideas to sink in, by giving them both barrels in a strange setting.

'Right, any questions, lads?' asked Tony, but, as there was no one coming forward, he shouted 'O.K. let's board the bus and get our job done.'

The players' journey to the Prent Park ground was in almost complete silence. Tony and Barrie discussed the game at Storr, Tony's evening with the Woodville party and the team talk at the hotel. Tony then talked to Grant Evans about his changes in the team, his pre-match hopes and his reaction to the Treecliffe manager, Sam Dyson's, comments, recently, that his team would win the league cup-tie comfortably. On this last matter Tony said, 'I'm always amazed at people who stick their necks out to predict a football result. I don't believe it can be done. If it could there would be pools winners every week and just how often have so-called experts fallen flat on their faces after seeing results go the opposite way to their pre-match forecast.' Grant Evans rushed back to his seat on the coach to prepare for the match report on the game.

Unfortunately, the town of Prent was not blessed with two good league sides. Prent Town were eighth in Division Three last season but had only picked up two points from their first four games. Prent Park, who were always the poor relations in the town, had never been out of the Fourth Division whereas Prent Town once held their own for three seasons in Division Two from 1964-1967. Prent Town averaged home crowds of 8,000 and Prent Park of 3,500.

It was a bright day with a blustery wind and The Park ground was freshly painted in the club's colours of yellow and light blue. It was a compact ground with one main stand, which was well maintained. The flags on the roof of the players' entrance fluttered briskly and the visitors' dressing room was spacious with a clean disinfectant aroma.

Back in Sharrington Penny Davidson had risen early so she could do all her shopping and household jobs before settling down in the afternoon to the local radio station's bulletins on the Sharrington game. She made herself a cup of tea and tuned in ready for the first report at 3.45 p.m. which would give the half-time result. She knew how anxious

Tony was of the game at Prent Park and she wondered how his team talk had gone at the hotel as he had phoned her during the morning to advise her of his proposals. She hoped there had been no problems. The music on the radio stopped and a voice gave the half-time report of the Rallingborough v Treecliffe league game. The score was 0-0. Another voice then spoke on the Third Division game between local area team Beckham Town v Collingwood. Penny heard the score to be 2-1 to Beckham Town. She now knew the next report would be on Sharrington's game, and so it was. The voice in the studio said, '*and now over to Prent Park to hear how the last of our local teams Sharrington are fairing.*'

There was a brief spell of crackling and then a distant voice was heard to say, '*Good news for Sharrington supporters they lead by 1-0.*' Penny cheered out aloud before listening to the details, '*Yes,*' the voice continued, '*it was a good goal scored by the old campaigner, Alf Henning, after sixteen minutes. Sharrington defender, Tommy French, broke down a Prent Park attack, squared the ball to young Graham Hart who cleverly beat Saddler and Hurt in the home team defence before crossing to the near post where Henning glanced the ball sharply past the outstretched had of keeper Gannon.*'

The voice now seemingly more distant than before summarised the first half. '*Prent Park are once again failing to find the back of the net although they have had three clear chances to score. Home, the centre-forward has missed two easy chances, and Pilling, the number 10, had a good volley saved bravely by the visitors' keeper Hawkins, near the foot of the post   Sharrington have attacked down both flanks and caused the Prent Park full-backs many problems. Anyhow as the teams take to the field again there is still everything to play for – Ian Gilmarsh returning you to the studio.*'

Penny switched off the radio and watched the Saturday afternoon T.V. film before tuning in again for the full-time result. She only hoped Sharrington could hold on for a win. The forty-five minutes passed slowly for Penny, perhaps because she had looked at her watch every two minutes. Four forty finally arrived and Penny turned down the sound on the T.V. and switched on the radio again. A voice was already summarising the Beckham Town game. They had won easily by 4-1. Then came the report on the Treecliffe game at Rallingborough, one of last year's relegated teams from Division Three. The home team had won 1-0 by a late goal from Fanthom. Eventually the voice in the studio said, '*Now back to Ian Gilmarsh at Prent Park. Have Sharrington held on to that goal lead Ian?*'

Once again the line crackled and a delayed voice said, '*No,*' and paused. Penny slapped her hand against the settee arm in disappointment and then heard the voice say, '*they've added another and won 2-0.*' Penny's expression quickly changed to one of delight. The voice of Ian Gilmarsh went on, '*a deserved victory for Sharrington. They soaked up Prent Park's early second half pressure and then controlled the game from the sixty-eighth minute when a corner kick on the left taken by Chaddock was floated into the home team's penalty area. Henning was challenged by centre-half, Amberling, who had a nightmare of a game, but the ball was missed by both of them, it fell to the ground, bounced and rolled over the line and into the net between a bewildered goalkeeper, Gannon, and full-back, Hurt. Sharrington played some good football and were particularly hard in the tackle. Prent Park should really have sewn the game up in the first half and, on reflection, perhaps Sharrington were a little lucky not to have conceded a goal for the fourth time in five games.*' The voice became almost inaudible but Penny had heard all she wanted. Sharrington had won and she knew the result would make her husband happy. She switched off the radio and concentrated on the T.V. Film.

Chapter 29

At 10.00 a.m. on Sunday morning the queues gathered outside the Sharrington offices to buy tickets for the first leg of the local Derby cup game at Treecliffe on the following Wednesday. The number of people waiting appeared to be far in excess of the Sharrington ticket allocation of 6,000. There were 1,500 stand seats and 4,500 ground tickets. The press had predicted a sell out of 18,000 for the game.

Sid Parkin replaced the telephone receiver and shouted over to Peggy Hollingsworth, 'That was Jim Smart at Treecliffe. He says there are huge crowds waiting for tickets.'

'Did you tell him it's the same here?' said Peggy, as she busily sorted out the tickets at the window cash point.

'I've never seen so much interest for this club,' remarked Sid as he stared through the office window at the multitude of supporters.

'I know why Mr. Davidson gave us Friday afternoon off now, Sid,' said Peggy.

'Yes, we needed that rest because you can bet it'll be hard work for the next few hours.' Sid looked at his watch and the office clock. 'Ah well, better open the doors and get cracking.'

The orderly crowds filed in and for the next four and a half hours the stand and ground tickets were distributed to all different types of people. Approximately 20 tickets a minute were sold by six members of the office staff and exchanged for pound notes, silver, coppers and hastily written cheques. When the last ticket was finally purchased Sid counted over 200 people still waiting in the queue. A total amount of £7,125 had been collected and was quickly deposited in the office safe after three individual counts. This would mean the total receipts would be £21,375 for the first leg alone.

'It might not have been the best draw for Sharrington but the gate receipts for the two games should top £12,000,' mumbled Sid as he locked the safe door.

'That will be welcome money for the club, and who knows, Sid, we might beat Treecliffe and draw a top club in the next round,' replied Peggy as she poured hot water from the kettle into a teapot.

Sid looked tired and stretched his arms into the air and yawned, 'Can't honestly say I enjoy selling tickets to the fair-weather supporters, and if we do well on Wednesday night we will be repeating the process but on a larger scale next Sunday.'

'I don't know why you complain, Sid. We haven't had this much work to do for years and I for one prefer to see this club on the up. If it means working hard to get success then Mr. Davidson will achieve it. You have only to look at the expressions on the, players' faces after training to see that they're not used to putting so much effort into each session. He is making them all fit and you know over the last few years most of them have had an easy time. I think he will do well for the club.'

Sid interrupted Peggy as she poured tea into his special mug, 'Wait a minute, Peg. The man's only been here six weeks and whilst I would openly admit the changes he's made seem to be for the better there's an awful long way to go.' Sid slurped at his tea before continuing. 'Don't forget he's never managed a professional club before and he won't learn the job overnight. I think he will find it harder going than he thinks.'

'What about the results this season, Sid. We've not been beaten in the league this season and you're not telling me that's a fluke,' argued Peggy, quite forcibly.

'I'm not arguing with you, Peg. Let's just wait and see what happens,' slurped Sid.

'I wish you would have faith in him. He needs as much help and support as he can get, and really I don't think you've ever liked him have you?' shouted a red-faced Peggy.

'Not so loud, Peg. I think you've overworked yourself this morning. Let's finish our teas and get off home.'

'Humbug, Sid Parkin. You will not face up to a subject which doesn't suit you. I just wish you would realise we are all on the same side, and personally I think it shows in your attitude that you don't care for the ability of Mr. Davidson. I just couldn't believe your offhand remarks about his policy decisions only last week and while I'm on this matter don't you think you could…'

The office door opened. Peg and Sid looked round quickly. Sid spilled some of the tea down his sports jacket. Peg's mouth fell open as she uttered, 'Oh, Mr. Davidson we didn't expect you to come in today.'

Tony remained in the doorway, holding his left hand on the doorknob. He paused for a moment and said, 'No, I wasn't intending to come in but I heard, on the radio, that large queues were building up for tickets. Have we sold our allocation already?'

Sid continued to wipe the tea off his jacket as he replied, 'Yes, Mr. Davidson. It's all gone very smoothly. We've deposited over £7,000 in the safe and had to turn hundreds of people away.'

Peggy felt embarrassed for Sid. Tony smiled and said, 'Very good indeed. I just hope we can give the supporters something to cheer about on Wednesday.'

Tony stayed to talk for some twenty minutes or so before returning home.

'I wonder if he heard you,' groaned Sid as they watched Tony leave the car park.

'I don't know but, if he did, it could have only confirmed what he knew already,' snapped Peggy.

'Don't be silly, woman. It's all in your imagination. I don't mind the chap,' said Sid condescendingly.

'Humbug again, Sid Parkin. You're a hypocrite. I'm going home.' She snatched her coat and bag and without turning to say goodbye to Sid left the office. Sid sat on his own for a while, contemplating the possible consequences if Tony had heard their argument. He didn't dwell on it too long as the phone rang. Sid answered it. It was a message for Tony Davidson from Phil Wade, the manager of Woodville, asking him to phone him on Monday morning. Sid couldn't see the importance or relevance but left the message on Tony's desk before going home.

Monday was a bank holiday; therefore, as a reward for his team's efforts at Prent Park, on Saturday, Tony had given them the day off. Tony arrived early to clear up some paperwork before facing the local press at 11.00 a.m. and travelling to the afternoon League Cup tie at nearby Third Division Leston United who were playing against the new Fourth Division entrants, Warworth United. Tony saw the message to phone Phil Wade but left it until he cleared his outstanding paperwork. In between time he recorded a note of his chat with John Briggs so he could raise the question of making a written offer for Baynes at the next board meeting. The telephone rang frequently and before completing his morning's work Tony organised three daily coaching sessions for local junior players on the 12th, 13th and 14th September.

The interview with Grant Evans and David Cassidy of the local radio station was brief but straight to the point. Tony refused to predict a result and would not be drawn into naming his team. As the interview progressed they reported to Tony that Sam Dyson, the Treecliffe manager, had specified Treecliffe would win by such a sufficient amount in the first leg that he wouldn't be surprised if Tony phoned him to concede the return game and avoid embarrassment. Tony smiled, knowing the reputation of Sam Dyson and his much publicised verbal comments of the past. The uncanny thing about many of his seemingly outlandish remarks were that he was usually proved to have been right. Tony, however, didn't let this latest prediction worry him and remained perfectly calm. The only reference Tony would make was to the current league form of both clubs. He said, 'Whilst my team is still in the experimental stage we have been playing well, particularly in defence. I am happy with the players' application to the games we have played so far and fortunately we remain undefeated with only two goals conceded. I haven't had the opportunity to see Treecliffe this season but I don't think Sam Dyson can be satisfied with only four points and two defeats from the first five games.'

The two reporters eventually left Tony's office. Tony quickly telephoned Phil Wade at Woodville.

'Hello, Mr. Wade. Tony Davidson of Sharrington here. I understand you wanted me to get in touch with you.'

'Ah yes, Tony, I've got a bit of news for you. I've heard on the grapevine that Neil Baynes is unsettled at Storr, and although their Directors are not keen on selling him, they may be forced to in the near future, as I understand there have been personal disputes between the player and manager,' came the sharp voice of Phil Wade.

'What's the problem; do you know?' enquired Tony inquisitively.

'It seems the only problem is a clash of personalities and it appears the strain is affecting the other players. Knowing the club as I do, the directors will almost certainly support John Briggs and agree to the transfer of Baynes,' Phil Wade continued, without hesitating. 'Unfortunately, Tony, to be perfectly frank with you, there will be an awful lot of clubs after his signature and I don't think Sharrington will have enough money to compete. I am sure they will be looking for, well… err, £75,000 at least.'

Tony didn't answer straight away. 'Mmm,' he mused, 'it's a shame indeed. If that's the money they want there is no way Baynes will end up here. We cannot raise that amount in such a short time and I can't see the bank loaning it us either.'

'Ah well, don't worry, Tony, in all honesty I couldn't see him signing for a Fourth Division club at this stage in his career,' said Phil Wade.

'There was a chance, Phil, just a chance. You see we played at the same club many years ago at Sprannon Albion and, in those days, we got on very well indeed, so I was confident of persuading him,' replied Tony firmly.

'You will just have to see what your board of directors say and then wait for Storr's asking price,' remarked Phil Wade.

'Yes, Phil. I think you're right. Thanks for the information anyway,' said Tony replacing the receiver.

Tony quickly left his office to pick up Barrie Trippett and Jack Elliott, in his car, before driving to the Leston United v Warworth United cup game.

There was no particular interest in the game for Tony. He was just anxious to watch as many games as he could, to learn as much as he could. There was an interest for them however, as John Turner, the ex-Sharrington centre-forward, was playing for the visitors, Warworth United. Leston United were an ordinary Third Division team who obviously treated the game too casually. Warworth were sharper and more positive and finally deserved to share the four goals. Tony remarked to Barrie and Jack that he would be content with the same result on Wednesday night.

Chapter 30

The interest for attending the Treecliffe v Sharrington first leg cup-tie was mounting. Tony, Barrie, Sid, Peggy, all the players and directors were constantly being pestered by the general public of Sharrington for extra tickets to the game. The pre-match interest was also seen on the local T.V. programme and heard on both local and national radio shows. The game was being built up to a climax. The town and local area had never known a game involving Sharrington have so much media coverage. The local derby cup-tie had been discussed by all connected to the two clubs and also by others who only shared a passing interest in the game. Every aspect of the game had been aired, and in one quarter or another argued about furiously. Only the players now could prove the point.

The Sharrington team bus arrived in Treecliffe at 5.30 p.m. It was decided to have the pre-match meal at the Shepperson Hotel approximately half a mile from the Treecliffe ground, so the team would not be delayed in getting from Sharrington to their near neighbours' ground. At 5.00 p.m. when the coach left Sharrington the tension was building up within the town. Some supporters were getting prepared for the evening game. Coaches, cars, trains and public buses would all be making the six-mile trip. All 6,000 supporters would be travelling to Treecliffe over the teatime period.

After the light meal, the Sharrington party looked out of the restaurant room window to find an endless crowd of home and away team spectators pursuing the same destination towards the Treecliffe Football Ground. The match pressures for the Sharrington squad of players clearly showed in their facial expressions. Tony Davidson had particularly kept calm, although he had admitted to Jack Elliott over tea that he was more nervous today than he had been on the day of his interview. He had also purposefully delayed announcing the team for the game. However at 6.30 p.m. before the players boarded the bus for the journey to the ground Tony quickly announced his team selection. There was no fuss, no apologies or reasons, simply the name of the players. He read out:

1. Hawkins
2. Bond
3. Smith

4. Fisher
5. French
6. Holland
7. Hart
8. Cracknell
9. Henning
10. Docker
11. Chaddock
Sub: Poole

Yes, it was the same team which had played against Prent Park. On arrival at the ground, the Sharrington supporters were wishing their team all the best while the Treecliffe supporters were chanting taunting remarks. By coincidence the Treecliffe coach arrived at the same time as Sharrington's coach, consequently there was a certain amount of confusion amongst all the supporters. The crowds blocked the players' entrance and it took some ten to fifteen minutes before all the players and officials had arrived in the changing rooms. The players quickly inspected the pitch, to resounding cheers and boos. The voice over the public address system announced both teams. Treecliffe's team was also unchanged from the previous game: 1. Hemmingway, 2. Angel, 3. Collins, 4. Tyke, 5. Simpson, 6. Bell, 7. Outhroyd, 8. Hope, 9. Villers, 10. Mexiban, 11. Bass, Sub: Anderson.

The ground was compact and covered on each side. The stand catered for 4,000 and the ground for 14,000. Tickets had been allocated sensibly so that all the Sharrington supporters were behind the Main Road goal and the home supporters scattered in the other parts of the ground. Even the Sharrington stand-ticketholders were positioned at the end of the stand nearest their fellow supporters. The evening was fine and calm, and the evening sky was cloudy and rather dull. The pitch was wet from an earlier rainfall and the floodlights were switched on. The scene was now set, and the patient, well-behaved fans awaited the teams.

The team talks were over, the night's tactics rehearsed and as the final bell sounded the players were doing their last minute behind the scene exercises to release knotted muscles and nerves.

Treecliffe took to the pitch in their strip of yellow shirts and black shorts, Sharrington in red shirts and white shorts instead of their normal black shorts. The atmosphere was typical of a local derby but there seemed to be an extra excitement in view of the game being a cup-tie. Simpson, the Treecliffe captain, won the toss and decided to kick towards the home supporters end in the first half. The teams changed ends at 7.30

p.m. Alf Henning kicked off at the sound of referee, Bill McLeod's, whistle. The tension within the ground was unlike any previous fixture between these two teams. There was a distinct silence but a feeling of partisan conflict. The lights in the stand went off in sequence and the game commenced at last.

Alf Henning's pass had no sooner got to the feet of Simon Docker when Bob Villers, the home side's centre-forward, chased frantically to dispossess him of the ball with a blatant body charge. Docker hit the ground and Villers bludgeoned his way down the pitch like a marauding pirate, skittling Fisher and Holland in a similar manner. Treecliffe's tactics were clear and Villers was particularly renown for his somewhat crude physical contact. However, the amazing point of interest was that the referee only blew for a foul after Villers' final rough tackle on young Steve Holland. The silence in the crowd turned to a raucous noise within seconds. The game was no more than thirty seconds old before both trainers were on the pitch attending to two Sharrington players, Fisher and Holland. The former was holding his right shoulder and the latter clutching his left ankle.

'Disgusting!' stormed Eddie Flannagan, 'I knew we would have problems with this referee. Three blatant fouls, two men injured and he only blows for one foul. If this is the way Treecliffe are intending to play the game tonight we will be lucky to field a fit team for the second leg.'

'He's not even taken Villers name, or for that matter, spoken to him about the incident,' echoed Bill Boothroyd, as he slapped his rolled up programme on his knee in an effort to press home his point.

The crowd was buzzing with excitement at the incident, during which time the two injured players were finally getting back onto their feet. Fisher was moving his injured shoulder in the air, like a spin bowler, and young Steve Holland was hobbling quite badly and judging from his grimace was in obvious pain. The game had been held up for three minutes. The crowd were now showing their impatience.

Tony Davidson finally ran out of the dugout and onto the pitch to learn of the seriousness of Holland's injury. The home section of the crowd was quick to make some snide comments, which were followed by outbursts of laughter. The referee now insisted Holland should be helped off the pitch.

'I think it's too serious for the lad to continue, Tony,' said Barrie as he pushed the pain-relieving spraycan back into his first-aid bag.

'How do you feel, Steve?' enquire Tony. 'Oh, it's bad boss. I can't put any weight onto it,' replied Holland. 'Maybe the tendon. Better put Graham on, Barrie,' stressed Tony.

In the meantime referee McLeod restarted the game. Allan Smith purposefully dawdled with the free kick to give Graham Poole time to strip off the tracksuit. He was warned by McLeod but after some further ten frustrating seconds he was booked, to his amazement. Tommy French was quick to remonstrate with McLeod and although Graham Bond attempted to pull him away the referee also booked French as well. By this time the crowd was acting wildly. The game was only four minutes old, and thirty seconds of play had been witnessed, one player was off the pitch injured, the substitute was ready to come on and two Sharrington players had been booked by referee McLeod.

'Utterly disgraceful. The man's nothing but a buffoon,' cried Flannagan as he rose to his feet in anger.

'Easy, Eddie,' shouted Steve King trying to make himself heard above the screaming crowd.

'But the man's hopeless, Steve. I just knew something like this would happen,' said Flannagan descending to his seat.

Graham Poole ran onto the field after receiving his playing instructions from Tony. Poole automatically went straight into the number six position vacated by young Steve Holland. The free kick was finally taken amid the chanting of the crowd. Steve Holland was helped to the dressing room by Barrie Trippett.

The game continued at a fierce competitive pace with both teams fouling quite blatantly at times. In the twenty fifth minute with the score still 0-0, Collins of Treecliffe and Paul Cracknell were both booked after a fracas on the right wing. As a result of the free kick from Graham Hart, Simon Docker drove the ball against the hand of Simpson in the home team penalty area. The Sharrington players demanded a penalty but McLeod waved away their protests as Treecliffe defenders cleared the danger. Tony Davidson put his head into his hands and shook it slowly from side to side. Steve King remonstrated with a Treecliffe director. Eddie Flannagan simply kept mumbling "Disgusting." Bill Boothroyd aimlessly shook his weakly clenched fists in the air.

With ten minutes remaining, Sharrington's attack developed down the left hand wing and a slip by Angel, the home team full-back put Sammy Chaddock clear with only goalkeeper Hemmingway to beat. He cleverly controlled the ball, took it into his stride and chipped it firmly over the sprawling keeper only to watch the ball fall onto the crossbar and out for a goal kick.

Sharrington were playing well but totally against the run of play and with only four minutes to play before half-time Treecliffe's right winger Outhroyd rounded Allan Smith, crossed the greasy ball into the visitor's penalty area, and watched Tommy French clear the danger with his head, but then to his own amazement he saw Jimmy Hope, volley the clearance through the crowded area and low into the net. Alan Hawkins never moved. The goal was an excellent one. The home crowd became ecstatic. At half-time the score was Treecliffe 1 - Sharrington 0. As the teams trudged off the clouds which had gathered over the ground suddenly produced a heavy rainfall.

Tony tried to settle his players down and raise their confidence after the goal out of the blue.

'Well played, lads. Now sit down and take a cup of tea. I've got no arguments on your play so far. The bookings were unfortunate but in your case, Tommy, you will learn that there is absolutely no benefit in arguing with referees. Admittedly he has made some weird decisions tonight but we cannot control his actions and we must learn to play to the decisions he gives, however unjust they may be. I know its hard work out there but believe me if we are going to achieve anything over the next few years you will experience much harder games. Stick to our plan for the second half and keep it tight. If we cannot penetrate their defence I will settle for 1-0. Now come on lads, try and keep calm but be positive.' Tony slapped each player on the back before they left the dressing room. 'Best of luck, lads. Just keep it going.'

Before Tony left himself, he enquired about Steve Holland. 'How's it feel now, Steve?'

'It's still sore, boss,' replied Holland now sitting on the treatment table in the centre of the dressing room.

'We had better get Dr. Ericson to check it first thing tomorrow morning, Barrie. Right, Steve, get bathed and changed,' said Tony as he and Barrie left the dressing room.

Just as they settled down in the dugout the game restarted. Quite evidently both teams were just as hard in the challenge for possession and the Treecliffe captain, Simpson, was booked for a late tackle on Alf Henning after ten minutes. Suddenly the wet conditions seemed to favour Treecliffe. They were passing more accurately and moving quicker to the loose ball. As the rain persisted the pressure on the Sharrington's rearranged defence began to tell. The home crowd got behind their team and the one goal advantage was stretched to two in the seventy-third minute. Bob Villers, the marauding Treecliffe centre-forward, was the scorer. He latched on to a bad pass by captain Graham Bond, raced towards the Sharrington goal and forcefully kicked the bouncing ball passed Alan Hawkins into the roof of the net. The Treecliffe players jumped up and down in delight. The home supporters did likewise. They knew that the second goal would destroy Sharrington's chances of progressing any further in this competition.

Tony and Barrie looked disconsolate and the Sharrington supporters were stood and sat in complete silence whilst all around them was chaotic with jubilation. Graham Bond, to his credit, did not let his head drop as a result of his own error. He made every effort to try and lift his colleagues for the remainder of the game. For a brief spell Sharrington did counter attack and create one good chance after excellent work by Steve Fisher but unfortunately Paul Cracknell slipped down just before touching the ball into the open goal. The opportunity had gone and Tyke cleared for Treecliffe.

With the home team supporters chanting their team's advantage, a harsh decision by referee McLeod led to a third goal for Treecliffe. He awarded a direct free kick for obstruction against Mexiban by Graham Poole. Before the Sharrington defence had had time to form a wall, Villers blasted the stationary ball, which struck Tommy French on the shoulder and deflected it passed Alan Hawkins into the empty goal. The goalkeeper could do nothing about any of the goals. The yellow-shirted players congregated in excitement around Bob Villers. Even a dozen supporters ran onto the pitch to show their delight. The Treecliffe spectators were delirious. Treecliffe were in a strong position for the second leg. Sharrington had been unlucky. The game finally ended at 9.20 p.m, some ten minutes later than it should have done due to injuries, bookings and time wasting. It had certainly been an exciting match but the result didn't reflect the true state in the ability of the two local teams. The return match should now only be a formality for Treecliffe.

As Tony left the pitch the thought which immediately came to mind was Sam Dyson, the Treecliffe manager's, pre-match prediction that his side would win so easily that the return game should be cancelled to avoid Tony's embarrassment. Tony knew a 3-0 deficit was a difficult obstacle for his team to overcome for a place in the second leg. Although the score line was not a true reflection of the game it would go down as the thrashing he had anticipated for his team.

The Sharrington dressing room was in total silence by the time Tony arrived there. The jubilation from the Treecliffe dressing room was sickening for the visiting players and officials. Tony knew he could only offer his sympathy, particularly as his team had worked hard but hadn't had their share of the luck. The after-match comments were therefore laconic. Tony left the players to congratulate Sam Dyson and his team. He then joined his directors before making the return journey to Sharrington. His only comments to the press were, 'We were terribly unlucky and will fight to the end.' The bottom had just been blow out of Sharrington's good start to the season. Sharrington needed to win the second leg to prove so many things to so many people.

'How on earth will we ever live that down?' questioned Bob Bennett from the rear of Frank Sneddon's car.

There was a silence. Neither Frank nor Eddie answered him.

'Come on, lads, speak to me, please. What went wrong tonight?' enquired Bob for a second time.

'Oh shut up worrying, Bob,' shouted Eddie as he pulled off his red and black bobcap to reveal his unruly hair.

'Let's face it, fellows, we were desperately unlucky,' commented Frank in his normal amiable manner. 'For a start Chaddock was unlucky not put us one up with that lob in the first half and who knows, if Steve Holland hadn't had to leave the game so early on, the defence may have held out.'

'I know all that, Frank,' snorted Bob. 'The thing is, how will we live a 3-0 defeat to Treecliffe down.'

'I don't know what you're so bothered about, Bob, we don't usually win at Treecliffe. In fact we have never beaten them at all in the history of the club,' stated Frank, as he carefully drove around the supporters on the main road.

'May be so, Frank, but 3-0 is pretty convincing for the first leg of a cup-tie. What hope have we of qualifying to the second round now,' said a disconsolate Bob Bennett.

'Who knows, Bob,' shouted Eddie, 'it's a daft game, football, and if the luck runs for us in the second leg maybe we will put three past Treecliffe; although, having said that, I can't honestly see it somehow.'

'We can only wait and see what happens next Wednesday,' reflected Frank as he finally drove out of the crowds and onto the road to Sharrington.

The three men made for the Village Arms to discuss the game in more detail.

Tony finally arrived home at 11.15 p.m. to the condolences of his wife, Penny, who had heard the result on the local radio station.

'We were unlucky, love, but credit to Treecliffe, they took their chances just at the right time,' remarked Tony, as he poured a bottle of milk into a glass.

'I'm sorry, dear,' said Penny sympathetically. 'I know just how badly you wanted to do well against Treecliffe.'

'Yeah, it was a night of tragic events. We had four players injured, three booked, some bad referee decisions against us, and to cap it all, the hardest core of Sharrington's spectators witnessed it all and suffered an embarrassment to their greatest rivals. I'll tell you what, Penny, this is a game where a manager can never be complacent or honestly admit to himself that his best will be good enough for the club he represents.'

Eddie Flannagan arrived home, walked straight upstairs, drank two stiff whiskies and fell asleep without speaking to his wife. Dolly, his good lady, assumed Sharrington had been defeated.

The gloom had returned to Sharrington F.C.

Chapter 31

'SHARRINGTON TAKE THE FIRST STEP OUT OF LEAGUE CUP' - *Daily Sport*. 'TREECLIFFE'S TREMENDOUS TRIUMPH'   - *Daily Globe*. 'LOCAL DERBY WITH A ONE-WAY TICKET' - *The Ace*. 'SHARRINGTON HAVE NO ANSWER TO VILLERS' - *Daily Eagle*.

These were some of the newspaper headlines on Thursday morning. The salt had been deeply printed into the Wednesday night wound as all those connected to Sharrington F.C. knew it would be. To be fair to Sharrington, all the newspapers categorically stated that the result was not due to a poor team performance but to bad luck on the night. The most annoying article was from *The Daily Sketch,* which virtually reported the game with the words of manager Sam Dyson who was his usual forthright self. Dyson was gloating over his team's 3-0 victory and suggesting the game went exactly to plan.

When other newspapers contacted Tony for his comments on the match he refused to be drawn into any verbal battles with Sam Dyson. He would only reiterate that the cup tie was not yet over and that Sharrington would hope to strike early in the return game to offset the three goal margin which would put the pressure on Treecliffe.

In the lunch time edition of the *Sharrington Echo,* Grant Evans had chosen the headlines of 'The First Defeat of the season is the one which hurt Sharrington.' He followed the headline up with a comprehensive report on the incidents of the match. He was most ruthless with some of the decisions made by referee, McLeod, and supported his arguments with sound reasoning. He concluded by stressing the importance of local support for Sharrington in the return game and how he would dearly love to see a resounding victory next Wednesday over the Treecliffe team to balance out the differences once and for all.

The players arrived at the ground at 12.30 p.m. for a team talk and treatment on any injuries. In addition to Steve Holland's bruised tendon, Simon Docker had a pulled muscle in his right thigh, Allan Smith, a bruised toe on his left foot, and Sammy Chaddock had a badly cut right knee, which required three stitches. All men were doubtful for Saturday's league game at home against Low Grove.

Once again Tony quickly skimmed over the Treecliffe game without making any scathing attacks on individuals. He knew they had all played to the best of their ability. The players looked tired and downhearted. He motivated their egos somewhat by discussing the good parts from the cup game before allowing them to go home at 2.30 p.m. They were told to report for training on Friday at 10.30 a.m.

Tony turned to Barrie, who was tidying up the first aid equipment, and said, 'We have definitely got a few serious injury problems for Saturday so I want us to give it a little thought now just in case we are faced with four absentees.'

'Yes, good idea, Tony, because to be quite honest I think Allan Smith will be fit enough to play on Saturday,' replied Barrie.

'Well if that's the state of affairs we will be well and truly struggling against a team of the calibre of Low Grove. Having said that I note that they only drew 1-1 against Holydice in the cup last night so perhaps they may be going through a bad patch after their good start to the season,' stated Tony optimistically.

The two men provisionally picked the following team, should the three injured players Barrie mentioned be unable to pass fitness tests before Saturday:

1. Hawkins
2. Bond (Captain)
3. Smith
4. Fisher
5. French
6. Thomas
7. Hart
8. Cracknell
9. Henning
10. Poole
11. White
Sub: 12. ? (the fitter of the three injured players or reserve goalkeeper Bates)

Tony looked down at the list of names and said in despair, 'There's no other option open to me, Barrie. I will have to get into the wheeling and dealings of the transfer market again and make every effort to buy three more players to strengthen our squad; although, I may have to sell one man to afford the three players the club requires.'

'What do you mean, Tony?' enquired Barrie.

'Simply this, Barrie. We have only 12 professional players and three part-time professionals. In the circumstances we now find ourselves in, we cannot name a full team and a fit substitute for our next league game. It is not good enough for a club who are out to gain a place in the top part of the division. I've given it quite a bit of thought recently, Barrie,' continued Tony, as he placed the team sheet in his inside pocket, 'and, entirely off the record, I've had an offer from a Second Division club for…' he paused. 'Guess who, Barrie.'

Barrie looked surprised at this information and studied momentarily. 'I've no idea, Tony. Who?' said Barrie.

'Would you believe: Steve Fisher,' answered Tony, slyly. 'Steve!' exclaimed Barrie. 'Yes, I got an offer in writing from the Second Division team Andlerstone United at £30,000,' commented Tony.

'But he's worth more than that Tony. He's played well this season and has been the most consistent player. I would have thought you would be wise to keep Steve, Tony,' insisted Barrie.

'I agree the offer is ridiculously low for a player of Steve's calibre, but if I could get £50,000 for him, I think I could use the money to replace him with at least two useful players,' mused Tony.

'Who have you in mind, Tony?' enquired Barrie, looking somewhat bemused.

'Number one would be a cash offer of £50,000 for Neil Baynes and number two would be £10,000 to £20,000 for young Micky Leighton, the reserve wing half with Blackway, in Division Two,' said Tony, confidently.

'When have you seen Leighton, Tony?'

'I knew that would be your next question, Barrie. Tell me, do you remember about four years ago when Baynes was at Trandon Rovers and scoring an awful lot of goals?'

Barrie thought for a moment and then nodded.

'Well, do you also remember a curly-haired youth who was in the same team and played a similar game to Baynes?' Once again Barrie contemplated the question and nodded.

'Good. Baynes was transferred to Storr and the curly-haired youth to Blackway within the space of two weeks and then the goals dried up for Trandon. The curly-haired lad was young Leighton.'

'Oh yes, of course. I'd forgotten all about him,' stressed Barrie.

'Exactly, and so have many others. Baynes and Leighton used to play very well together and in fact I sent Jack Elliott to watch Leighton play last week. The report on him was good. I also heard a decent report on Leighton from Phil Wade, the Woodville Manager, only the other week,' explained Tony.

'I can see what you are driving at, Tony, and if you could bring both these players back together again, who knows, they may do for Sharrington what they did for Trandon Rovers. But, to be honest, I can't see you pushing Alderstone United up to £50,000 for Fisher,' reflected

Barrie, now sitting down after completing his duties.

'I agree there is much wheeling and dealing to be done, but you can take it from me I will refuse to release Steve Fisher for less than a realistic figure.'

'Have you anyone else in mind?' enquired Barrie.

'Only a full-back at the moment. As you know we have only two full-backs at the present time and a serious injury to one of them would mean we would require a replacement immediately.'

'Who's the player you have in mind?'

'Another youngster, Barrie. Do you recall Paul Brooke the Leston United right full-back in their game against Warworth on Monday?' Barrie nodded. 'I thought he played well and I liked his style of play particularly.'

'Yes, he worked hard and stood out with some fine tackles.'

'Mmm, his tackling was positive, but I'd like to see him play again before jumping in with an offer,' said Tony.

'Do you suppose he'd be for sale?' asked Barrie.

'Again, Barrie, I don't know at this stage, but I'd like you take in their return game at Warworth next week and make a few subtle enquiries,' stressed Tony.

'The only problem is he is a right full-back and so is our club captain. Would a new signing suggest there is no room for Bondy?' quizzed Barrie.

'My main concern is getting cover for the full-back position. It will add to the competitive spirit of playing for a place in the team and hopefully for the money we can afford he is the best player for that position that I've seen and is realistically available for our club.'

The two men left the dressing room still discussing the transfer situations open to Sharrington.

Chapter 32

Barrie Trippett's prediction on the injury situation had been confirmed. Only Allan Smith passed a fitness test on the morning of the league match. The team was announced as the one earlier selected by Tony and Barrie. The substitute was Bates.

Low Grove were Sharrington's visitors. Although they had finished in fourteenth position last season, one place below Sharrington, their early form had been impressive. They were undefeated after five games, three of which had been draws, and two, victories. The previous Saturday they had beaten the exciting Seamingway team in a home game 3-2 but had faltered in midweek in their cup game against Holydice-on-Sea, a team Tony and Barrie had witnessed them beat convincingly in the second league match of the season. Low Grove manager Paul Taylor had introduced a youth policy to the club three years ago and the results were now taking shape. It was not going to be an easy game for the depleted and dejected Sharrington team.

The somewhat fickle Sharrington supporters had seemingly rejected the team after the embarrassment from the result in the local derby. The terracing was thinly populated. The visiting supporters were gathered in large numbers behind the bottom end goal. The attendance of 5,630 was over 2,000 down on the last home match. The weather was bright and humid and the flags on the roof of the stand were motionless.

Low Grove, kitted in all light blue, were first out onto the pitch. They looked a young, fit and confident team. Their supporters greeted them wildly. Sharrington players ran out onto the field to a mild murmur from the crowd. If a stranger had been in the ground not knowing which team was which he would have guessed that Low Grove were the home side. Sharrington had won last season's fixture but the odds today seemed to be stacked against them.

Tony had made every effort to motivate his fit eleven players to maintain their unbeaten league record. He had cajoled them by highlighting the strong points from their game against Treecliffe and the other games during the season. He particularly stressed that this was a character-testing time as, in view of the injuries, they were entering the stage where the better teams of the league were all coming at once and squashed in between was the return game against Treecliffe. Tony made the point that they must all pull together as a result of these difficulties.

Within seven minutes of the first half the much more confidant Low

Grove team were leading 1-0. Sharrington were caught too square in defence and Udderholm, the visitors' inside-forward had sprinted through into a good position to easily beat Alan Hawkins. After twenty minutes the Low Grove forwards had mesmerised the Sharrington defence only to see their efforts either judged to be offside or miss the goal by inches. Tony, who was sat in the dugout, was quiet thinking of a way in which to offset the visitors' superiority. Suddenly, after a brief consultation with Barrie Trippett he issued instructions to Graham Bond for more aggression amongst the team. He also brought Alf Henning back in defence to help stamp a bit of his experience on the game and put the Low Grove forwards out of their stride. Tony White was moved from outside-left to centre-forward to harass the opposition. The tactics worked successfully almost immediately and although Sharrington still trailed 0-1 at half-time they had gradually worked their way into the game with one or two narrowly missed chances.

Tony realising the possibility of getting a result from the game looked down upon his weary players with great enthusiasm. 'Much better lads. The effort has been good. We can get two points today. You're all pulling together now. Alf, I want you back up front playing alongside Tony. Graham, I want you to be the extra man in defence for the first ten to twenty minutes depending how it goes. Play it hard. Let's take the game to them now, lads, and don't give them a chance to settle in the second half. I want to see some character from you all now. Come on, lads, let's push it up an extra gear.'

The players were lifted by Tony's half-time speech and left the dressing room with revitalised determination. The evidence of the team talk was clear to the spectators. Sharrington challenged for possession on every occasion and slowly they were taking control of the game. Alf Henning was masterful in the air and young Tony White in his first league match was impishly distracting the Low Grove defence with his ceaseless running and challenging.

After seventy-six minutes Sharrington were on level terms. The constant attacks finally wore down the Low Grove defence. The move was started at the back by Steve Fisher and worked forward by Paul Cracknell. He drew the Low Grove midfield of Lennon and Williams before passing the ball accurately to Allan Smith who was overlapping on the left wing. Smith took the ball in his stride, side stepped two challengers before firing the ball hard and low from twenty yards around Ellison in the visitors' goal. There was great delight amongst the home supporters but tragically it was ruined by an opportunist goal from Bridge, the Low Grove right-winger, with only six minutes of the game remaining. He beat French, Thomas and Smith cleverly in the space of four yards, dribbled into the penalty area and stabbed his shot with the outside of his left boot. The ball ran awkwardly past Hawkins' outstretched fingers, onto the far post and spun agonisingly, for the Sharrington team and supporters, slowly over the line. That goal destroyed Sharrington and the end result was a defeat by 2-1. It was another undeserved result for an unlucky Sharrington. The outcome, however, was their first league defeat, but another performance of fighting spirit and effort.

Tony had admired the way in which his team had played. He was unhappy that they had not held on for a point but he could see the steady improvement in his squad of players from game to game. He was undeterred about criticism that came his way from the small band of hecklers in the crowd. He could see his players developing to the style to which he was guiding and training them and he knew that if he was given the opportunity to see out at least one season with the club then the results and performances would surely come good in the end.

Chapter 33

Treecliffe had defeated Harloft 2-1 in their league game and moved within one point of Sharrington. In view of the first leg result and both teams' respective last league results it was decided not to make the second leg game an all ticket affair. The attendance was not expected to be high and Grant Evans had suggested there would be more Treecliffe supporters than Sharrington fans on Wednesday evening. Sam Dyson was quoted as saying, 'Well if the Football League insist upon the second leg being played we might as well prove the first result wasn't a fluke.' Tony Davidson was unconcerned. All he would say to the press was, 'This is a classic situation where everyone expects us to be dead and buried. I really believe if we can get a couple of early goals then Treecliffe will have their work cut out in keeping us out of the next round. Don't forget if the aggregate score is level at full time there is extra time and we must surely put this to our advantage being on our home ground.' Both men had done all they could to promote an interest for this return game, bearing in mind the 3-0 score line from the first leg.

Barrie Trippett had witnessed Warworth dispose of Leston United 3-0 in the second leg on Monday evening. He made the reason for his visit known to the Third Division club's manager, Jim Freeman. The latter was annoyed at his team's exit, from the League Cup, especially to the new league club Warworth and by such a convincing defeat. Young Paul Brooke had again played well and Freeman told Barrie to put any offer in writing but he stressed the directors would be unwilling to release him unless the offer would help to remove Leston's deficit to the bank. Barrie knew Sharrington's offer would not be the figure Leston had in mind. He did not commit Sharrington in any way but left saying he would report to Tony Davidson, as Freeman was certainly not in a mood for discussing the matter in detail. Barrie did report to Tony accordingly.

Only Sammy Chaddock was fit enough to add to the squad of players for the return game against Treecliffe. Tony Davidson decided to drop Graham Poole to substitute, replace Sammy Chaddock to the left wing and brought young Tony White to inside-left. Otherwise the team from the previous Saturday was unchanged. Grant Evans' suggestion that the visiting side would be better supported than the home team was proved to be correct. The attendance, for the 6.45 p.m. kick-off, was 9,500, of which some 5,000 plus appeared to be in the colours of Treecliffe. The evening was cool and dry but the pitch was still damp from the weekend rain. The Treecliffe team were unchanged from their last four games. The referee this time was Alex Maddon of Beckham, who was not as controversial a figure as Bill McLeod.

The game started just as sensationally as the first leg at Treecliffe had done. Alf Henning had kicked off but instead of to either Cracknell or White he found Graham Hart on the right wing. Hart was quickly into his stride and passed Bell and Collin with two neat body swerves. At the edge of the penalty area, with Cracknell in support, he played a one-two with him and struck the ball through the crowded goalmouth. With the Treecliffe defence running towards their own goal the low cross caught Geoff Tyke on the right foot and flew into the corner of the net to put Sharrington 1-0 in the lead within the first forty seconds. The few home supporters were soon chanting their team's name with great excitement.

'That's one back already, Tony. That's fantastic,' shouted Barrie jumping up from the dugout. Tony smiled but remained calm.

'Well I'll be blowed. What a start for us,' murmured Bill Boothroyd, who was sitting in the directors' box in the stand.

'Hooray! Come on lads, let's give them what for,' shouted Eddie Flannagan, who was stood up trying to antagonise Sam Dyson in the visitors' directors' box.

No sooner had the pandemonium calmed down than Treecliffe restarted the game and attacked down the centre of the field. Jimmy Hope cleverly evaded a lunging tackle from Mike Thomas but the ball ran away from him and out of play. As the players waited for the ball to be returned into play, referee Maddon, ran into the area and pointed to the penalty spot. The Sharrington players were dumbfounded. The Treecliffe supporters jumped up and down wildly.

'Would you believe it?' screamed Steve King throwing his programme on the floor.

'Not a penalty, surely,' whimpered Bill Boothroyd. Eddie Flannagan was transfixed with shock.

Sam Dyson stood up and caught Flannagan's stare before shouting, 'You're not back in this game yet, Eddie, so calm down old man.' Flannagan remained standing with a vacant expression on his face.

Angel scored from the penalty kick. The score was 1-1 after only five minutes, and 4-1 on aggregate to Treecliffe.

The game went from end to end with exciting incidents in each goalmouth but the score remained 1-1 at half-time. The players trudged off to a great reception from the crowd.

'Well played, lads,' said Tony encouragingly as the players sat down around him. 'It was a shame Maddon thought your tackle was unfair,

Mike. I can think of some referees who would have just got on with the game. Anyhow, let's keep on playing the way we have been and I'm sure the goals will come.'

All the players discussed the game with Tony and Barrie before leaving the changing room for the second half.

Treecliffe played defensively straight from the re-start and Sharrington tried everything within their attacking capabilities to break them down. With twenty minutes remaining Tony substituted Paul Cracknell for Graham Poole as he felt the youngster was tiring rapidly as the game progressed. The change certainly gave Sharrington the advantage. Within seven minutes Poole started a move which ended with Graham Hart crossing high to the far post and Alf Henning heading hard passed Hemmingway in the Treecliffe goal. Sharrington led 2-1.

The action was still restricted to an endless stream of Sharrington attacks. The Treecliffe players did not venture into the home team's defence. They appeared to be content with their two-goal advantage on aggregate. When Sharrington added their second goal there was only thirteen minutes remaining and time was quickly running out for them. The Sharrington crowd was right behind their team but the Treecliffe supporters were quiet and checking their watches anxiously. Sharrington were playing well as a team by working hard for each other, running sensibly into free positions for passes and giving encouragement.

From a throw in on the left by Allan Smith to Tony White the ball was played back to the full-back who chipped it to Sammy Chaddock. The winger stylishly dribbled passed Angel, the visitors' full-back and penalty scorer, before laying the ball back into the path of Tony White who shot on target only to see Hemmingway palm the ball away into the six-yard box. No sooner did the ball bounce than Alf Henning moved his burly frame in between two defenders to side foot it over the goal line to make the score Sharrington 3 v Treecliffe 1. The aggregate difference was now only one goal with four minutes remaining.

'Come on, lads, stick another one in,' yelled the red faced Eddie Flannagan.

'You can do it, Sharrington,' cheered Bill Boothroyd.

'Let's get rid of these Treecliffe fellows once and for all,' sang Flannagan in the direction of the silently seated body of Sam Dyson who was now clasping his hands together so tightly his knuckles were white.

The Sharrington team were quickly back into their positions waiting eagerly for the Treecliffe centre-forward, Villers, who had had a surprisingly subdued game, to restart the game. The referee waved to Villers and demanded he kicked the ball without any further delay. Villers stalled even longer and was booked for his trouble. By this time the initiative had been taken away from the anxious Sharrington players. The focus was directed upon Villers by the section of Sharrington supporters. When the ball was eventually kicked by Villers, his gamesmanship, although far from sporting, had thrown the young Sharrington players off the main objective of scoring another goal. As soon as the referee's back was turned Alf Henning collided with Villers leaving him prostrate on the floor. The commotion from the visiting supporters drowned the noise of the home spectators but the referee failed to take any notice. The linesman waved his red flag furiously but all to no avail.

Treecliffe played a time wasting game when they had possession of the ball and after one or two anxious moments in their defence their final relief came when referee Maddon blew shrilly on his whistle to end the game and cup tie between the two local teams. Treecliffe had won 4-3 on aggregate, but it had not been as easy for them as they had thought. The Sharrington team had redeemed themselves and were unlucky not to force Treecliffe into extra time and a possible replay. However, Sharrington failed to qualify into the second round of the League Cup again; although, admittedly this was the nearest they had ever been to reaching the next round. If the disappointment of losing on aggregate to their near neighbours was not enough for the Sharrington club they had to travel some 370 miles to play the league leaders Seamingway in two days time for the important league game on Saturday.

Chapter 34

At the weekly board meeting, on the Thursday evening, all were present with the exception of Steve King who was bedridden with flu. The Treecliffe games were discussed and also the home league match against Low Grove. It was agreed the team had been unfortunate not to qualify to the second round of the League Cup. All the directors had stated how impressed they had been in seeing Sharrington beat Treecliffe for the first time. After everyone had aired their views on the local League Cup derby, Tony got to his feet to change the subject.

'Gentlemen, as you are all aware last Saturday I only had 12 players available to select a team to play Low Grove and one of those was young part-time goalkeeper, Alan Bates. Admittedly, we had three injuries after the first game at Treecliffe but it could so easily have been four. Hopefully, this bad luck will not continue but I must stress the urgency to sign some more useful players.' Tony paused before continuing, 'I do have three players in mind. They are Neil Baynes of Storr Town, inside-forward, who is available I understand at around £60,000, an ex-colleague of Baynes, Mick Leighton of Blackway, wing-half at around £25,000 and finally a young full-back, Paul Brooke, of Leston United, who I would assess at £30,000. Obviously, gentlemen, that is a great amount of money but one consolation is I have had an increased offer of £45,000 for Steve Fisher from Andlerstone United. I should be grateful if we could discuss this situation.' Tony then sat down not knowing really what to expect from his directors. First to talk was, as usual, Eddie Flannagan.

'Tony, you have done well for Sharrington in the two months you've been manager here, but, from what I've seen of the players currently in your squad, I personally feel the three players, of the calibre you mentioned, are not essential at this moment in time for us,' said a sober-faced Eddie Flannagan. 'Can't you find any players at lower transfer fees who will do a good job over a shorter period of time?'

'I take your point, Mr. Flannagan, but whilst I would gladly do as you suggest I feel it would be economical for the club to sign the three players now,' remarked Tony confidently.

'But, Tony, we are talking about an outlay of £115,000, at the least, with an income from any future transfer of Steve Fisher of only £45,000. Surely a loss of £60,000 would be frowned upon by the bank although our current deficit with them is down from a pre-season figure of £50,000 to £13,000. A total of £73,000 owing to the bank is really not on and I will not agree to giving you the go-ahead to sign these three players. I must also point out that Steve Fisher is playing well enough to help put this club up the league and is possibly as good a player as one of the men you want to sign,' commented Eddie Flannagan quite bluntly.

Tony sat calmly biting his bottom lip awaiting the most predictable Bill Boothroyd and without too much delay he heard Boothroyd stand up to say, 'I must agree with Mr. Flannagan, Tony. We can't be in debt to the bank by that much money. I'm sorry, I cannot agree to your move into the transfer market for these three players.'

Tony still sat motionless. Chairman Jack Elliot finally stood up to summarise. 'Thank you, gentlemen. Well, Tony, without Steve King it is difficult to say if he would have agreed with you or not but personally as the casting vote I would agree with Eddie and Bill. I do not feel we can put the club to that expense at this moment in time.' Jack looked up and caught the eye of Tony before continuing. 'Tell me, Tony, can't you go for young Brooke now, keep Fisher and see what transpires as the season develops.'

There was a silence around the room. Barrie Trippett looked at Tony for his reaction to the board's refusal. Before Tony could speak Eddie Flannagan got to his feet again. 'Good point, Jack. I'd go along with that suggestion. We only have two full-backs and this youngster Brooke sounds a good lad. He would be good cover for us and a fine prospect for the future. If you can get him for £30,000, Tony, I would O.K. that.' Eddie smiled. 'After all, Tony, this is the first refusal you've had from the Board, and in your first season as football manager you've responded tremendously to the faith we put in you, so don't take it too bad. I know your heart's in the club but I am sure deep down you know we couldn't approve the three transfers.'

Eddie nodded towards Tony as if to say 'there's no hard feelings, it was worth a try but I will prevent you from running before you can walk.' Tony acknowledged Eddie Flannagan's words and held his right hand aloft as he finally said, 'All right, gentlemen, I can appreciate your reluctance to my proposals and you are right, Mr. Flannagan, this is the first time you've all gone against me. I accept a deficit to the bank of some £70,000 may be too big a burden for the club to carry but I know how valuable Baynes and Leighton would be for Sharrington. I am so sure I could get both their signatures and in fact if I cannot sign them soon it could mean the difference between promotion this season and another one or two seasons in Division Four.' The directors and Barrie sat patiently as Tony continued, 'I do not mean to pressurise you into reconsidering your decision but if I do not act quickly I am certain

Baynes will have joined another club within the next two weeks and he is just the player this club needs.' Tony looked determined to get the directors' O.K. He didn't wait for anyone to speak, 'As for Leighton he would be a snip at £25,000 and the perfect playing partner for Baynes. They are both excellent footballers with good habits and ideal for the future success of Sharrington.' Flannagan opened his mouth to speak but Tony raised his voice louder and spoke quicker to avoid the interruption. 'Steve Fisher is not a bad player and I agree he has done well this season but I would rather give him the opportunity of playing Second Division football and replace him with Micky Leighton, who is in my opinion a more versatile player, and, don't forget gentlemen, about five years younger. I would like to conclude by stating young Brooke is also important for the future of the club but if you insisted that I could only make one signing I would gladly attempt to sign him particularly as the full-back position is under strength at the moment. I do appreciate your reservations and in fact I took the liberty to raise the financial aspect of the pending transfer deals with the bank manager only this morning. I must say he felt as reluctant as yourselves but after accepting the club had cleared £37,000 of its debt in two months and also my assurance that I would not sign any more new players in the foreseeable future, he agreed to the deals on the condition the club could repay £50,000 by the end of the season. Gentlemen, I request you, for the reasons I have just explained, to reconsider your decision. Thank you.' Tony fastened the centre button on his jacket breathed in deeply and sat down to await the directors' comments.

There was a noticeable pause. What could the directors say? Tony had seemingly covered all the angles. Eddie Flannagan stared at the ceiling, Bill Boothroyd fidgeted nervously with the papers in front of him and Jack Elliott tapped his fingers lightly on the top of the table. Barrie Trippett sat nervously on the edge of his chair. The silence was embarrassing to all concerned. Jack Elliot contemplated commenting but he stopped short before making any sense. Eddie Flannagan changed his stare in the direction of the boardroom window. Bill Boothroyd was now busily looking through his papers as though he expected to quote from a paragraph to fill the void. If he intended to do so he never found the appropriate passage. Tony obviously sensed the embarrassment and rose to his feet again. 'Gentlemen,' he said trying to get everyone's attention, 'it may be advisable if I left the room while you discussed…'

'No, it won't be necessary, Tony. I think you've got our approval to proceed with the transfer negotiations,' interrupted Jack Elliott.

'Aye, go ahead Tony, you're the most organised manager I've known at this club. There seems to be no stopping you once you've made your mind up. Just don't get drawn into any higher figures than the ones you've discussed here tonight, unless it is an increased fee for Steve Fisher,' remarked an unusually humorous Eddie Flannagan.

Bill Boothroyd nodded in agreement as he joined in the joke. Barrie Trippett sighed with relief. Everyone now seemed at ease.

Tony knew he had persuaded his directors to see things his way but he felt sure their decision would enable him to bring success to Sharrington sooner than he had anticipated. The meeting ended with all present in good spirits after Eddie Flannagan had made the point to Tony that he had been testing him, in the meeting, to see just how much he had the future of the club at heart. Tony smiled and shook his hand. Jack Elliott had known Eddie's earlier loss of words to be a submission to Tony's proposals. It was just Eddie's nature to make a feasible excuse so he could keep his credibility.

Chapter 35

At 9.00 a.m. on Friday morning all the Sharrington players reported to the ground for the journey to Seamingway. Tony agreed that all the playing staff should travel; although, Stephen Holland and Simon Docker were still unlikely to be fit for the game. Seamingway had only been relegated to the Fourth Division at the end of last season and this meant Sharrington would have to travel further for this league fixture than any other during their history. Seamingway had never been in the Fourth Division before and at no time in the same league as Sharrington. They had recently sacked Ted Meersbrook from the manager's post at the end of last season and brought in chief coach Paul Royston as his replacement. Since that change at the helm of the club Seamingway had never looked back. They were currently top of the Fourth Division and had won their first round of the League Cup on aggregate 4-2 against Third Division Collingwood. The seaside resort of Seamingway was expecting a big crowd for the visit of Sharrington.

To make the journey as quick as possible the board had agreed for the party to travel by rail. The train departed at 11.30 a.m. from the station in Sharrington and after an eight hour journey the party arrived at the Seamingway Central Hotel for the weekend stay. The party of fifteen players, three directors, Barrie, Tony and Grant Evans, were to return home on Sunday morning. The total bill to cover the travelling and hotel costs was £1,134. Tony hoped the holiday resort would give his players a much-needed break and an enjoyable evening out after the game. He felt the players would relish the comforts of the luxurious hotel and change of surroundings. But it was business first and after a delightful evening meal it was curfew time by 10.30 p.m. The players were tired after the long journey and quite willing to retire to bed before the stipulated time. Tony, Barrie, Jack Elliott, Eddie Flannagan, Bill Boothroyd and Grant Evans remained in the hotel lounge to discuss many stories involving Sharrington's journeys over the years. After a bracing walk on the sea front everyone was ready for bed before midnight.

'Right, lads, settle down,' shouted Tony to the playing staff in the club's private hotel room. 'Before we board the coach to the ground I want to read out the team for today now we have had a chance to test Steve and Simon for fitness. Unfortunately,' Tony went on, 'they have both failed; therefore; the team will be the same today as it was last Wednesday evening.'

The players listened to the tactics from Tony and were warned not to be frightened of the Seamingway team, just because they were the top of the league and a high scoring side.

'Keep it tight from the start and play it hard,' said Tony demonstrating with his clenched fists. 'If you can maintain the work rate from recent games and the constructive attacking moves we have discussed in training I can't see us leaving here without at least a point. Don't forget, lads, we need to get back on course after last week's set back and a win today will make it a much more satisfying evening for you tonight!'

The team left by coach to the ground well in time for the 3.00 p.m. kick-off. The Seamingway side was announced as unchanged for the ninth time. They had not had any serious injuries since the season started. The crowd was recorded as 11,500, their highest for almost two years. The ground was similar to Sharrington in that it was open on three sides but the cantilever stand was a splendid construction which seated 4,000 supporters. The surrounding paintwork on placards, fixtures and fittings were all in the Seamingway club's colours of blue. The sun was shining brightly and the corner flags were waving gently in a cooling wind as Sharrington and the home team took to the pitch. There was no evidence of any Sharrington supporters having made the extremely long journey.

Surprisingly, for the first twenty minutes the majority of attacks had been by Sharrington, and the league leaders had not troubled Alan Hawkins. Sharrington were using both wings to build attacks but the home team defence did not have any trouble clearing the high and low crosses. The Seamingway danger men Lincoln, centre-forward and Fox, inside-forward, were well marshalled by Tommy French and Mike Thomas respectively.

However, possibly due to the ease in which Sharrington were finding their opponents, they fell a goal behind to a long-range shot by right-winger Aston. He had not been picked up by Allan Smith and was allowed to turn and run at Thomas before curving a right-footed shot past Hawkins' left hand and into the net. Before Sharrington had time to settle down they were once again hit by a solo effort. This time the Seamingway inside-forward Fox dispossessed Paul Cracknell in the centre circle, dribbled twenty yards upfield and beat Tommy French outside the penalty area before firing the ball over the advancing Hawkins and high into the roof of the net.

Within three minutes, after being in control of the game, two individual efforts had virtually put Sharrington in a hopeless position.

The half-time whistle blew with the score 2-0 to the league leaders. The home crowd were voicing their approval and shouting for a repeat score of the third league match of the season in which they thrashed Prent Park 6-0. Seamingway had not so much played as a team but more like a side of skilful and talented individuals.

During half-time Tony was quick to point out the goals arose from slack marking and poor tackling. He expressed his annoyance and chose to highlight the poor efforts of Allan Smith, Paul Cracknell and Tony White. The players were obviously upset by Tony's fury but whether this was the reason for a more wholehearted second half display or not it was difficult to say, but after eight minutes of the restart, a determined run at the home team defence by Tony White resulted in the ball running free and into the path of Graham Hart who side-footed an easy goal into an empty net.

Sharrington played very well in phases throughout the second half but the third piece of individual Seamingway play by Lincoln, the high scoring centre-forward put a two goal difference between the two sides again. He controlled a left wing cross from Sergeant on his chest, screened the ball passed Mike Thomas and chipped it out of the reach of Hawkins to make the score 3-1. Shortly after this, Hawkins saved brilliantly from a ferocious volley by the same striker and Aston had been tackled superbly at the last minute on a run towards goal by Allan Smith.

As Sharrington pushed forward to get back into the game, centre-half Tommy French rose high above the Seamingway defenders and headed a Sammy Chaddock corner powerfully into the net.

The home crowd were anxious, as Sharrington's team play brought them forward time and time again in the remaining nine minutes of the game. Good efforts by Alf Henning, Paul Cracknell and Tommy French again rocked the league leaders, particularly when the former's effort cannoned off the bar and was cleared desperately off the line by captain Powers.

With only a minute to go Lincoln almost put the game out of Sharrington's reach when he also hit the crossbar with a diving header but it was the referee who finally ended Sharrington's nail-biting efforts to equalise when he blew the full time whistle. Sharrington had lost 3-2 to the league leaders but they were applauded off the field. They had, once again, proved their fighting ability and teamwork effort when the chips were down. Tony had no complaints at the end of the game. He told them, 'things were beginning to take shape,' and rounded off by telling his squad to go out and have a good night on the town as they had given the league leaders a game to remember.

Chapter 36

On the following Monday, Tuesday and Wednesday, Barrie and Ray Walton, the youth coach from the local town club, were extremely busy organising the junior coaching sessions at the Sharrington ground. In fact Tony's programme over these three days was as follows:

8.00 a.m.	- Office
9.30 - 11.30	- First team training sessions
11.30 - 12.30	- Lunch and office
12.30 - 4.30	- Junior coaching sessions
4.30 - 5.30	- Home for evening meal
4.30 - late	- Office and transfer negotiations

The junior training sessions were a great success to all concerned and a future date was arranged for the early new year over the weekend 14th, 15th and 16th January, 1978.

Transfer negotiations got under way during the return journey from Seamingway. Tony had mentioned the offer the club had received from Andlerstone United to Steve Fisher. The player was interested in Second Division football and promised he would discuss the matter with his wife and let Tony know his answer on the Monday.

As Andlerstone was only 60 miles or so from Sharrington, Steve confirmed to Tony he and his wife would be keen to meet their manager to discuss contractual terms before making a final decision. Fred Hayes, the Andlerstone United manager, was notified of Steve Fisher's wishes and an appointment for Tuesday was agreed. Jack Elliott offered to take Steve and his wife to Andlerstone. Tony also agreed with Fred Hayes a transfer figure of £50,000 should the player accept the Second Division club's terms. On Tuesday evening Steve Fisher had signed to become an Andlerstone United player.

During this transaction Tony had sent a telegram to Storr Town making a £50,000 offer for Neil Baynes on Monday morning. By Monday evening there had been no response from the Second Division club. Tony had also telephoned Bernard Pointer, the Blackway manager, during his lunch break on Monday.

'Hello, Mr. Pointer, my name's Tony Davidson, manager of Fourth Division Sharrington.'

'Ah well, I suppose someone has to manage them,' replied a flippant Bernard Pointer. He was renowned for his sense of humour.

'Yes, it's a good training post for me,' said Tony half laughing and half seriously. 'I would like to discuss with you the possibilities of the transfer of Micky Leighton, your young reserve midfield player.'

'Surprise, surprise, Tony. I wasn't expecting that. You know he's not made the first team this season nor for that matter has he been a regular member of the team since we signed him some three seasons ago,' remarked Bernard Pointer. 'I thought you may be enquiring about John Temple our experienced centre-half who may be useful to your club.'

'No, my only concern is young Leighton. Is he for sale, Mr. Pointer?' enquired Tony, wishing to get on with the phone call as quickly as possible.

'Mmm, very good. A positive man are you, Davidson?' mused Bernard Pointer.

Tony didn't answer. There was a brief silence. 'Well, I must honestly say the lad's not done well here and I rather doubt if he ever will, but a good player, definitely and very skilful.' There was another brief silence. 'To be quite frank, I would be prepared to release him for a reasonable figure.'

'Can I come and discuss further details with you and Leighton on say Wednesday evening about 7.30 p.m,' stressed Tony, sensing a deal could be arranged sooner than he'd expected.

'Yes, that should be fine. I'll arrange for the lad to be here in my office for 7.30 p.m. Do you want to stay overnight, Tony?' asked Bernard Pointer considerately.

'No thank you, Mr. Pointer. It's only some 140 miles and I will have to get back as things are hectic here at the moment and I have a lot to do. I would have got there earlier but we have some junior training sessions on throughout the day. I will see you on Wednesday at 7.30 p.m,' said Tony hurriedly.

'Bye, Tony,' replied Bernard Pointer but Tony had rung off, so he could contact Jim Freeman the Leston United manager.

Tony rang several times but there was no reply. When he eventually got through to Leston on Tuesday lunchtime the switchboard girl informed him Mr. Freeman was not expected at the ground until Thursday morning. She confirmed Mr. Freeman would phone him back on his arrival. Tony later heard Jim Freeman had been sacked by Leston United, in view of their poor results. The negotiations for Paul Brooke would have to wait, as it was not normal practice for clubs to deal in the transfer market in the absence of a manager. Tony watched the developments at Leston closely.

On Tuesday evening at 10.30 Tony received a telephone call at home.

He had just heard about the Steve Fisher deal but on the other end of the phone this time was Jim Briggs, the Storr Town manager.

'Thanks for the telegram, Tony. I just thought I'd let you know your offer will go in front of the board at tomorrow's meeting. I will keep you posted,' said Jim Briggs. Tony acknowledged the call and expressed his eagerness for the signature of Neil Baynes.

On Wednesday evening, Tony had travelled to Blackway and spoken to young Micky Leighton about the transfer. He had explained the possibility of the signature of Neil Baynes but after two hours no decision had been reached. Leighton said he was interested in joining Sharrington if it meant he could join up with Baynes again but he would prefer to see what transpired before making a decision. Tony made every effort to convince Leighton to join Sharrington but he didn't succeed. Leighton requested he would want an £80 per week wage if he accepted at a later date. Bernard Pointer also stressed his club would be looking for £25,000 to clinch the deal.

As Tony drove back home at 9.30 p.m. he realised the players he needed were not as eager to join the club as the players at Sharrington were to leave it. It looked doubtful whether Baynes or Leighton would sign for Sharrington before Saturday's home league game against rivals Treecliffe. Tony now realised his error in agreeing to the Steve Fisher deal before at least ensuring replacements were guaranteed. If Docker and Holland were still considered unfit he would really be desperate to field a strong team on Saturday. He was too busy mulling over the whole aspect of the club that his return journey seemed to take half the time. He concluded that the press and supporters would demand a few explanations. His only lifeline was that the Storr Town Board would give the go-ahead to Baynes' transfer. That deal would surely secure the signing of Leighton. He could only wait patiently, but he felt on edge with the situation he'd created.

As Tony walked into his home, Penny rushed up to him to greet him. 'Darling, I've got a message for you from Jim Briggs. The Storr Town Board have agreed to the transfer of Baynes but he wants you to know your offer has been matched by two other clubs.'

'Who are they, did he say?' asked Tony impatiently.

'Yes it was… er, here it is… Hill Wade United and Dabrook,' replied Penny, reading the names from the telephone notepad.

'I thought Hill Wade were interested in him,' said Tony scratching his head slowly. 'It's not too far from Storr either and as they're a Third Division club he may prefer them. I'd better make an appointment to see Baynes first thing tomorrow morning. This fish is just too big to let go now.'

Tony sat down to eat his supper and discussed the events of the day before retiring to a well-deserved sleep.

Tony was awake early on the Thursday morning and instead of telephoning Jim Briggs he made the journey by car to Storr. He arrived at 9.00 a.m. and received permission from Jim Briggs to speak to Baynes about the transfer on his arrival at the ground. By 10.30 a.m. Baynes and Tony were in discussion privately. As the two men were old friends there were many things to discuss. At 11.15 a.m. Jim Briggs interrupted the two men to say Tommy Raylor wanted to discuss the transfer with Baynes in the afternoon. Then quite by surprise to Tony, Neil Baynes spoke up, 'That won't be necessary, Jim. I've decided to accept Tony's terms and sign for Sharrington.'

Tony was astonished, as he had only briefly outlined his ideas for Sharrington and his efforts to sign Leighton. At no time had he discussed the wage, bonuses and housing accommodation. However, he was delighted to hear Baynes' commitment to join Sharrington.

'Just a minute, Neil. Hill Wade have increased the offer to £55,000,' retorted Jim Briggs.

Tony didn't need time to think about this problem and quickly blurted, 'O.K, Jim, I'll give you £60,000 to settled the deal now.'

Jim Briggs thought about the figure briefly before nodding in acceptance, 'I'll tell Raylor, Neil's signed for Sharrington for £60,000.' He then left the office.

'Tell me why did you say you'd agreed to our terms when we hadn't discussed any?' enquired Tony immediately.

'I just knew Sharrington was the right club for me now. I've been following your progress closely since they appointed you manager, Tony. I like what I see and I don't think you will fail. Even without Leighton I would have joined you. I think I can offer great help to Sharrington. As you know I'm not married and I'm a free agent to move where I want. I will accept my normal wage of £85.00 per week plus the club bonuses. I'm not greedy, as you know, Tony; I just need a decent standard of living. Can we agree?' stated a happy-faced Neil Baynes.

'You bet, Neil. It's a deal. I'm sure it will work out just fine,' said Tony whilst shaking his new signing's hand firmly.

Although the papers were signed there and then it was too late for Baynes to play in the local derby league game against Treecliffe on Saturday. Sharrington's new club-record signing was quickly announced to the press. Tony thought he'd let the story get around before contacting Leighton again.

Chapter 37

With half an hour to go before the kick-off against Treecliffe, Frank, Eddie and Bob had taken up their usual position on the terracing at the Sharrington ground. The game was not all-ticket. The crowd had slowly built up to about the same as the second leg of the League Cup-tie. The clouds were heavy with rain and there was a mist surrounding the ground. It was a miserable afternoon. However, the local derby atmosphere was building up as the supporters of each team gathered together. The game had not been publicised to the same extent as the cup games and the activities on the transfer market also pushed the derby game into the background. Both teams were level on seven points, with Sharrington having the better goal difference. They were positioned in the middle of the league.

Frank Sneddon carefully lit a cigarette as he turned to Eddie and Bob before saying, 'Well, lads, don't you think Davidson's dropped a bit of a clanger by letting Steve Fisher go before getting Baynes to sign in time for this game.'

Eddie Fisher was quick to comment, 'Maybe so, Frank but I think he's made a good deal, don't you?'

Frank paused before answering. 'I must say Steve Fisher was playing well this season and I'm not surprised a higher league club came for him.' He paused again as he drew on his cigarette. 'I've not seen Baynes for a few seasons but he was a good player in those days. If he's still as good now then I think Davidson will have made a good deal. We will have to see how he fits in with the other players.'

'I was amazed when I heard the news about Fisher joining Andlerstone United but I was delighted when I saw the papers on Thursday night. I think Davidson's planning for the future and rightly so,' remarked Bob Bennett.

'Yes, Bob, I'll go along with you about planning for the future. It's just that I think he could have planned the negotiations better to avoid leaving the club a player short for today's game,' commented Frank.

'We don't know the full facts, Frank. Maybe it couldn't be helped,' said Eddie as he jumped up and down to try and keep warm.

'Oh I think it could. Managers can usually organise their transfers to suit them and not the other way round. I mean he's still green at the job isn't he, so what can you expect,' sneered Frank.

'Hold on a bit, Frank,' interrupted Bob, as he tapped him on the shoulder with his programme. 'Give him a break. He's done very well so far. Let's judge him again later on in the season. Alf Henning was a good deal and Neil Baynes can't be…'

Eddie Fisher interrupted Bob, 'Hold on. Hold on a minute. They're announcing the teams.'

The voice over the public address system was heard to say, 'The Treecliffe team is as printed in the programme. The Sharrington team will be, in goal Hawkins, No. 2 Bond, No. 3 Smith, No. 4 Poole No. 5 French, No. 6 Thomas, No. 7 Hart, No. 8 Cracknell, No. 9 Henning, No. 10 White, No. 11 Chaddock, Sub. Docker.

'That's not a bad side, Frank. Poole's come in for Fisher. The rest of the team is the same as the last two games with Docker, back after injury, as substitute,' said Eddie.

'No, it's not bad. I just hope they can finish the game with the same result as they did here in the cup game,' remarked Frank as he stubbed out his cigarette.

The three men discussed the transfer deals with the Sharrington hardcore supporters around them before the kick-off.

As the game started the rain began to fall heavily. The players were soon saturated as they all skidded, and slipped for possession of the ball. There were three or four early fouls as both teams tried to settle down. The referee had obviously appreciated that it was a derby game and had therefore not taken any action against the offenders. The rain had certainly dampened the high spirits of the supporters. A mist was still present and visibility was limited, but not poor enough to abandon the game.

'I wish Poole and Thomas would push up to support young White and Cracknell. The gap seems enormous,' said Frank Sneddon.

'Aye, and Treecliffe are exploiting the middle of the pitch,' remarked Bob Bennett.

'Get up in support, Pooley,' shouted Eddie Fisher.

'I like Graham Hart's wing play. He is improving with every game. Just look at the way he beat that man,' enthused Bob Bennett.

'Yes, he's good and so will young Paul Cracknell be, in a few years time, once he gets a bit more experience under his belt. He's certainly looking a good find,' stressed Frank Sneddon.

'It doesn't look as though either team will break the deadlock today fellows,' cried Bob Bennett above the noise from the crowd.

'No, there haven't been any clear-cut chances,' agreed Frank.

The rain continued and the players became more and more downhearted as the first half neared an end. The score remained 0-0 at half-time. The men discussed the game.

'I think one goal will win it today, Frank,' said Eddie, slurping at his Oxo drink.

'I feel we will be lucky to see a goal at all,' said Frank doing likewise.

'Look at that, men,' said Bob pointing over in the direction of the half-time scoreboard. 'Crookaby are beating Seamingway 2-0. That's a shock.'

'I'll say it is. Crookaby are having a strange season so far. They seem to beat the teams they shouldn't beat and lose to those who they should do well against. To say it's their first season in a professional league I guess they'll be happy with the results so far,' summarised Frank.

'Yes, all the teams seem to be on a par with each other and my guess is that it will be a close thing for promotion this season,' yelled Eddie so he could be heard above the cheers of the crowd as both clean-kitted teams ran out onto the pitch. The rain had eased and the supporters settled again for the start of the second half.

'Eh! Look at that,' shouted Eddie, 'Davidson's put Docker on for young White. I wonder if that's a tactical change or what?'

'I didn't notice any injury to White,' said Frank as he closely watched the visitors' first, second half attacking move.

Docker appeared to be playing a similar role to White but his greater experience was easily recognisable. In fact he was playing well for the first game after his thigh injury. He was moving sharper than he had been doing before the lay off and was getting more involved in the game than usual.

The mist was thickening and without any floodlights the spectators were finding it difficult to pick out the players when the play was at the furthest part of the ground from them. The yellow shirted Treecliffe players were easier to see than the dark red shirts of the home team. The local derby was a battle in the mist.

'Only fifteen minutes left,' said Bob anxiously. 'It looks like a goalless draw as you said, Frank.'

'Yes, it's certainly been a stalemate this afternoon,' replied Frank.

'I can't see some of the goalmouth action at the Treecliffe end. When our lads put the crosses over I just lose sight of the ball altogether,' mumbled Eddie as he squeezed his eyes up to try and see more clearly.

'Aye, it's getting more difficult to see what's happening every minute,' sneered Bob as he peered in the direction of the play.

'I just hope the mist doesn't stop the game. I wouldn't fancy another game against Treecliffe so soon,' remarked Frank.

'I think both teams would settle for a point now, lads,' commented

Eddie.

'Just a second Eddie this looks like a breakaway for Treecliffe to me,' shouted Frank. 'Oh no, Outhroyd's got round Smithy… I've lost sight of the ball… He's crossed it into the area… I've lost sight of it again…'

'It's in the net. The referee's pointing to the centre circle. I think it was Jimmy Hope who knocked it in but I'm not sure,' cried Bob.

'We've thrown it away and with only a few minutes remaining as well,' stormed Eddie.

'Would you believe it, they've got one upon us again. The lucky so and so's,' gesticulated Bob furiously.

'Just listen at the Treecliffe supporters. They certainly have all the luck when they play Sharrington, don't they?' said Eddie in a downhearted tone.

No one answered him. The section of supporters on the terrace remained quiet. Some even began to wander out of the ground but they were still looking over their shoulders as the Sharrington team restarted towards the Treecliffe goal.

'This is our last chance surely,' stressed Eddie as the Treecliffe supporters whistled loudly for the referee to end the game.

'Come on, Sammy, give that full-back a run for his money,' shouted Bob as Chaddock controlled the ball and sprinted down the left wing.

'He's got the ball across. Come on stick it in, lads,' raged Eddie. 'They've cleared it,' murmured Frank. 'Not very far though,' answered Bob. 'It's gone straight to Thomas.'

Before anyone else could speak the young wing-half swung at the loose ball and it rifled through the packed goalmouth, disappeared from view momentarily, then flashed into the Treecliffe net.

'It's there! We've done it! What a shot!' roared Eddie.

'Fantastic goal, Thomas!' cheered Bob waving his arms above his head jubilantly.

'What a beauty. We deserve it eh, lads,' clapped Frank, with excitement written all over his face.

'What a time to get an equaliser. The referee's looking at his watch already,' said Eddie wildly.

'Come on, ref: before the mist ends it for you,' jeered Bob.

The referee suddenly blew his whistle as though he'd heard Bob's cry.

'Thank goodness for that,' said Eddie breathlessly. 'A point's a point and, in the end a good result for us.'

The three men left the ground in jubilation.

Chapter 38

Neil Baynes was introduced to his new colleagues after the match against Treecliffe. He had a likeable manner and could always find something pleasant to say to people he did not know. He was 29 years of age, blond haired, five foot ten inches tall and eleven and half stone in weight. He had kept his youthful looks and taken great pains to maintain his physical fitness during his playing career. He explained to the Sharrington players how he was looking forward to playing with them in the Fourth Division and helping the club to promotion. The players, who were feeling rather pleased with the afternoon result, took an instant liking to Neil Baynes. Tony was particularly happy with the introduction of his new signing and, of course with the 1-1 draw against rivals Treecliffe.

Although the Treecliffe game had been hard-fought there was no time for any rest. Sharrington were to play away from home against Braman in a league fixture on Monday evening. The journey was 132 miles to the south east of Sharrington, consequently the team would have to travel during the day which would give them no time for a training session before the game. Tony did not wish to bring the players in for training on Sunday. The players were told to report at the ground at 11.30 a.m. on Monday morning. The team was not announced at the time but everyone was keen to learn who Tony would drop for Neil Baynes.

As there were no serious injuries from the Treecliffe game, Tony had made his decision on Sunday of the team to play at Braman. Braman had only missed promotion by three points during the previous season and finished in fourth position. They had beaten Sharrington 5-1 in the same fixture last season. They were a young skilful side who were determined to get promotion this season. Their manager Bob Heard was an ex-Braman player and had promised the local supporters Third Division football next season. Unfortunately, his team had not got off to the start he had predicted, mainly due to five draws in the first eight games. However, they had only lost one game in the league to Ellistart. The main disappointment was their exit from the League Cup to the Third Division team Hillwade by 4-3 on aggregate; the reason being that they had played extremely well to draw 2-2 in the first leg away from home only to go down and out 1-2 on the second leg in front of a 16,000 crowd. Their defeat to Ellistart followed the Hillwade game and they could only draw 2-2 against Low Grove in the last league game after leading 2-0 with twenty minutes of play remaining. Tony hoped his team, with the added skill of Neil Baynes, could surprise the Braman team while they were still recovering from a lean period. His team selection was 1. Hawkins, 2. Bond (capt.), 3. Smith, 4. Poole, 5. French, 6. Thomas, 7. Hart, 8. Baynes, 9. Henning, 10. White, 11. Chaddock, Sub. Docker. The change was simply Baynes for young Paul Cracknell.

The team arrived at the ground at 6.00 p.m. after a two hour stay for lunch on the journey down. The kick-off was 7.30 p.m. Braman's ground was on a larger scale to any Sharrington had played on this season. The ground was covered on three sides, two being modern stands and the other a covered kop, behind one of the goals. The floodlights were towering metal structures in each corner of the ground, with more lights positioned on the roof of each stand, which ran along the length of the pitch. Braman was a busy industrial town and their attendances were usually well above the Fourth Division average.

The weather had improved considerably from the previous Saturday. It was a mild evening and a clear sky. The darkness was drawing in around the ground as the game started. The crowd was 8,447 of which only an estimated amount of 200 or so were Sharrington fans.

Braman in their bright blue shirts and white shorts were the first to attempt shots at goal. They played possession football in defence and then moved the ball quickly through midfield and into attack. They had a talented right-winger by the name of Oakes who had interested many First Division clubs over the seasons and who was valued at over £100,000. The Braman team played the ball to Oakes more than to the team's opposite winger Bridges but Allan Smith was playing well and not allowing the gifted danger man too much room. Oakes had scored six goals in the league this season but although he produced ample evidence of his trickery and speed he did not look like adding to his tally this evening. Sharrington were beginning to blend together as the first half progressed and Baynes had shown some excellent control and thoughtful distribution of the ball to his new colleagues. The Braman defence were finding it more and more difficult to hold possession of the ball as the Sharrington forwards advanced quickly to pressure them into mistakes. With the game evenly balanced as half-time approached a Sammy Chaddock corner was headed from a crowded penalty area and the ball looped gently over the home team keeper and dropped casually into the netting. The Sharrington players swarmed to congratulate the scorer and it was not until half-time that the name of Tommy French was credited with the goal. French was beginning to make quite a name for himself as a scorer from corner kicks.

'Good play, lads,' said Tony cheerily as his team arrived in the dressing room at half-time. 'It's a close match and the second half won't be easy for us. They are bound to come at us during the first twenty minutes, so if we can keep it calm at the back and look out for a quick break while they are pushing defenders forward I think we can get back to winning ways tonight, lads.'

'Yes, let's keep it played out wide when we are going forward,' urged Graham Bond as he was towelling the beads of sweat from his forehead. 'Their two full-backs seem weak to me.'

'We've got to pick their three midfield men up a lot quicker,' remarked Barrie Trippett as he was massaging Graham Poole's right thigh.

'I think we are beginning to put our game together now that we are learning Neil's style of play,' commented Mike Thomas.

'Aye, he's not a bad player but if he's worth £60,000 I must be valued at twice that amount for the way I'm snuffing superstar Oakes out of the game,' joked a cheeky-faced Allan Smith waiting for the new club member's reaction. There was a brief pause and the slightest signs of tension.

'Well, I hope you're joking, Smithy, because to be perfectly honest I think young Oakes is playing you off the park,' said the straight-faced Neil Baynes. There was another brief pause before Baynes broke out into a high-pitched laugh and pointed to Allan Smith. 'Oh,' he snorted, 'if only you could see your face. One up to me, Smithy, eh?'

Allan Smith had been worried that Baynes might not be used to his sense of humour or think he was showing off but he smiled, winked at his new colleague and slapped him on the back playfully. The tension was gone.

'O.K, lads, that's enough of the acting around. Let's get out there and put some serious football uppermost in our minds,' said Tony quite deliberately making sure his players were prepared for a tough second half.

Fortunately his team had not gone off the boil during half-time and they played as Tony had suggested. Braman did attack during the early period of the second half but the Sharrington defence kept cool. Alan Hawkins had saved two long-range shots which were heading for the top corner of the net and Graham Bond marshalled the team magnificently. The captain played his best game of the season. After seventy-five minutes, a Sharrington attack involving Poole, Baynes, White, Baynes again and Henning ended with winger Graham Hart firing a volley passed the Braman keeper, Dawson, to make the score 2-0. The home team scored a consolation goal from full-back Houseman after good work by Oakes but Sharrington comfortably held on to their second away win of the season. The players were in good spirits after the game and enjoyed their hotel stay in Braman knowing that in the first instance the evening's performance was of good quality, secondly that to win at Braman was a rare occurrence for most teams and finally that the confidence was beginning to build within the team as a result of Tony Davidson's fine example as a dedicated manager who was keen for the success of his players and the club as a whole.

Chapter 39

Tony was back into the transfer market on his return to the office on Tuesday afternoon and by Wednesday evening his negotiations with Blackway had been finalised with Micky Leighton signing for Sharrington F.C. for £15,000 and a further £10,000 after the completion of twelve first team games. Tony was happy with the deal. Leighton accepted a £75 per week wage plus the normal club bonuses.

Leighton was a single man, 22 years of age, 5'8' tall, stockily built with dark, curly hair which fell just below the bottom of his neck. He was a strikingly attractive young chap and dressed in the latest fashion. He was an experienced player for such a tender age but his transfer to Blackway from Trandon Rovers had never spurred him to greater heights. He was pleased to join up again with Neil Baynes but he had stressed to Tony that he was anxious to get back to his old form and help Sharrington win promotion. Tony had no doubts as to Micky Leighton's ability on a football pitch but he knew he would have to curb the player's fancy for the bright lights. Leighton certainly had a reputation for nightclubs and the like but Tony purposely hadn't mentioned this aspect to Leighton before he had had a chance to learn the truth himself. He could only wait to see how the player settled.

The news of yet another new signing intrigued the Sharrington supporters. Tony had also made it known that he was interested in another player to strengthen his squad but he refused to give any indication of the player in question, his club or position.

The training sessions on Thursday and Friday had gone well and although Leighton had fitted in with the other players, Tony and Barrie thought he lacked the fitness of the other players. It was therefore agreed to keep the same side as the one which beat Braman, with new signing Leighton sitting it out. Tony told Leighton of his reason for leaving him out of the team but he did not inform the press. There were a variety of comments in the press on Tony's decision to leave Leighton out of the team but Grant Evans of the *Sharrington Echo* stated that he was not surprised with Davidson's choice particularly when the team had played so well at Braman. He had concluded his article by reporting that Tommy French was off the transfer list. Tony Davidson was quoted as saying, 'Tommy has buckled down to his game this season and his playing has impressed me so much so that I feel he should be withdrawn from the transfer list.' There was a photograph of both manager and player shaking hands. French was reported to be "much happier following the club's decision" and that "he hoped to keep the No. 5 shirt for the remainder of the season." There was also a brief comment on the two recent goals scored by French, the credit for which the player gave to the coaching of Alf Henning.

The Saturday league game was away at Crookaby, some 190 miles from Sharrington. The team travelled during the morning to give them plenty of time for relaxation before the kick-off at 3.00 p.m. Leighton, Bates and Holland were the travelling reserves. Bill Boothroyd and Eddie Flannagan were the only members of the board to make the journey. Jack Elliott, Steve King and Paul Cracknell were all flu victims. Steve had been ill for over two weeks and although he was almost recovered he thought it in the interests of the playing staff if he stayed away from this game. He had, on Tony's request, gone to watch Rallingborough, Sharrington's next league opponents, play at home to Low Grove.

Steve bought a programme so he could follow Sharrington's score on the half-time board. He was only partially interested in the Rallingborough game but he made note of a few important points on their style of play, which he thought would help Tony in preparing for Sharrington's next game. At half-time the Rallingborough team were leading 1-0 following a thirtieth minute goal by Solley. During the half-time period Steve waited patiently for the scores to be shown on the scoreboard placard. Eventually a man in a long white coat commenced to allocate numbers to letters, the latter of which corresponded to the games in the programme. The letter for the Crookaby game was N, therefore Steve waited a considerable time for the Sharrington result. The man with the numbers finally put a nought against the home team (Crookaby). Steve smiled to himself knowing his club at the least could only be drawing. The score-man fumbled with the numbers before placing another nought against the away team. A goalless half-time score suited Steve. He knew Sharrington tended to score the most of their goals in the second half. He watched the players troop onto the field and concentrated on the start of the second half.

Jack Elliott sat comfortably in an armchair in front of a large blazing fire. There were three fat white pillows wedging him in an upright position. There was a small table which had bottles of pills and medicines scattered on it. He sniffed and sneezed into a huge red and white spotted handkerchief. With his other hand he held a small black transistor radio to his left ear. Jack had heard the half-time report of the game at Crookaby and was confident Sharrington could turn their advantage into goals. He waited eagerly for the next local report on the game. At approximately 4.25 p.m. the local Crookaby commentator announced, *'Still a stalemate here at Crookaby. Sharrington are still on top but they have been unable to force the ball into the net. Crookaby have had one or two chances but Hawkins in the visitors' goal has made superb saves. I think that the first team to score should hold on to win this game.'* The voice trailed off and the voice from the studios remarked that they would rejoin the Crookaby reporter for the full time result at 4.45 p.m. Jack Elliott slowly pulled himself up from the chair to go to the kitchen and make himself a cup of tea before the final result came through. He was optimistic Sharrington would get a good result from the game.

Some ten miles from Jack's home, Paul Cracknell, the young part time professional was laid in bed listening to the same radio programme. He was keen for a win by Sharrington. The other local results had been announced and reported upon. Rallingborough had defeated Low Grove 1-0. Treecliffe had beaten Aldway 3-1. Paul was now awaiting the Sharrington report frantically. After a few further moments the Crookaby reporter was on the air again. The noise from the crowd around the commentator's voice was loud and the reporter had to shout to make himself heard. Paul sensed something sensational had occurred. The voice was high pitched, *'What a tremendous turn around we've had here. After the visitors had dominated most of the game Erich Lazackerlich, the Crookaby winger, was left with the simplest of chances to sidefoot the ball into an open goal to give the home team a shock 1-0 win.'* Paul punched his fists deep into the blankets in his frustration. The reporter continued to give an account of the game but Paul was so disappointed with the result he couldn't listen to the commentary. He wondered what had gone wrong and why they had failed to score after being so much on top. It was a bad result for Sharrington.

Jack Elliott also wondered the same and was disappointed with the final result, so much so, he suddenly felt like telephoning Crookaby to speak to Tony but decided not to do so.

Steve King heard the Sharrington result over the loud speaker at Rallingborough, after their game had ended. There was a sarcastic cheer from the Rallingborough supporters who had stayed on after the game. It was not the result Steve had hoped for. As he walked slowly from the ground he also contemplated telephoning the Crookaby ground for a match report but, like Jack, thought it best to wait until the weekly board meeting for the full details.

Sharrington's brief return to the winning way in the league had been short lived and the defeat at newly promoted Crookaby was totally unexpected.

Chapter 40

At lunchtime on the following Monday the F.A. Cup 1st Round draw was made. This round involved all 16 teams from the Fourth Division and 80 non-league clubs (all amateur). There was one game only, unlike the League Cup 1st Round, where an aggregate result would be taken from two games. It was a straightforward knock out cup competition and Sharrington's last chance to progress on to meeting First Division opposition this season. The F.A. Cup was a prestigious cup competition and although Sharrington F.C. were not expected to advance further than the 3rd or 4th Round it was an opportunity for them to make the headlines and earn some valuable gate money.

Training had been hard during the morning. It had been a programme of five miles running, short sprinting tests, stomach and leg muscle exercises and, finally, shooting practice. The players were physically tired but eager to hear the cup draw for Sharrington's opponents. They were in good spirits as Tony had congratulated their overall performance in the Crookaby game. They had dominated much of the match but Tony simply put it down to, 'just one of those days when the ball would not go in the net'. The players knew for themselves that it had been a good team performance. They were caught by some slack marking with only minutes of the game remaining but they should have scored enough goals during the game to have won easily by that stage. Four efforts were cleared off the goal line; Henning and Chaddock had hit the bar with two solo efforts. Hart's early second half corner hit the inside of the far post and was scrambled away and the home team goalkeeper, Jacks, saved marvellously from goal bound shots by Henning, Smith, White and a sensational overhead kick from Baynes. Crookaby had been extremely lucky not to have suffered a heavy defeat.

'Who do you think we will draw, Smithy?' shouted the burly Alf Henning towelling himself dry.

'One of those tiny little non-leaguers will do me, with a right winger about 40 years old so I can concentrate on my goal scoring ability,' quipped Alan Smith as he emerged from the huge white-tiled rectangular bath.

'I hope it's not Treecliffe again. I don't think I could go through another game with them so soon,' butted in captain Graham Bond.

'Don't mention them. It's forced to put a jinx on us if you do,' said Tommy French, tying his tartan patterned tie.

'Well surely it's odds-on to be a non-league side; after all there are 80 of them in the hat,' remarked Alf Henning.

'Yes, I'd go along with that, Alf, and a home draw too. I don't fancy some of those tiny little pitches they play on,' shouted Graham Poole above the radio announcers statement that the draw was now taking place.

'Ssshhh! lads it's on,' squealed Mike Thomas.

Eddie Flannagan sat in the main office at the abattoir listening to the cup draw. Scores of teams were called out, many of whom Eddie had never heard of before, but although Sharrington were not mentioned in the first part of the draw, Treecliffe had been drawn out to a non-league club by the name of Freeway Raiders. The draw continued in its usual officious manner but then suddenly Eddie heard the name Sharrington. It was a home draw. He waited patiently for the name of the visitors. A number 27 was drawn from the velvet bag at league headquarters and the corresponding name given was Hooper Brook Rovers. It was a non-league team but not a well-known one. Eddie quickly checked his non-league team booklet and found that Sharrington's first round opponents were from the South East Premier League and had been formed sixteen years ago. It was a small village with a population of 2,000 and near to Chemwick, a town famous for its fruit produce and a well-established First Division team. Hooper Brook Rovers had not enjoyed any success and were not known for any giant-killing act during the previous F.A. Cup competitions. Eddie was pleased with the draw and was of the opinion Sharrington should qualify for the 2nd Round, which included all the Third Division teams, without too much difficulty.

'Have you heard the cup draw?' asked Barrie Trippett as he burst into Tony's office.

Tony was listening to someone on the telephone but motioned Barrie to come and sit down. After a while Tony spoke into the mouthpiece.

'I'll certainly consider it, madam, and if we have any problems with accommodation I will get in touch with you. Thank you for phoning.' Tony replaced the receiver and put his head in his hands.

'What's the matter, Tony?' enquired Barrie.

'You might not believe it, Barrie, but that is the sixth telephone call I've received this morning from landladies offering their home to Micky Leighton as a place to stay until he finds somewhere permanent to live,' mumbled Tony. Barrie smiled to himself. 'It's ever since his photograph appeared in the *Sharrington Echo*. It also appears his reputation has spread further than I'd thought it had. Well I've decided,' continued to Tony, 'to send him to Mrs. Maxwell's as she has had a spare room there ever since

Greg Hanby left. Now let's see: Graham Poole's there, Simon Docker and Sammy Chaddock has another two months in digs before he gets married. I know they are all quieter than Leighton but if we don't send him to Mrs. Maxwell's, who can I trust to keep him in order, I just don't know what would happen to him.' Tony scratched his head. 'However, let's hope he keeps on the straight and narrow. The trouble is he will be the most eligible bachelor in and around Sharrington. I'll explain the position to Mrs. M,' remarked Tony before pausing.

'Have you heard the draw?' repeated Barrie.

'Oh, yes, Barrie,' answered Tony, 'Sid told me only a few moments ago. It's certainly one we should win without any doubts. If we can't beat a non-league team on our own ground we don't deserve a second chance. Anyway, Barrie, the way the lads are starting to play I wouldn't like to be in Hooper Brook's shoes. I can't imagine how the non-leaguers will cope with the likes of Alf Henning, Neil Baynes and company, can you? I'm totally confident.'

'I suppose you're right, Tony, but don't forget the shock results over the years in this competition,' answered Barrie rather seriously.

'Don't worry, Barrie, we will get the players in the right frame of mind before the game starts. My main concern at the moment though is preparing for our next game at Rallingborough. We can't afford to lose too much ground in the league at this stage of the season and a win on Saturday is imperative. As you will see from my weekly list I want us to spend more time on shooting, set pieces and two-touch football. Our approach work is good but I feel it is a little deliberate and we can use two-touch to develop this aspect of our game. The defence is playing well, Alan Hawkins in particular, but we must stress the importance of concentration for the full 90 minutes to the lads. If we had maintained the same concentration as we had shown during the first 88 minutes, Crookaby wouldn't have scored such a soft goal. Graham must keep… ' Tony was stopped in his tracks by the sound of the telephone. 'Oh no, not another obliging landlady, I hope.' He picked up the receiver and listened, then grimaced. Barrie laughed aloud and left the office for Tony to sort the matter out.

Chapter 41

The following Wednesday evening, Tony, Barrie and the whole squad of players drove to Ellistart to watch their 2nd round League Cup, first leg game against Third Division opponents Hill Wade United, the team who were after the signature of Neil Baynes at the same time as Sharrington. The interest in the game was mainly due to Ellistart being the next visitors to Sharrington. They had had a good season, so far, and after ten games were positioned second in the league. In the first round of the League Cup they had defeated Third Division Trandon Rovers, who had been relegated from Division Two at the end of the previous season by 3-2 on aggregate. Ellistart were said, by manager George Tranter, to be confident for the cup game, in view of their recent away draw at league leaders Seamingway. They were at full strength. Their new £50,000 centre-forward, Deighton, from Ranchley Athletic had scored six goals in five games and was the danger man as far as Hill Wade were concerned.

Within ten minutes, the white-shirted Ellistart team had broken down the Hill Wade defence on two occasions. First Fenning, the home team No. 10, scored from 30 yards and then Deighton bustled his way through at speed to make a goal for No. 11 Smith. In the second half Deighton scored the third himself and, to put the tie beyond the Third Division side, Brand the No. 8 fired a penalty into the roof of the net to make the final score 4-0. Ellistart's 14,000 supporters rejoiced long after the game was over and the Sharrington party left the ground knowing much more of the Ellistart side and their style of play. Tony immediately rated them as the best side he had seen from the Fourth Division that season but he thought Sharrington were capable of beating them in the home game in two weeks time.

Before the Sharrington coach set off for Rallingborough on the following Saturday Tony gave his pre-match talk. 'Right lads, we've worked hard this week and over the last few weeks you've certainly improved as a team. I know last Saturday was an unfortunate result for us but we can't afford to throw this game away today through missed chances and slack marking on one occasion due to a lack of concentration.' Tony paused as he stroked his hair away from his eyes. 'As you know, lads, Rallingborough were relegated last season and after a reasonable start this season they have lost twice in their last three league games, not to mention the 4-0 thrashing to Mirth Cross in the 1st round of the League Cup. As we have already discussed this week they are a side who rely upon high crosses to the far post for either, Greene, Bright or Solley. They have a fast winger in Fanthom and a solid defence. No one has scored more than two goals against them in the league so far this season but, having said that, they do not score many either. We will have to be patient, building from the back, through midfield down the wings or making breaks towards their goal.' Tony broke off momentarily before continuing. 'It will be hard again, today, but I am confident we can come back with two points if we keep our heads, continue to play as a team and take our chances. And don't forget it's the 1st round of the F.A. Cup next week and I don't want us to lose any more ground in the league at this stage. I have selected the following team today.' Tony straightened the knot of his tie before reading from the team sheet. 'No. 1 Hawkeye, 2 Graham Bond, 3 Smithy, 4 Micky Leighton, 5 Tommy, 6 Mike Thomas, 7 Graham Hart, 8 Neil, 9 Alf, 10 Simon, 11 Sammy and sub Graham Poole. I've decided to rest you today, Tony,' he said to young Tony White, who was looking a little surprised by his manager's decision to leave him out of the team. 'You have played well for the club but we have been putting together some important moves this week in training and I want us to try them out if possible today.' Young Tony White nodded slowly. 'Don't be discouraged, Whitey, you, like the other part-timers are doing what is required of you when I throw you in at the deep end, and, after all, you have age on your side.' There was an easy atmosphere as the players had learned that Tony Davidson made it his policy to talk of his viewpoints in front of the whole squad whether the comments were complimentary or critical. The players led the way out of the dressing room to the bus followed by Tony, Barrie and the travelling members of the squad who were not chosen for the game at Rallingborough. Those concerned were Steve Holland, who was being kept out of the side by Tommy French, Alan Bates, the reserve goalkeeper, Tony White and Paul Cracknell who had now recovered from flu.

The journey to Rallingborough took only 50 minutes, as it was only 22 miles away from Sharrington on the main north road. There were fifteen coaches of Sharrington supporters, which helped to swell the crowd to 9,000. The green-shirted Rallingborough took to the field first to a loud reception. The Sharrington team in their characteristic red shirts and black shorts started the game and after the first quarter of an hour they found themselves defending furiously to keep out the on- form Rallingborough forward line. The home team were playing hard and after twenty-two minutes a late tackle by centre-half Grimes brought Alf Henning crashing to the floor and earned himself a booking from the referee. The visitors' centre-forward had injured his shoulder in the fall and this greatly incapacitated his movements. If this wasn't enough, Sinclair, the tough home team's defender, ruthlessly injured Graham Hart after the winger had clearly beaten him. He also was booked. Hart had to be helped off the field with a right knee injury and was replaced by substitute Graham Poole. Fanthom the home team right-wing hit the crossbar with Hawkins well and truly beaten, Docker had a shot blocked on the line, Bright, a big broad centre-forward was brought down on the edge of the Sharrington penalty area by French but the referee gave a free kick instead of a penalty. Allan Smith was booked for a handling offence and the play went from end to end at a tremendous pace.

Then, after thirty-nine minutes, with Sharrington struggling on the right flank due to Hart's departure, Neil Baynes proved his worth to the club. He won possession in midfield and drove the ball to the left to Sammy Chaddock. Chaddock had trouble in beating his marker so Baynes ran to the left hand side to support him. He received a short pass, played a tight one-two with the incapacitated Henning, feigned to his left but quickly pushed the ball to his right to dribble past captain Wellings and fired a low shot to the right of keeper, Tye, to put Sharrington 1-0 in the lead. It was a good solo goal and even sections of the Rallingborough crowd applauded Baynes' play. At half-time the score remained 1-0 but Mike Thomas had been booked for a bad tackle on the home winger Fanthom.

During half-time the referee warned both managers and captains to calm the aggression. As the players took to the field for the second half Barrie Trippett counted six injured players in all, three of whom were Henning, Docker and of course Hart who had a swollen knee. Rallingborough attacked from the re-start and were unlucky not to draw level when a shot by Bright deflected off of Graham Bond's outstretched leg, past the unsighted Hawkins and slowly shaved the outside of the left upright. Rallingborough forced four corners in succession but to no avail. Summerton, the lanky defender, sent a 30-yard shot on target only to watch Hawkins drop the ball and a desperate and tired Sharrington defence eventually hook the ball to safety.

Henning and Docker were taking less and less active participation in the game due to their injuries and the workload on the other nine players was taking its toll. In sheer desperation French fouled left-winger Moon to hopefully slow the pace of the game. He was booked for his trouble. Solley, the skilful No. 10 for the home team, beat his marker repeatedly only to see his efforts wasted by his colleagues or cleared by retreating Sharrington players. With Sharrington building fewer and fewer attacks and with the constant and pressurised onslaught by Rallingborough the equaliser looked inevitable. With six minutes remaining the weary, battleworn Sharrington players trooped back into defence once again after a free kick was given for a foul by Leighton on Solley. The shot by Greene, some 25 yards out cleared the heads of the wall and was headed on by Bright to Sinclair to force the ball over the line. The equaliser had come, but when the Sharrington players noticed the linesman standing with his orange flag raised high in the air, they insisted the referee should go and speak to him. He eventually did to the dissatisfaction of the Rallingborough team and crowd. The two men talked for approximately ten seconds before the referee ran quickly to the Sharrington goalmouth and signalled the goal to be disallowed and awarded a free kick to the visitors for some offence which was not evident at the time. The Rallingborough players bombarded the referee with questions and some physical force. He remained firm although he booked one more player and sent off Grimes for persistent arguing. The crowd were incensed. They had seen their team equalise only to witness the goal disallowed through something for which they didn't understand.

The reduction of the home team by one man helped Sharrington to pull themselves back into the game and whilst the crowd were still cat-calling the referee, Leighton and Chaddock linked well together only to see a shot from the new signing skim the crossbar. With eight minutes added on to normal time, Alan Hawkins clawed the ball to safety in the last seconds only to have his right hand trampled upon by marauding Rallingborough forwards. As the referee's whistle blew for full time Hawkins had to have treatment on his damaged hand long after the teams had left the field.

It had been the most brutal and physical game Tony had witnessed for a long time but apart from the crop of injuries he was well satisfied with the 1-0 victory, so much so he cancelled the following Monday's training session, which was most unlike him, simply as a reward for his team's brave efforts.

Chapter 42

On the following Thursday evening Barrie Trippett and Dr. Ericson entered Tony's office.

'Come in and sit down, gents,' remarked Tony as he continued to pour out some coffee from a flask into the three cups on his desk. 'How's the injuries, Doctor?'

Dr. Ericson was of Danish descent but spoke perfectly good English. He was a small man, dressed in a blazer and flannels, with greying hair and a thin, jawline grey beard. He sat down, crossed his right leg over his left knee to reveal a pair of bright black and white checked socks. He spoke in a light voice, 'Actually it's not very good news for you, Tony.' Tony passed the coffee to Dr. Ericson and Barrie before sitting down to listen to the Doctor's opinions. 'If I can start with the most serious injury, I would say Alan Hawkins is the worse. As you know it was not certain whether his index and second fingers on his right hand were broken or not, but the x-rays have now confirmed a hairline break in each finger. I would guess, as he is the goalkeeper that this injury will keep him out for about four weeks.'

Tony drank from his coffee cup but showed no reaction to the Doctor's news. He simply nodded for the Doctor to continue. 'I would say Graham Hart will be out for a period of three or four weeks. He has a patella injury which can only be rested. It is a painful type of injury and will require elasticated strapping for the first two weeks.' The Doctor paused and sipped at his coffee before continuing. Barrie Trippett was jotting notes down on a piece of scrap paper. 'Turning to Alf Henning, I feared on Saturday evening that he may have dislocated his shoulder but fortunately it was only jarred and badly bruised. He is a strong man and I don't foresee the shoulder injury should incapacitate him after this weekend but I wouldn't recommend he played on Saturday. I don't feel he would be 100% fit, but having been in this man's company over the last few days I cannot imagine him expecting to miss the cup game for what he considers to be such a "trivial knock." Finally, Simon Docker's pulled muscle in his right thigh has recurred again and I would suggest a two-week lay off with infra-red treatment daily.' The Doctor placed his file of papers on the floor and sat upright in his chair to await Tony's comments.

'Thank you, Doctor. As you said it is not good news. The only consolation is that we are playing a non-league club on Saturday and hopefully we can progress through to the next round with the players who are fit,' stressed Tony optimistically.

'Do you propose to play Alf?' enquired Barrie Trippett.

'I'm not sure just yet. I think I'll leave the decision until lunch time on Saturday,' replied Tony.

'Will you select the team at the last minute?' asked Barrie.

Tony paused briefly before replying. 'Well I propose to make it clear to young Alan Bates that he will be playing and I won't change the defence. However, with the other injuries restricted to forwards it will really depend upon whether Alf considers he is fit enough to play, but if he isn't I will choose…' Tony paused again as he flicked through the papers in front of him '…number 7 Cracknell, number 8 Baynes, number 9 White, number 10 Poole, number 11 Chaddock with substitute either Henning or Steve Holland. We've certainly had our share of injuries this season. Having said that at least it's given the part-timers a chance to acclimatize themselves to the pros, and the Fourth Division. It is good experience for them and possibly even better for the club as it keeps everyone happy and makes my job easier.' Tony smiled to himself as he locked the papers in his desk drawer. He turned off the desk light. Barrie and Dr. Ericson joked about Tony having the easiest job at the club as all three men left the offices for their respective cars which were parked in front of the ground. 'Don't fool yourselves, men. It may be easy now but wait until all the playing staff are fit and you'll just see how difficult this job of mine will become.'

'Maybe you are right, Tony, but I'm sure you will cope admirably,' commented Dr. Ericson as he closed his door, started the car and drove off slowly waving his right arm through the open window.

'I'll second that, Tony. You'll take this club a long way,' smiled Barrie as he also took his leave.

Tony sat in his car for a moment contemplating the sudden compliments which had been showered upon him. He eventually put the car into first gear and drove home wondering if he had got off to a lucky start with his new job or whether there were bad times ahead. He knew everything had got off to a relatively smooth start, his team were higher than they'd been for many years, the players responded well to him, the directors and chairman were pleasantly surprised with the club's early success, the transfer negotiations had all been free of problems and the supporters were coming back in thousands through the turnstiles. Where was the catch, he thought to himself? Although the injury situation was poor he could still manage to field a reasonably good side of youth and experience and at no time before had the young players let him down. He sensed everything couldn't continue so smoothly but without trying to sound so pessimistic, the only cloud in the sky to halt the steady progress of the club was for a shock defeat in the F.A. Cup on Saturday and a run of bad results in the league. If that happened the job would become intolerable and then he wouldn't have a friend in the world. As he finally approached his home he realised what he was thinking. For some reason he was being negative in his outlook. He knew it was unlike him but the doubt had entered his mind somehow. Was this part of the precarious job as soccer manager? He didn't know. He parked his car in his driveway and slammed the driver's door as though to be rid of the worry on his mind which had needled him during his journey home. Perhaps it was tiredness. It had been a busy week. The doubts persisted until he eventually fell asleep.

Chapter 43

Saturday was a bright day although the wind was gusty and forceful. Tony had arrived in the office at 10.30 a.m. Sid Parkin, in his ragged and stained sports jacket ran to greet Tony as soon as he had heard him. 'Mr. Davidson, Mr. Davidson,' he squeaked breathlessly.

'Yes, Sid, what on earth's the matter?' replied Tony quite matter of fact.

'It's the Hooper Brook Rovers' bus,' he paused momentarily. 'It's broken down just outside Fillingway.'

'What? When did you hear that? Why have I only just been informed?' asked Tony sternly.

Sid was taken aback. He'd never heard Tony raise his voice before. 'I've only just heard myself. Not more than five minutes ago,' replied Sid stroking his hand over his greasy hair.

'What are you doing about it, Sid?' urged Tony picking up the telephone receiver.

'Well, their manager, Walter Harriott, told me they were waiting for another bus to be sent from their home town. It was apparently setting off about five minutes ago. It had all been arranged,' mumbled Sid reading from his telephone note pad.

'But Fillingway's almost 100 miles from Sharrington and Hooper Brook is approximately 60 miles further south. I know it's mainly motorway from Fillingway but they will be cutting it fine,' said Tony as he looked at the map which was hanging on the wall behind him.

'He said he would phone again when they eventually boarded the replacement bus,' said Sid.

'Let me know as soon as he phones again, Sid. I want to speak to him.' Sid nodded. 'In the meantime I am going to telephone Directory Enquiries and get the number of a taxi firm in Fillingway so, if the worse comes to the worse, they can get three or four cabs to the ground. I can warn the taxicab to be ready to pick up the players at a given time, at least. Other than that I don't know what else we can do,' stressed Tony as he dialled the Directory Enquiries number.

At 11.50 a.m. Walter Harriott telephoned to say the replacement bus had arrived but it was overheating rather badly. Sid relayed the information to Tony. 'Put him on to me,' demanded Tony. Sid handed over the receiver quickly, 'Mr. Harriott, my name's Tony Davidson, manager of Sharrington F.C.,' said Tony politely.

'Oh hello, Mr. Davidson. I'm pleased to speak to you. I'm afraid we're in a bit of a mess. Isn't it amazing the day all our players have been dreaming about and two coaches break down on us. It's most frustrating. We are…'

Tony butted in Harriott's conversation. 'I'm afraid time's running out on you, Mr. Harriott. If you can tell me exactly where you are located,' *beep beep beep beep beep beep beep beep beep* 'Oh quick, man, put some coins in!' shouted Tony into the phone after the beeping sound had stopped. 'Hello, hello, are you still there, Harriott?'

'Yes, I'm still here. I thought my money had jammed in the coin box. It's certainly not our day today. What a carry on…'

'Mr. Harriott, please tell me where you are located as I have arranged for some taxis from a nearby firm to pick you up and bring you to Sharrington,' demanded Tony.

'Well, I understand from our driver, the first one that is…' (Tony put his hand over the mouthpiece and mouthed to Sid Parkin, 'We've got a right one here.') '… that we are at junction 27 on the main north to south motorway on the slip road for the northerly route. It's very good of you to arrange this on our behalf, Davidson. It'll be a bit of a rush but…' Tony butted in again and, as time was pressing on, kept his question to a minimum.

'How many of you are there?' quick-fired Tony. 'Now let me see there's the team, plus…' dithered Harriott. 'Just a number PLEASE,' stressed Tony anxiously. There was a brief pause.

'49 exactly,' replied Harriott.

'49. Oh no! I can only get five taxicabs from the firm I spoke to. This will, at least get your team, trainer and yourself here won't it?' Before Harriott could reply there was the familiar *beep beep beep beep beep*. Tony turned to Sid. 'You won't believe this, Sid, but I think he has run out of coins. The beeps are just continuing. Ah! wait a minute. Nothing! It's just cut off. I've never known anything like it. The way he's carrying on you'd have thought they were coming for a week's holiday. I mean there was just no urgency in his voice at all. After all it is the first round of the F.A. Cup and the kick-off is 3.00 p.m. today and not next Saturday,' Tony shouted as he dropped the receiver back in disgust. 'I'll telephone the taxi firm and ask them to send five cabs to pick the players up and get them here as quickly as they can.' Sid smiled to himself whilst thinking of the farcical situation.

At 2.35 p.m. the five taxis arrived at the ground. The spectators who were queuing to get in the ground wondered what on earth was happening as twenty men jumped from the cabs and ran towards the players' entrance carrying balls, bags and kit.

Tony had explained the position to the referee and both men were highly delighted when they saw the Hooper Brook Rovers team rush into the visitors' dressing room. Walter Harriott apologised profusely, but Tony was not keen to hear him relate the whole story at snail's pace, so suggested they talked after the game. The bald-headed, plump little man disappeared into the visitors' dressing room, as if in a trance, carrying an old-fashioned briefcase under his arm.

A good crowd had turned up for the game hoping to see Sharrington progress into the next round. Alf Henning had opted to play so Tony White stepped down to substitute. The wind was still strong and Tony urged his players to keep the ball on the floor for better control.

The amateur team had changed briskly into their all white strip and gone out onto the pitch at 2.50 p.m. They were a side of small stature who were obviously surprised with the 8,107 crowd, which had been recorded, and also perturbed by the events of the unfortunate journey.

The game started at a furious pace with the Sharrington team looking the much fitter, more skilful and busier. Hooper Brook Rovers couldn't seem to keep possession and the makeshift home team were creating all the chances from the errors. In fact, after 14 minutes a clever move by Smith, Thomas, Chaddock and Henning ended with Paul Cracknell scoring a simple goal, his first for the club. The visitors recovered slightly from this early goal and kept the score to 1-0 until six minutes from half-time when Baynes thumped a cross ball from the right to the left and Graham Poole leapt high to head the hovering ball into the net. Sharrington led 2-0 at half-time. Alan Bates had an easy baptism for his first game.

During the second half the visiting amateur team looked drained and tired. Their big day had got off to a bad start and being 2-0 down away from home to an obviously stronger and more professional team, didn't give them any incentive to try harder. Although they defended bravely the constant Sharrington pressure wore them down. After 66 minutes Alf Henning scored with his head from a good corner by Sammy Chaddock. Three minutes later Graham Poole added his second with an excellent thirty-yard shot which swerved in the high winds. The visitors were still trying to attack but they were thwarted time and again by the hard-tackling Fourth Division team. The spectators were appreciative of Hooper Brook Rovers' efforts. The end finally came when Alf Henning, who hadn't looked to have an injured shoulder, intercepted a cross-field pass by the visitors' left full-back and ran unhindered to round the sprawling goalkeeper and casually stroked the ball into the empty goal.

Sharrington won the game 5-0. It was an easy game for them but it showed Tony how much his team were improving when comparing this game to the earlier friendly game against amateurs Anster Heath.

Hooper Brook Rovers finally departed by coach from Sharrington at 7.30 p.m. Tony received a telegram from Walter Harriott to thank him for the club's hospitality and to confirm they had arrived home safely at 11.15 p.m., very tired, a little more experienced, financially better off; and with an offer to Sharrington to play a friendly in preparation for the next season.

Tony acknowledged the telegram confirming he would keep the offer in mind but suggested that if he could arrange the game to be played at Sharrington, then Hooper Brook should travel by train or alternatively beep beep beep beep beep beep beep. He hoped Harriott would understand the attempted humour.

Chapter 44

'Sharrington drawn away to Western amateur team in next round!' shouted the newspaper seller in the centre of the town.

'Who have they drawn?' enquired Bob Bennett as he passed by. 'Buy a paper, mate,' snorted the newspaper seller. 'Oh come on, fellow. Tell me,' said a sad-faced Bob.

'Look, mate, if I told everyone the main lunchtime news I wouldn't sell a paper at all would I,' lectured the determined newspaper seller.

'O.K, here's the money,' replied Bob hoisting his mackintosh as he searched for the correct amount.

'Thanks,' mumbled the newspaper seller.

Bob frantically looked at the stop-press to see who Sharrington had been drawn against. As he looked down the 2nd round draw list he noticed Treecliffe were at home to another non-league team, Bayscroft Utd, Rallingborough away to Seamingway, Third Division leaders Summerstone Albion at home to ex-Fourth Division team Brookfield United. Eventually, three quarters of the way through the list he noticed the fixture Lepperton Trinity v Sharrington. Bob did not feel too happy at the thought of the away game to the Western Area's amateurs. He knew they had beaten amateurs Craddock Town in the 1st round by 2-1 and he was also aware that the Trinity team had beaten Verrington in last season's 1st round. They played on a tiny ground and the crowd had to stand around the touchlines. He had an uneasy feeling about Sharrington's chances. He stuffed the paper deep into his mackintosh pocket and pulled up the collar before striding off down the street.

'Mr. Haydell, there's a Mr. Davidson, the Sharrington football manager to see you,' said a pretty young girl as she entered the plush office.

'Ah good! Tell him to come in,' replied Mark Haydell, the well-dressed business executive of Gold Star Promotions.

'This way please, Mr. Davidson,' announced the young secretary politely. Tony walked briskly into Haydell's office. The two men shook hands.

'Pleased to meet you, Mr. Davidson,' remarked Mark Hayden.

'Hello, Mr. Haydell. Thank you for allowing me some of your time,' answered Tony.

'Tell me what can I do for you?' asked the business executive as he hitched his trousers before sitting.

'I'll come straight to the point,' said Tony doing likewise. 'I have one or two ideas about raising money for the club through weekly ticket sales, or a lottery of some sort. I would be interested to hear of what lines you have and which type you feel would be advantageous to Sharrington F.C.

'Well, first of all, there is no doubt that football clubs are turning to both types you have mentioned and finding the revenue from these ventures a great help towards supplementing the club's funds,' explained the genial Mark Haydell.

'Oh? Do you promote for many football clubs?' enquired Tony.

'Oh yes, we do a tremendous amount of business with them. This is, of course, not all from this branch but as a healthy total of our overall sales within the organisation. The weekly "Spot Prize" ticket is popular or alternatively our special "Gold Quest" card game is proving very successful indeed, since its introduction last year. On the other hand the lotteries we operate up and down the country, which as you are aware offer better cash rewards than the weekly tickets, are our leading product at the moment,' explained Mark Haydell.

'Could you explain to me the facts in detail. I mean the minimum ordering level you would require, our profit margin, the best product for a club such as ours, payment systems.' Tony paused for a second. 'In fact the whole operation behind the ticket scheme,' summarised Tony with a broad smile.

Mark Haydell lifted a pile of literature out of his desk drawer and proceeded to explain carefully the "Gold Spot" products to Tony for a period of one and half hours. At the end of the discussion Tony confirmed he would raise the "Gold Spot Promotions" products at the next board meeting and promised Mark Haydell the club's final decision in the next few weeks. Mark Haydell had been very helpful and Tony was satisfied in his own mind the lottery would bring valuable revenue to the Sharrington club. He didn't foresee any problems from his board of directors but preferred to seek their permission before giving the go ahead to launch the lottery scheme.

Chapter 45

'E-L-L-I-S-T-A-R-T E-L-L-I-S-T-A-R-T,' chanted the visiting supporters as they thronged together behind the right hand goal. Sharrington's younger supporters replied a sarcastic moan of WHO? WHO? WHO? WHO? WHO? WHO?

Another good crowd had assembled for this important home league match against currently second placed Ellistart. The shock news of the day was that star striker Deighton and right winger Turpin were both unfit to play following injuries in the 1-0 home win against Prent Park in the F.A. Cup 1st Round the previous week. The replacements were Fletcher and Grant respectively. The cup match had been a hard fought battle particularly after the 2-2 draw away to Hill Wade in the League Cup replay only three days beforehand. Ellistart were now through to the 3rd Round and had drawn a plum tie with Collingwood of the 3rd Division.

Tony was aware of the difficulties ahead for Sharrington in this game but in view of the injuries to two of the visitors' better players he had asked his team to work hard and give Ellistart no time to get into their stride. 'If you can put them under pressure from the start of the game, lads, and keep their forwards from running at you from midfield positions, I think we can do well today. Don't let the crowd worry you. You are playing better every week and lying in a good position in the league and two points today will put us on to 14 points and in contention for the top three places. You have all seen Ellistart play and, make no mistake about it, they are a good side but they will also be worrying about us. We are only two points behind them and a win today is as good as four points for us. We are getting a reputation as a hard team but, be that as it may, we can also play some good football, so let's show 'em. Get out there and prove to me you can cope with a bit of pressure,' said Tony with great encouragement. The players ran out onto the pitch to a good reception.

During the week the three injured players were progressing well and Alf Henning's shoulder injury had cleared completely. Tony had therefore relied upon the same team that had defeated Hooper Brook Rovers. He was a little anxious about how young Alan Bates would perform in his first full league game. Ellistart were obviously aware of the goalkeeper's inexperience and would no doubt test him early on. Tony knew his defence would guard Bates as much as possible but he could only wait and see how he dealt with direct shots and crosses. Although

Tony, Barrie and Alan Hawkins had worked hard on Bates' training during the past two weeks it was totally up to the young lad himself on how the occasion affected him. Alan Bates was an agile confident goalkeeper, six foot tall, weighed 12 stones and Tony rated him as a brave player with a great future.

Tony took his seat in the Directors' Box for the first half. All Sharrington's directors were present for the game.

'It's a good crowd again, Tony,' stated Steve King as he buttoned up his camel-coloured overcoat.

'Yes, I would estimate above 10,000. Although the Ellistart supporters must make up for a third of the total,' answered Tony as the two teams changed ends so they would be kicking towards their own supporters in the second half. Young Alan Bates received a good ovation as he ran towards the goal he would be defending during the first half.

'How's the young goalkeeper feeling?' enquired Bill Boothroyd timidly. 'He's a little nervous but I'm sure he will do his best,' replied Tony. The Ellistart team kicked off.

'Of course he'll be nervous. That's a good sign. After all it's his first league game isn't it? He looks a big lad and judging by the way he handled the ball during the kick in, he doesn't look too overawed by the occasion to me,' blurted Eddie Flannagan. 'By the way, Tony,' he continued, 'I like the look of Baynes. He's a skilful player and what a workhorse,' enthused the ruddy faced director.

Tony nodded in agreement but didn't take his eyes off the game. Ellistart looked sluggish in comparison to the performance Tony had witnessed two weeks beforehand. They were clearly missing Deighton and Turpin. Likewise Sharrington did not seem to be able to raise their game after the sluggish start. The play was concentrated in the middle of the pitch and both teams were making stupid passing errors. As the first half wore on Tony found the game tiresome to watch and judging by the talking going on around him, other people were of the same opinion.

Just prior to half-time Bates made a full length save from a 20-yard shot by Fenning, the visitors No. 10. From the resultant corner Bates produced a positive punch to clear the ball from danger. The first half ended goalless and neither team had deserved a goal. It was a lack-lustre performance all round.

Tony met Barrie Trippett just before going into the home team dressing room. 'I just can't understand them all, Tony,' he said. 'They are playing as though they haven't the slightest interest in the game at all.'

'Yes, it's pathetic isn't it. I'm sure going to stir things up a bit,' said Tony angrily. He burst into the dressing room. All the players looked up in surprise at his entrance. He slammed the door and shouted, 'What do you think you are all doing out there?' pointing in the direction of the pitch. 'You were shocking! A disgrace! There has not been an ounce of effort from one of you during that first half. What's wrong? Can someone tell me?' There was no comment from any player. There was an embarrassing few silent moments. Tony shouted again, 'I know we've had a few good wins of late but that is no reason to rest on your laurels. I was bored, 10,000 supporters were bored and even the goalkeeper was bored for the simple reason he had nothing to do!' There were a few chuckles from the players. 'It's nothing to laugh at, you three,' stormed Tony pointing to Smith, Thomas and Leighton, who were sitting in the far corner. 'It's perfectly true. On today's showing you deserve your wages stopping and if the second half is anything like the first, I'll make a point of docking one week's money from each and everyone of you. Now get out there and start doing some work. I know the referee's bell has not sounded yet, Mr. Poole, just get back onto the pitch and graft.'

The players trooped out, thoroughly shell-shocked. 'And get your heads up,' echoed Tony's voice as they ventured down the tunnel.

'If Ellistart's manager has given his players an outburst like that, we are in for a cracking second half,' commented Barrie picking up his sponge and bucket.

'I just won't stand for it, Barrie. I know it's not always possible to play to pre-match plans but I cannot tolerate a total lack of effort and a disregard for paying spectators,' explained Tony.

'Are you going into the Stand for the second half?' enquired Barrie.

'No, I'm not. I'm going to sit in the dugout and remind anyone personally if he falls back into apathy,' urged Tony.

The two men and substitute Tony White took up their places alongside the pitch. 'Get ready, Tony, I might decide to substitute someone shortly. Go and have a few runs up and down the touchline,' stated Tony. The youngster nodded his head and exercised as he had been instructed.

The second half opened with the Sharrington players taking the upper hand. It was evident that Tony's half-time message had had its effect. The red-shirted players were running, tackling and generally playing with more effort. Tony kept on at certain individuals to ensure they knew he was still there. Ellistart were still ineffective in front of goal and Bates was having a relatively trouble free afternoon.

Sharrington were starting to build attacks from defence and constructively through to the attack. Henning and Baynes had gone close to scoring in the first fifteen minutes of the restart. The Ellistart supporters were noticeably quiet as the home team launched attack after attack. Cracknell and Chaddock were dominating their respective wings and Leighton had two excellent long-range shots well saved by Bernards, in the visitors' goal.

With only thirteen minutes remaining, Tony substituted Graham Poole, who was having a miserable game, for young Tony White. The youngster was quick to make his mark on the game. Following a pass from Graham Bond he dashed into the heart of the Ellistart defence with electrifying speed and passed a fine, angled ball to Paul Cracknell to run onto. The winger's cross was to the near post and Alf Henning's lunging header hit the goalkeeper's knee and shot quickly across the area into the path of Tony White who joyfully thumped the ball high and hard over the prostrate keeper and hit the back stanchion on the inside of the net. Within the space of being on the pitch for three minutes, Tony White had scored his first goal for Sharrington. The crowd jumped up and down wildly to greet the goal. Tony was also on his feet applauding White's goal. Barrie Trippett threw the towel into the air in delight. The Ellistart team coolly tried to work their way into the game and their professional approach was refreshing. They did not show any dissent against being a goal behind. They simply continued to try and play football, but it was too late. Sharrington kept control of the last few minutes and ended the game on a high note by firing some excellent shots and creating some exciting goalmouth incidents. The game ended 1-0 in favour of Sharrington, and substitute White was the dressing room hero. Tony congratulated his team's much improved second half display but only stayed for a few moments in the dressing room before departing to the directors' bar.

'What on earth did you say to those lads at half-time?' quizzed a delighted Steve King.

'Yes, it was the most sensational transformation I've ever witnessed,' rejoiced Eddie Flannagan, raising his pint mug to his mouth.

'Oh, I just made a few crucial comments,' said Tony coyly.

'I bet you did!' laughed Eddie. 'Whatever you said, it paid off and it's another two points in the bag for us. It also puts us level on points with Ellistart, and, with two relatively easy games against Verrington and Warworth in the next two weeks, we could be on top by half way through the season.'

'I'll not jump the gun by saying we will win against these two lowly clubs. For instance look what happened at Crookaby,' announced Tony mildly.

'Don't be modest, man! You know you'll take this club up to Division

Three in one season,' prattled Eddie. Tony didn't answer. He smiled momentarily before going to speak to Ellistart manager George Tranter, who was in the company of Jack Elliott.

Chapter 46

During the following week's board meeting it was agreed to launch the Gold Spot Promotions lottery which would offer ten cash prizes ranging from a top prize of £500 to the last prize of £5. Total payout would be £1,050. It was anticipated that 200 ticket sellers should sell 100 tickets per week. The total sales should amount to £2,000 and of that amount Sharrington were expected to pocket £600 per week, on the assumption all tickets were sold. The board agreed to advertise for ticket sellers before fixing a date with 'Gold Spot Promotions' to start the regular order of tickets. It was hoped that some small businesses would advertise the lottery and assist where possible.

'Well, if all goes to plan, gentlemen, the £600 profit per week could be put to good use,' commented Jack Elliott.

'Aye, it's a good idea all right! If we can keep it in operation throughout the close season as well, I calculate we will make £30,000 a year and that would be invaluable to us. Who knows, if we have understated the allocation of saleable tickets we may be able to add to that figure,' enthused Eddie Flannagan.

'If we get a good response to our advertisement we should be able to launch the scheme by the end of this month,' remarked Bill Boothroyd gleefully.

'That would be optimistic, I think, Bill, but I think we should be planning definitely to implement it by the end of November,' stated Eddie adamantly.

'Perhaps that date is more realistic on reflection,' said Bill polishing his glasses on his large white handkerchief.

'We will just have to wait and see what response we get to the advert and plan from there on,' summarised Steve King.

'Yes, I agree Steve. I will arrange for Sid to ensure that the advertisement will be shown in the *Sharrington Echo* tomorrow evening and I'm sure we can all contact our business friends to see if they will help us out with this new venture,' concluded Jack Elliott.

All the directors nodded in agreement.

The meeting progressed swiftly. The manager's report of the home game against Ellistart had been given. The Fourth Division league table and results were analysed, the financial position was read out, the list of repairs to the ground was discussed and agreed upon and the arrangements for Saturday's visit to lowly Verrington were clarified.

During the last item on the minutes headed "Any Other Business," Tony raised the 2nd round draw of the F.A. Cup against Lepperton Trinity. Although this matter had been discussed during the previous week's meeting Tony looked apprehensive as he stood up to address the board of directors.

'As you are all aware, we have to travel to Lepperton Trinity in three weeks' time to play the 2nd round F.A. Cup tie.' Tony paused briefly. 'And also a fact of which you are all aware, is that our friends from the Third Division enter the cup competition at this point in time. What I'm getting to is that (a) I would like to sign young Paul Brooke from Leston United before they have a cup run and refuse to release him until it is over and (b) I want him for my squad now, just in case we progress well in the competition. Also, but more important, I feel that if we wait until Leston United appoint a new manager then the player will either be not for sale, or, if he is, then it will be for a much higher fee,' said Tony seriously.

'But we said you could sign him a few weeks ago, Tony. What's the problem?' interrupted Eddie Flannagan light-heartedly.

'No, I'd not forgotten. It's just that I've spoken to the club's caretaker manager and while he is not one of Brooke's most ardent admirers he is looking for strikers to help them from their current slump and goal starvation,' replied Tony, half-heartedly.

'Well what's this leading up to?' enquired Eddie again.

Tony delayed his reply briefly. He looked anxious, as though he was wording the next sentence carefully inside his head, but fearing the response of the directors. He finally spoke. 'He has asked if we would agree to a part exchange deal of Graham Poole for Paul Brooke, with Sharrington paying a balance of £15,000.'

'That is a surprise,' stressed Steve King immediately.

'It's a shock to me too!' chirped Bill Boothroyd, as he sucked on his mint sweet.

'It's more than a shock. It's another of our manager's cunning deals if you ask me,' laughed Eddie Flannagan. He continued, 'I mean, who for one moment would expect the likes of Graham Poole to increase their team's goal scoring ability. He may be only a caretaker manager but surely he is aware Pooley's not the fire power he needs to set a Third Division team back on the road to success. Can you honestly say, Tony, that this stand-in manager asked you about Poole specifically?'

Tony smirked slightly, 'May be I recommended the player in our conversation, but as he seemed to know of Poole's ability and experience I think we should accept the deal as it was put to us before it is retracted.'

'It seems a bit harsh on Graham in some respects,' murmured Steve King as he clicked the end of his biro repeatedly.

'Yes, I agree it does but this player Brooke is the one I want, and with respect to Graham Poole he simply does not have the overall qualities I'm looking for in my players for Sharrington F.C. Admittedly he has worked hard in training and tried his utmost but as you will recall from last Saturday he lacks the competitive spirit and total involvement in the game. I must say that he has played in a different role to which he is used to, but his ability is lacking. Let's face it, he may do well for Leston United but, after all, we are running this club for success and not for sentimental reasons. I simply feel we cannot afford to miss this golden opportunity to sign Brooke and I would hope you'll give me the go-ahead to try and finalise the deal tomorrow.'

'What if Poole doesn't want to move to Leston, Tony?' enquired Steve King.

'Oh, I think he will agree to the move. It is, of course, a move to the Third Division, a forward attacking position again, and no doubt a move so close, as one to Leston, will not cause too many problems for him,' stressed Tony officiously.

'What about Brooke? Is there any guarantee he will want to come to Sharrington?' mused Eddie.

'Oh, I don't think there will be any problem there either,' said Tony confidently. 'Let's look at the facts. For a start Leston are struggling. Secondly, the name of Sharrington is starting to attract some interest in the football world. Our results are improving all the time, our new signings are respected players in the game, our attendance on Saturday was 4,000 more than Leston's last home crowd. We are a club who are going places and finally a move from Leston is not so great as to make the lad feel homesick for his parents.'

'Well, that doesn't seem to leave much to be said, gentlemen, as usual,' remarked Jack Elliott. 'All in favour? O.K, Tony: go ahead.'

The following day, the transfer deal was announced to the two players concerned and by Thursday evening both had agreed to the transfer. Paul Brooke signed for Sharrington at his parents' home after Tony had cleared one or two delicate points with Mr. and Mrs. Brooke and Graham Poole signed for Leston United after saying to the press that: 'the transfer came out of the blue but I am pleased with a move back to the Third Division.'

Tony was quick to point out to the press that Paul Brooke was bought to strengthen the full-back position, as the club only had two recognised full-backs on the books. He made the point that Brooke had not been bought for the future only, but would get his chance as soon as Tony thought he deserved the opportunity. Tony was quoted as saying: 'I would eventually like to field a settled team, but with the constant problem of injuries it is a very difficult thing to do for over a set period of time. I am therefore bringing players to the club who are prepared to fight for their place, compete hard and fair, entertain the crowds with their skill, work and play as a team unit, with a team spirit, and, most of all, I am building a squad to take Sharrington out of the doldrums and into the First Division!' Tony did not comment on the position of Graham Bond, as captain, but he knew a meeting with him was inevitable shortly.

Chapter 47

'Come on, Bob, we'll be late for the kick-off,' shouted Eddie Fisher as he popped his head out of Frank Sneddon's car passenger window. Frank pipped the car hooter loudly. Bob stumbled out of the front door and awkwardly fell into the back seat of the car, clutching a bacon sandwich in his right hand and holding a batch of newspapers under his left arm.

'Sorry, men,' blurted Bob, spraying the backs of his friends with food.

'It's about time you were here ready and waiting when we call for you,' commented Eddie sarcastically.

'I've said I'm sorry, haven't I,' stressed Bob before pushing the sandwich back into his mouth.

'That's all well and good but we have to wait for you every time we arrange to pick you up at home. I mean it's not much to ask for you to be ready once in a while, surely,' argued Eddie.

'O.K, both of you. This could go on all the way to Verrington,' said Frank, trying to stop the men from bickering. 'Let's get on our way pretty smartish as no doubt there will be a lot of support for the team today. I mean Verrington's only 40 odd miles away and we're late already.'

'Yeah, and we know whose responsible for the delay don't we,' quipped Eddie.

'Oh, don't start that again, you.' Frank interrupted Bob's sentence by switching the car radio on full blast. All three men laughed and began to settle down on their way to Verrington.

'I'm surprised to see Davidson hasn't made the new boy Brooke substitute today,' commented Eddie.

'It's not his style is it Eddie? He prefers to let his new players have a week or so getting to know the rest of the team before launching them into action,' reflected Frank.

'And quite right too,' agreed Bob, 'He didn't play Baynes or Leighton straight away and just look how well they have fitted into the side, Eddie.'

'That's true, but all other managers are usually quick to blood their new signings, aren't they,' asked Eddie.

'Ye,s but I think Davidson is handling himself extremely efficiently as a manager and by instilling into players that they must have the team spirit and knowledge of their new colleagues' style of play before being given a chance in the team, it makes for… er… er… well, a better all-round feeling within the club,' suggested Frank as he pulled out to overtake a line of slower vehicles.

'Well , Frank! That seems to be exactly how the club is running at the moment. There's a good atmosphere amongst the players, the supporters and from what I've heard the directors are highly delighted with Davidson's positive and dedicated approach to the club,' urged Bob from the back seat.

'How far are we from the ground now, Frank?' requested Eddie.

'Not far now. The last signpost said "Verrington six miles",' answered Frank.

'It says here, in this newspaper article, that Verrington's manager, Albert Fisher, thinks his side have "turned the corner" now that they have beaten Prent Park and drawn to the league leaders Seamingway, in their last two home matches,' read out Bob.

'He must be kidding! More like a bit of good luck to me,' suggested Eddie scratching his head.

'They have had a bad start to the season and are currently bottom club on seven points if my memory serves me correctly, but like all games now, for them they have got to fight their way clear. It is up to Sharrington to continue their own winning run here today, so it will certainly be an interesting match tactically, I feel,' mused Frank, carefully lighting a cigarette.

'Well, at least they won't have to face both our ex-players transferred to Verrington earlier this season. It says in this report that Braddock is injured and will miss the game but Sanders will be out to prove a point against his old club,' laughed Bob.

'Can you see all right from here, men?' shrieked Bob, pushing his way behind the visitors' goal.

'Yeah, it's a good view, but I'm a bit squashed,' muttered Frank.

'There's not much room in this section of the ground. It seems they've packed all of the Sharrington supporters in here,' said Eddie as he watched the game.

'Fancy missing the start of the game,' moaned Bob.

'No comment, Mr. Bennett,' said Frank and Eddie in unison.

'Oh, good ball, Neil, …good run Sammy… nice cross… good header Alf… it's in… oh no! Excellent save, keeper,' shouted Bob as the Sharrington supporters clapped their team efforts.

'Baynes and Leighton are putting on a good display again,' said Frank.

'Yes, and the two wingmen, Cracknell and Chaddock, are giving those two full-backs some problems,' remarked Eddie pointing down to the touchlines.

'It's all Sharrington! They are playing with so much confidence,' said Bob excitedly.

'They've been on top for the last twenty minutes,' commented Eddie.

'Oh, what a glorious pass. It's split their defence wide open. Alf's onto it… yes… it's there… brilliant goal,' cheered Bob. The three men laughed out aloud as they clapped and shouted their delight at the goal to Sharrington.

Before Verrington had time to settle from Henning's 32-minute goal, a loose ball ran from a packed home team goalmouth and Alan Smith struck a fierce left footed shot into the top right hand corner of the net.

'Two-nil – yeah… yeah… Smithy you're a beauty,' chanted Bob Bennett as he danced deliriously up and down.

At half-time the score was Verrington – 0, Sharrington – 2. In the second half the play continued in the same vein with Sharrington dominating the game in every department. 'Only ten minutes left to play, men,' stressed Frank, looking at his watch. 'Did you see that? It was brilliant. The way Leighton beat those two men. It's so easy,' raved Bob. 'Ooohhh! Hard luck, Whitey. Good effort,' shouted Eddie.

'This is clever play. Come on, Thomas, make your tackle… oh he's round him… Good shot lad… it's bounced off of French… oh no would you believe it? it's fallen to old Basil Sanders… it's in… 1-2,' said a sullen-faced Bob.

'Well he couldn't miss that, could he? My missus could have scored that open goal,' muttered Frank in disbelief.

'Fancy Sanders scoring against us, eh? How long left, Frank?' asked an anxious Eddie Fisher.

'About four or five minutes, I make it,' replied Frank.

Straight from the restart Baynes beat two men before sending an accurate pass to the right wing for Cracknell to cross to the penalty area, only to see a Verrington defender, Potter, head out for a corner.

'Come on, lads. Let's make sure,' shouted Bob, 'Good corner, Paul. It's in! It's in! It's French from the corner again.'

'Now that was an excellent header. The goalkeeper didn't stand a chance with that. It went like a rocket from French's head,' praised Eddie. 'That's it now, lads. What a time to get back a two-goal advantage. Just when Verrington could have pressed for an equaliser as well,' shouted Frank above the wild cheering crowd.

'The ref's blown. 3-1! An excellent result, lads. Let's get back home and do some celebrating shall we?' asked a delighted Bob Bennett as he patted his two friends heartily on their backs.

The three men ran from the ground laughing and dancing like three young children. At last they felt as though Sharrington was a team competing for success, and after today's performance they visualised Third Division football next season.

Chapter 48

'I see Treecliffe had a good win at Seamingway on Saturday,' said Barrie Trippett reading from the Monday morning edition of the *Sharrington Echo*.

'Yes, I understand Paul Simpson played the captain's role for them by scoring in the last minute,' laughed Tony waiting for a voice at the other end of the phone.

'Aye, he chose to take the penalty instead of young Stuart Angel,' remarked Barrie. Tony nodded and suddenly spoke into the phone: 'Bob, it's Tony Davidson. Hello.' He paused. The two voices discussed things generally at first then Tony asked numerous questions about the Lepperton game from the previous Saturday. The answers were short and straight to the point and after some five minutes the conversation ended and Tony replaced the telephone receiver.

'That was Bob Vincent, an old friend of mine, who has volunteered to watch Lepperton Trinity for us before our cup-tie. Apparently they won comfortably last Saturday against the leaders in the league. I understand they play hard and have some good midfield players with an excellent centre-forward by the name of Sharkey. He scored both goals from corner kicks. Bob will watch them again next Saturday, in their away game, at Swanton Athletic,' said Tony.

'I'm glad you've had them watched. I didn't fancy taking our team to an unknown team and unfamiliar surroundings,' commented Barrie.

'I thought it would be advisable also to get some idea of the task ahead, Barrie,' stated Tony writing an entry into his desk diary. 'Now that I know that aspect is covered, I want us to concentrate on training this week. As you know we've got Warworth United here on Saturday and although we're on the crest of a wave at the moment, I don't want to ease off on training this week. Here's an outline of the sessions for this week,' continued Tony, passing a list of handwritten notes to Barrie. Both men followed the details as Tony expanded with the help of gestures from his hands.

(am) Monday – five mile run – hot bath – afternoon off
(am/pm) Tuesday – five mile run – exercises – sprinting – shooting
(am/pm) Wednesday – set pieces – specialised training – new moves
(am/pm) Thursday – " " " " " " "
(am) Friday – short sprints – exercises – two-touch football
(am) Saturday – short sprints – exercises

The two men discussed all the aspects of training in the list then went to start Monday's session.

'Could I have a word with you, boss?' enquired Graham Bond at the end of Monday's training sessions.

'Yes, sure, Graham. Do you want to come up to my office?' asked Tony reassuringly.

The two men finally arrived and sat down. 'Now what's the matter ,Graham?' said Tony as he relaxed in his chair.

Graham didn't answer immediately. He swallowed slightly, adjusted his seating position then crossed his legs. He finally spoke, 'I don't know how to say this boss but I'm a bit worried about my position at Sharrington now that you've signed young Paul Brooke. I mean the press are suggesting you might be considering transferring me.' He paused briefly. 'To be perfectly honest I am enjoying my game at the moment and feel that I can still offer Sharrington…' Graham couldn't finish his statement because Tony interrupted him in no uncertain terms.

'Graham, don't say any more. I'm going to give you my views so we both know exactly where we stand,' said Tony firmly. 'In the first place, I bought Paul Brooke for two reasons: (a) he is a good young player with a bright future, and (b) I hope he will be a useful stand-in for us should we suffer an injury to you or Smithy this season. After all, you two were the only full-backs on our books as you were only too aware.' Tony leaned forward placing his hands palm downwards on his desk. 'Graham, you are the team captain. You are a fine example to the rest of the lads in the club. To be honest I was not too happy with you at the start of my career here but I'm delighted to say you have improved with every game and proved my earlier thoughts wrong. You are only 30 years old aren't you?' Graham nodded. 'Well, Graham I've no intention of transferring you from the club, nor for that matter do I propose to replace you immediately with Brooke. Having said that, I want everyone to fight for their place, as you know, but you can rest assured I want you involved at this club as long as I feel you can contribute to its stability and success. Don't worry, Graham, I've no intention of putting you out to grass yet,' said Tony smiling slightly.

Graham Bond looked happier as he said, 'That's what I wanted to hear, boss. I accept what you say and hope I can prove to you that I'm worthy of captaining the team on the field.'

The two men discussed the affairs of the club in the capacity of manager and captain respectively before leaving the ground.

Tony was glad to have spoken in earnest with Graham Bond and confirmed to himself that he was a good professional and conscientious man.

Graham Bond felt likewise following his conversation with Tony. He had been delighted to hear that he figured largely in the future of Sharrington F.C.

The week's training continued most satisfactorily as far as Tony and Barrie were concerned. They were particularly pleased with all the players' efforts and their dedication to the work in hand. There was an excellent atmosphere amongst all the players although it was apparent they all knew that they were fighting for a regular place in the team.

The three injured players, Docker, Hart and Hawkins, were unable to take part in any of the week's training sessions but Dr. Ericson had told Tony that the first two players would be fit for the following week. However, Hawkins was unlikely to be fit for another two or three weeks.

Tony spent three evenings of the week specially training the three part-time players, Bates, White and Cracknell. They responded well to his coaching but he regretted that they couldn't get the benefit of full-time training with the professional players. He realised how difficult the task was for each of them now that they were three important members of the current team. He knew though that everyone would have time together to discuss the moves, plans and methods of the week's training session before the game on Saturday, during the pre-match training session and talk-in.

Chapter 49

BAYNES THE HERO, AS WARWORTH FALL

Tony Davidson, Sharrington's young manager must tonight be celebrating without a care in the world. This afternoon he witnessed his newly assembled team of existing players, youngsters and experienced men convincingly defeat newly promoted Warworth United by 5-2. Not only should he be happy with the results of late but more so with the way in which Neil Baynes so skilfully stamps his great ability and presence on the team.

From the start of the game Baynes was the Sharrington star. After only 90 seconds of the game he took a return pass from Alf Henning to lob the ball over the helpless goalkeeper, Clubb, and into the empty net. Before the visitors had time to settle down again, Baynes drove a perfect free kick into the path of his colleague of old, Micky Leighton, who volleyed the ball into the back of the Warworth net, to record his first goal for the club. It was Sharrington 2 , Warworth 0, after only six minutes play.

Warworth, who are having a mixed season so far, couldn't cope with Sharrington's exciting play. Baynes, White and Leighton were linking well together, young Cracknell and Chaddock devastated the wing play, Henning was his menacing best and the defence was solid, hard-tackling and quick to recover. The blend was excellent and the transformation in the team over a short period of time is unbelievable. Bates, the young part-time goalkeeper was untroubled. Sharrington controlled the first half and after their first two early goals they created enough chances to have trebled the score but fine saves by Clubb and the woodwork prevented any addition. Henning, Chaddock and White saw their shots saved by an acrobatic Clubb, and Baynes had a glancing header hit the crossbar and a direct free kick smack against the upright.

However, after 41 minutes, a rare cross by Warworth's right winger, Hardy, caught young Bates cold and the keeper dropped the ball at the feet of ex-Sharrington centre-forward John Turner who nudged it over the line to make the score 2-1.

That was the half-time score. At the restart, Sharrington took complete control of the game before Warworth used the goal before half-time as an incentive to their play. After 56 minutes of continuous pressure by the home side, a skilful run by Cracknell beat two defenders leaving them flat-footed and off-balance, and he was left with the simplest chance of side-footing the ball past the advancing Clubb and into the corner of the net.

Baynes was the master. His work-rate was second to none and when matched with his natural skill he really looked a player capable of holding a position in a First or Second Division side. It was Baynes who strode majestically through the bemused Warworth defence beating four players easily, and carefully striking the ball sweetly out of the reach of the goalkeeper to make the score 4-1 after 77 minutes.

The crowd of 10,300 were delighted. They chanted 'Easy, Easy, Easy,' continuously, and, as a reward for their efforts, Baynes again started a move which switched play from the left of the field to the right. Cracknell jinked to sidestep the advancing Jackson and centred into the crowded goalmouth. There was a mix-up in Warwor-th's defence and young Tony White stabbed the loose ball into the goal to make the score 5-1.

The remainder of the game was, in the main, Sharrington showing their ability to keep possession of the ball, but in between time, after 84 minutes the visitors' left full-back, Seekard, fired in a 35-yard shot which rifled under the crossbar, with Bates well and truly beaten.

Sharrington deserved their 5-2 victory and were given a standing ovation at the end of the game by the spectators. It was not a happy return for John Turner but there will be no doubt in his mind about the complete transformation in the Sharrington team over such a short period of time.

Sharrington are now on 18 points after 14 games and joint top with Harloft. If they can continue to keep their current form going until the end of the season then Tony Davidson should guide his team of Sharrington to Third Division football next season, at his first sensational attempt.

by Grant Evans
(match reporter)

'What's all the trouble down there?' shouted an irate middle-aged man leaning out of his bedroom window.

The commotion stopped immediately. There was a brief silence. Suddenly the noise started again. A dustbin was knocked over and the sounds of fighting broke out again. There was a scuffle, grunts and growls.

'Right! That's it! Whoever you are, I'm going to call the police. I can't stand any more of this!' yelled the man from upstairs to the intruders. He disappeared inside. A few bedroom lights, in close proximity, flashed on to investigate.

'Who are you? What are you up to down there!' enquired another neighbour. Before he could say any more two figures ran from the shadows at the side of the road, quickly disappearing from the view of the neighbour and running in the direction of the Sharrington town-centre. The neighbour could hear a further scuffle break out once the two figures, who he recognised as male youths, got out of sight.

After a period of ten minutes a police car arrived and was met by both men and a number of inquisitive neighbours. Two officers were quick to get out of the panda car.

'What's the problem then?' enquired the driver pulling his notepad from the breast pocket of his uniform.

'Well, I was woken up with a noise from outside. In fact it sounded like two men arguing and fighting,' said the first man.

'What time was that, sir?' said the other officer.

'About twenty minutes ago, I think,' replied the neighbour pulling his overcoat collar over his neck.

'That would be two-thirty then,' checked the driver looking at his wristwatch.

'Yes,' stammered the first man nodding his head.

'What happened then?' asked the driver.

'Well, I shouted down to them and for a moment it went quiet but they knocked over a dustbin, by the sounds of it, which was followed by another commotion. I then ran indoors to phone for you,' mumbled the first man as he fumbled with a cigarette.

'Do you know where they went?' enquired the second officer.

'I saw them run off in that direction,' said the second neighbour pointing towards Sharrington. 'No more than ten minutes ago. I only saw them fleetingly but they looked like two young lads of average height. They didn't look as though they were wearing overcoats, just jackets and trousers.'

'Well, we'll not waste any more time. We might see them along the road if we hurry,' said the driver.

'Yes, we might catch them. May I suggest you go back to bed now. I doubt whether you'll be seeing or hearing from them again tonight,' shouted the second officer returning to the car.

'Goodnight,' shouted the neighbours. The two officers acknowledged and drove off at speed towards Sharrington.

After driving for some twenty-five minutes the driver nudged his passenger, 'Hey, George, look at this fellow here.' A young curly headed youth was slouching along the pavement wavering slightly from side to side. He was dressed in a jacket and trousers with a tear on his left sleeve.

The police car crawled slowly passed the young man then stopped. Both officers got out of the car and approached the youth cautiously.

'It's a bit late, son, for walking the streets isn't it?' enquired the driver.

The curly haired youth nodded his head but didn't speak.

'Torn your sleeve as well. Been involved in a fight have you?' continued the driver.

The young man checked the ripped sleeve as if he wasn't aware of the damage.

'Have you been drinking, lad?' asked the second officer.

'Yes, I've had a few tonight, I suppose,' replied the young man casually.

'Drunk, eh? Had a bit of a scrap, eh? A few miles up the road. Caused a disturbance? Mmmm. Where's your mate?' quizzed the driver.

The young man looked askance at both the officers. He didn't answer.

'What's your name, eh? Where do you live?' asked the second officer.

'Mick Leighton and…' he paused slightly before continuing, '… in digs just down there on Brown Street,' mumbled Leighton.

'What number then?' said the second officer.

'Number 54,' replied Leighton immediately.

'Better make sure, hadn't we?' asked the driver. Leighton nodded. The two officers and Leighton walked to 54 Brown Street. They knocked on the door and after a while Mrs. Helen Maxwell answered the call. After all being invited inside, the two police officers grilled Leighton a little longer before explaining to him the reasons for their investigations. Leighton denied the allegations that he was involved in a fight. He told the officers he had been to a nightclub and met a girl. He had had too much to drink so he left his car in the car park at the club and walked the girl home. Although he was unable to give exact details of the girl's name and address the two officers eventually left Mrs. Maxwell's home after warning Leighton to get home a bit earlier in future, particularly bearing in mind his responsibilities.

Micky Leighton knew the officers had recognised him to be a Sharrington footballer but he wondered whether the incident would be reported to the club by the police or Mrs. Maxwell. He was a little worse for drink but he knew he had not been involved in any fight. Before he finally fell asleep the only thing that bothered him was how he had torn the sleeve on his jacket?

Chapter 50

'Let's treat the lads to a couple of days at the seaside, eh, Barrie?' asked Tony, light-heartedly.

'That will be bracing at this time of year. Where have you got in mind and when?' replied Barrie, inquisitively.

'I thought we might see if the board would approve taking the whole squad to Castlebay after training on the Thursday, do some light training on Friday morning and travel on to Lepperton's ground on Saturday morning. I think the distance will be about 40 miles or so,' answered Tony looking at the map on the office wall.

'It sounds like a good idea to me but what would you estimate the cost to be?' stressed Barrie, hopefully.

Tony didn't answer straight away He looked into mid air as though he was calculating the costs in his head. He shook his head slowly before answering, 'Well, the whole playing squad of sixteen men plus, you, me and a driver should cost the club about £400 or so.'

'Do you think the club can afford that sort of extravagance?' asked Barrie.

'I don't see why not. It'll certainly give the lads a much needed tonic and it will also give me plenty of time to get them in the right frame of mind for the game on Saturday,' said Tony, confidently.

'I'll be interested to hear the Board's decision tonight,' smirked Barrie.

'I do hope they will approve. Things are certainly going extremely well for us at the moment and I will have to express my concern that it is vitally important for the team before a game of this nature. That is, should they throw out my proposal in the first place, Barrie. If they give the go ahead I will announce it to the players tomorrow. I feel they deserve a few days away, and, good grief, after their efforts so far this season, £400 will, to my mind, be well spent,' said Tony sharply, 'I will let you know their decision later tonight.'

The two men left the manager's office in discussion about the possible problems facing Sharrington in the forthcoming F.A. Cup tie against Lepperton. It was clearly going to be a difficult game for Sharrington.

'How did it go tonight?' asked Barrie after picking up his telephone receiver at 10 p.m.

'You'll never believe it Barrie but as soon as I suggested the idea, the board immediately agreed and gave their wholehearted support and good wishes,' said Tony enthusiastically.

'Oh great? What are the arrangements?' exclaimed Barrie.

'Well, we are to travel at around 4 p.m. on Thursday afternoon, arrive at the Ship Hotel at 6.30 p.m., train Friday morning on the beach, use the rest of the day as leisure time and have a detailed talk about the game and our opponents about 10.30 before lunching and travelling to the ground at 12.30 p.m,' answered Tony running through the details rather quickly.

'That sounds good to me. I'm sure the lads will enjoy the break,' commented Barrie.

'I think they will, Barrie, and I will enjoy it even more if we can come out of the game with a victory,' replied Tony before signing off for the night.

The party, which included part-timers White, Cracknell and Bates, set off to Castlebay at 4.45 p.m. and arrived at 7.15 p.m. They enjoyed an evening meal and retired to their rooms around 11 p.m. The hotel was compact, comfortable and the staff were friendly and fussy. The players were well behaved and remarkably well suited to each other in their social company. Tony had gathered not only a fine group of players but also a sociable crowd amongst themselves and with strangers. The blend in their characters was perfect. Newcomers like Brooke, Leighton and Baynes fitted into the group as easily as the part-time players or the old Sharrington campaigners. Tony knew the club atmosphere was essential for the success of the club, in fact Barrie had commented that the spirit within the club was the best he had ever witnessed in his playing career.

When the men assembled for breakfast on the Friday morning they were amazed to find that there had been a two or three inch covering of snow overnight.

'Oh No! Just what we needed,' said Alf Henning on looking out of the dining room window. 'If this keeps up it will give Lepperton just the tonic they need. There's nothing like snow for levelling up both teams, regardless of their status.'

'That's if the ground will be fit to play on,' answered Graham Bond, also looking out of the window.

'It's stopped now but I don't like the look of those clouds,' commented Sammy Chaddock peering over the captain's shoulder.

'I've never known it snow so early, have you?' enquired Alf Henning now sitting at the long breakfast table.

'No, I haven't, and if I'm not mistaken it's bonfire night tomorrow isn't it?' replied Tony White as he joined the party in the breakfast room.

'Oh, yes it is. That'll cause a few damp squibs eh?' joked Allan Smith ladling hot porridge into his mouth.

'That's quite a surprise,' remarked Tony Davidson as he walked into the dining room along with Mike Thomas, Neil Baynes and Tommy French. 'I'd better get in touch with Lepperton after breakfast and find out what the weather's been like there.' Tony sat down. 'At least, lads, the snow won't affect our training on the beach, will it?'

'With a bit of luck lads the tide might have been in when the snow fell and frozen it solid,' laughed Allan Smith, which caused plenty of good cheer around the gathering.

Tony Davidson smiled and winked at Smith before chipping in with a brand of his own humour: 'Well if that's the case you can set off an hour before the rest of us and thaw it out with some of that red hot humour of yours.'

Allan Smith jokingly laughed at his manager's comment before licking his right index finger and stroked it in mid air saying, 'One up to you boss!'

After breakfast Tony decided to take training before contacting Lepperton. At around 11.30 a.m. the players ventured out for a two mile run to the beach. Tony and Barrie conducted training until returning to the Ship Hotel at 1.00 p.m. The session had not been too strenuous but good fun on the heavy sand and in the turbulent waves. There was, however, one unfortunate incident when Mick Thomas turned sharply from a challenge by Alf Henning, during a game of six-a-side football, and twisted his left ankle. After a few minutes treatment from Barrie Trippett he continued with the training but on his return to the hotel his ankle was swollen and immediately bathed it in hot and cold water before being strapped up.

Tony telephoned the Lepperton ground and discovered that they had also suffered a thin covering of snow but the only problem was that it had drifted to a height of about six or seven inches in one goalmouth and down the length of the goal line. He was told that volunteers had arrived at the ground to move the drifted snow and that a local referee was to inspect at around 4 p.m. He was also told the local weather station had predicted a cold night with a frost but that Saturday was expected to be dry with maximum temperatures around four or five degrees centigrade. Tony agreed with the Lepperton official that the match referee should be contacted with a view to inspecting the pitch early on Saturday morning.

As the leisurely day progressed Tony received a message on Friday evening that the local referee had passed the ground fit now that the drifted snow had been removed to behind the goal. It all depended on whether the snow and uncovered ground froze during the night. They could only wait for the match referee's decision at 10.30 a.m. in the morning.

On Saturday morning the players gathered in the lounge and waited for Tony to relay the referee's decision. At 11 a.m. Tony walked confidently into the room and announced, 'The referee's passed the ground fit. The match is definitely on. I understand the pitch is covered in an inch of snow but the ground underneath is hard but thawing rapidly and should be ideal by the 2.15 p.m. kick-off.' Tony sat on the edge of a comfortable chair before continuing his pre-match speech to get his players in the right frame of mind. He left his players with no uncertainty as to the job in hand. At the end of his talk, he announced his team for the game. 'In goal – Alan Bates, right back – Graham Bond, left back – Allan Smith, No. 4 – Micky Leighton, centre-half – Tommy French, No. 6 today will be Stephen Holland. Unfortunately Mick's ankle is still swollen and he is not 100% fit. No. 7 – Graham Hart. I've decided to make you sub today, Paul, for the reasons I explained to you last night. No. 8 – Neil Baynes, centre-forward – Alf Henning, No. 10 – Tony White and finally outside left – Sammy Chaddock. Best of luck lads. Now let's get our gear together and go and do a good afternoons work,' stressed Tony positively.

The Sharrington team arrived at the tiny Lepperton Trinity's ground at 1.15 p.m. There was a good crowd gathering outside the ground chanting the name of Lepperton, enthusiastically. The weather was cold but dry, and, as the Fourth Division players inspected the ground, they discovered a snow-covered pitch. The ground, underneath the snow, was still reasonably hard and the players decided to play in rubber-studded boots. The ground was open on all sides. The wind was brisk and bitterly cold but this did not deter the partisan home crowd from congregating together behind the roped sections, a few feet outside the blue markings around the pitch.

The Lepperton Trinity team ran out onto the pitch, from the rickety changing rooms, to an incredible reception. They were kitted in red shirts, black shorts and red socks. Sharrington were forced to change their strip but instead of their normal second colours of white shirts, black shorts and black socks, Tony thought the white shirts might lead to certain difficulties with the snow covered pitch. He therefore obtained, with the Lepperton Manager's approval, the host teams away strip of blue shirts.

The game began in a cautious manner and, for the first fifteen minutes, the players on both teams were adjusting to the ground conditions. Lepperton's forwards were quick to race at the Sharrington defenders and the home team's centre-forward, Sharkey, had a header saved well by young Bates.

Sharrington were defending against the strong wind, and, with the snow blowing from the surface on the pitch, the amateur team were taking full advantage as the game moved up to the half hour. Following a free kick, on the edge of the Sharrington penalty area, a headed clearance by Tommy French dropped at the feet of Wayne, the Lepperton starlet, who jabbed the ball through a melee of players in the penalty area. The ball ricocheted from a player and passed Bates and made the score 1-0 to Lepperton. The crowd went wild. Two dozen youngsters quickly dodged under the rope behind the goal and ran onto the pitch to cheer their heroes. There were also one or two firecrackers set off to celebrate the goal.

Lepperton continued to attack the Fourth Division team but taking into consideration the odds against the visiting defenders they did remarkably well to keep out a greater deficit although the lively raiders for the amateurs went close on two or three occasions.

Just before half-time a move between Leighton, Baynes, White and Chaddock saw the winger crack the ball against the upright and frantically cleared by the amateur defenders.

During half-time Tony urged his players to catch the home team defence cold. He praised his defence and asked his forwards to do their bit in the second half.

'Look, lads, we may be a goal down but let's face it they've had all the advantages.' He counted on his fingers as he stressed, 'the cold wind, the slope, the enthusiastic crowd and the blowing snow. Now let's hit them hard early with a quick goal. Their defence hasn't had anything to do yet. Let's give them a rough time. Keep playing the ball long and if possible deep for our forwards to run onto. The snow will slow it down for you. One goal should put us right back on top. This is the time to prove you are a class apart from this amateur team. You've got the fitness, the greater incentive and, most of all, the club's and your own pride at stake. Come on, lads, let's wrap it up and get off home. We don't want a replay if we can help it, do we?' The players all nodded before trooping out for the second half.

After ten minutes of the restart Sharrington were pressing forward but, surprisingly, the amateur defenders were holding them comfortably when a right wing cross by Graham Hart was headed by Alf Henning into the path of Tony White. The youngster took the ball in his stride when a seemingly fair sliding tackle by big centre-half Walker cleared the ball from danger. To the amazement of the home team and supporters the referee ran into the penalty area and pointed to the penalty spot.

Suddenly he was thwarted by protesting Lepperton players. The crowd jeered furiously at this decision. The referee remained firm and after a hold up of three minutes and three bookings for home defenders, Graham Bond handed the ball to Neil Baynes. The No. 8 placed the ball on the blue penalty spot, stepped back five paces, ran up to the ball at speed and drove the orange ball hard and high with his right foot to the left of the diving goalkeeper. The ball brushed the goalkeeper's left hand but the power of the shot carried the ball into the roof of the net. The score was now 1-1 and the penalty goal was just the incentive Sharrington needed. While the home team was still suffering from the referee's controversial decision, Sharrington pressed even harder. Just six minutes after the equaliser, a high corner from Chaddock was met by the unchallenged Tommy French who guided his header out of the reach of the goalkeeper. Sharrington led by 2-1 and the amateur team's players' heads went down. They had allowed the penalty decision to affect their confidence.

The home crowd still tried to raise their team and with only eight minutes remaining a rare defensive error by Allan Smith let in the Lepperton's outside right. The winger was amazed to find the ball at his feet with his marker out of position. He slipped and slid into the Sharrington penalty area before firing the ball across the face of the goal and into the path of the centre-forward, Sharkey, who steered the bouncing ball over the line with the Sharrington defence at sixes and sevens. Lepperton had equalised out of the blue. The crowd went delirious again with more youngsters chasing onto the pitch this time. They sensed a late victory but Sharrington didn't let the amateurs' equaliser affect their game. They soaked up two or three attacks, and broke quickly out of defence through Baynes, Leighton and White and into attack. Sharrington were looking dangerous as they attacked and, although the equaliser had temporarily raised Lepperton's game, the Sharrington players' fitness was proving too much for them. The visitors were quicker to the ball, harder in the challenge and running faster for loose balls. With only two minutes remaining and the wind blowing stronger into the Lepperton defenders' faces, a neat pass by Leighton found Henning who shielded the ball before laying it to Tony White at the edge of the area. The young part-timer lifted his head momentarily, judged the situation and carefully chipped the snow-covered ball under the crossbar leaving the goalkeeper hopelessly beaten. It was a goal of sheer class and the youngster was mobbed by delighted Sharrington players. The visiting supporters were relieved with the goal. The Lepperton team was dejected and disillusioned with the Sharrington late winning goal. The professionals had beaten them just when a draw looked almost certain.

Back in the dressing room the Lepperton manager was going off alarmingly at the referee so much so that he failed to hear Tony Davidson's comments. Sharrington were through by the skin of their teeth. It was not one of Sharrington's best performances but, having accepted that the referee's strange decision put them back in the game, they were delighted to have won the game, without a reply. The luck of the cup game went to Sharrington and they left the small town of Lepperton to jeers and cat-calls from the supporters of the home team. Sharrington were through to the 3rd round of the F.A. Cup.

Chapter 51

'Right then, Gentlemen, I confirm that the club will begin the Gold Spot Promotions lottery from week commencing 28th November 1977,' said Jack Elliott, after the board had discussed the project in detail. Now let's move on to the manager's proposal for the board to contemplate full-time professional contracts being offered to Tony White, Paul Cracknell and Alan Bates. The Chairman, who was looking tired and strained, sat down to listen to the discussion on this subject.

'Before we give a decision on this matter, can you give us your reasons for this request, Tony,' asked Eddie Flannigan.

Tony, as usual, stood up to address the Board. 'Basically, gentlemen, I feel these three young men have all proved to me that they are capable of making the grade as professional footballers. As you are all aware I have had to bring the lads in at difficult times and they have done everything I have asked of them, in fact they have all performed better then I expected of them. They have all given 100% and showed great ability and promise for the future. I would also stress that all their performances have been after evening training sessions only and a professional status would not only be beneficial to the players in question, but to the club as a whole. We have a professional squad of thirteen players, which in my opinion is on the low side. When I took over there was a squad of fifteen players and personally I think sixteen professional players is the ideal number for a one team club.' Tony placed his hands in his jacket pocket 'To close, gentlemen, with these three players on professional terms I will have completed the first stage I set myself in bringing experienced and young players to the club, which to my mind is the right balance for the future.' Tony finished speaking and sat down before reaching for the bottle of water and pouring it into a glass.

'Would the signings of these three young lads complete your activities in the transfer market for this season?' asked Eddie Flannigan.

'I can safely say that it would, barring serious injuries of course,' stressed Tony before drinking from the glass of water.

'I like the look of Tony White particularly,' added Steve King.

'And I think young Cracknell has done extremely well. I like his style of play,' echoed Eddie Flannigan.

'Yes, I would agree with both your views, but I think the young goalkeeper came in at a difficult time and has shown some good form,' indicated Jack Elliott.

'It looks a straightforward matter then. What do you think, Bill?' asked Eddie Flannigan.

'It seems unanimous to me also. I like the players who have been brought to the club since the beginning of the season. Our league position speaks for itself and credit to the Manager. I think the young part-time players should make good pro's,' said Bill Boothroyd.

'There you are then Tony, the board have given you the go-ahead to sign White, Cracknell and Bates on professional terms,' summarised Jack wearily.

'Finally, tonight, gentlemen, as all of Sharrington is only too aware we had the misfortune to draw Second Division Woodville away from home in the third round of the F.A. Cup.'

'Yes, after a difficult game last Saturday at Lepperton I was hoping for the reward of at least a home draw,' explained Tony.

'It is a huge disappointment for the club. A home draw would have been a big attraction and obviously a chance to test our current form with a team from a higher division,' stated Steve King as he looked through the list on the 3rd round draw. I see our friends Treecliffe have got a good home draw against Third Division Mirth Cross Town. They are having a lucky season.' 'Hopefully Steve we will be able to judge our progression with a useful result at Woodville. I have seen them once this season and rate them as a good team with an excellent chance of promotion to the First Division. It will not be an easy game for us but I don't think for one moment that Phil Wade, the Woodville Manager, will be treating it as a simple game. He is a true professional and will cover us in great detail before the game. The only thing which worries me is that the game against Woodville comes at a time when it is essential we don't lose our confidence. A big defeat or humiliation of some sort would take us into the last third of the season on a low note. Obviously, I don't like to talk like this but it is going to be a crucial game for us in many ways. We will need to consolidate them but you may rest assured we will not be going into the game expecting a defeat. We will go there to win, not to sacrifice the cup run to concentrate on the league,' urged Tony.

The meeting lasted a further twenty minutes before closing at 9.45 p.m. 'Are you coming for a drink to our club, Tony?' asked Eddie Flannigan.

'No, I am sorry, Eddie, I can't. I've got to call on one of the players to discuss a personal matter,' said Tony apologetically.

'Who's the player? Anything we should be able to help him with?' asked Eddie inquisitively.

'No, I don't think so at this stage. It's purely a manager and player matter. It's nothing serious,' stressed Tony, hoping Flannigan wouldn't delve into the situation any further.

'Ah well, you know where to find us if you need any assistance,' replied Eddie.

'Thanks, Eddie, but it'll be all right,' mused Tony. Everyone left the boardroom and ground at 10 p.m.

Tony drove straight to Mrs. Maxwell's home to speak to Micky Leighton. On his way Tony knew he had to act strongly against his new signing after receiving notification of the alleged street-fighting incident from the police constable. Although he knew the police had no evidence to charge Leighton, Tony felt he ought to clear the matter up for his and the player's peace of mind. Tony could not allow rumours from this unsavoury incident to spread around the town, and more importantly the football club. As Tony knocked upon the door at 54 Brown Street he adjusted his tie nervously. Mrs. Maxwell invited Tony into the front room where Micky Leighton was sitting watching television. Fortunately for Tony, Simon Docker, the other player who lodged there, was in his own room listening to his records.

'Hello, boss, this is a surprise!' said Micky Leighton, knowing his heart had missed a beat as he anticipated why his manager had called around to see him.

'Hi, Micky' stated Tony in a confident manner. 'Have you heard how Seamingway and Rallingborough have gone on in their replay?'

'Yes, it's just been on the news. Seamingway have won 2 - 1 after extra time,' replied Micky.

'Well, I should imagine you two will want to be left in peace. I'll nip off and made a cup of tea for you both,' interrupted Mrs. Maxwell in her usual pleasant manner. She left the room closing the door firmly behind her. 'Look, Micky, I am sorry to have to trouble you at home but I heard from the police last night about an incident in which you may or may not have been involved in a week last Saturday.' Micky Leighton tilted his head backwards so he was looking up at the ceiling. 'I thought it would be better to have a discreet chat with you before the matter affected you and your game. I can see from your reaction that you knew this would come out into the open sooner or later'. Tony scratched his chin whilst waiting for Leighton to speak. 'How about telling me your version of the evening's events, Micky,' stressed Tony considerately. Leighton didn't speak straight away After some ten seconds he thumped his fists, into the pillow on his knee and then covered his face with his hands. Leighton was clearly distressed. Eventually he spoke to Tony.

'I knew… I just knew the police wouldn't let the matter drop?'

mumbled Leighton quietly. 'I wasn't involved in a fight that evening. I just… well, I seem to attract trouble everywhere I go.'

'I know you're upset about it all, but let's have your story so we can get it over with, then we can let the matter drop,' said Tony briskly, trying to encourage Leighton into a more responsive mood.

'What are the police proposing to do?' asked Leighton sullenly.

'They won't be taking the matter any further, Micky. The police constable only informed me about it because… well because, believe it or not, he is a Sharrington supporter and said, quite openly to me, that he didn't think you had been involved in a street fight but he was concerned about the drunken stupor his officers found you in at 2.30 in the morning. I honestly believe he reported it to me so we could clear the matter up between us and, deep down, he didn't want it to affect the good results the club has been getting this season. However, Micky, I'm glad he did report it to me. I want to know everything which involves my players, in or out of the club. We have a responsibility to the footballing public and whilst I don't mind my players having a fling from time to time, what I do mind is for my players to be roaming the streets drunk. I won't be patient when players step out of line in this way.' Tony felt he was making his point to the wayward star. 'Now look, Micky, I bought you to do a job for Sharrington and by hook or by crook you will continue to do so, or, failing that, I will be forced to list you. The club is the important factor here. I will not allow my players to upset the rhythm of the club. Before, I conclude, Micky, you have fitted into the set up here remarkably well and I want you to be here to help us to challenge for promotion and, more importantly, I see you as the future of the club. Now then let's hear the full story now you know how I and the Police feel about it?' concluded Tony, forcefully.

For the next twenty-five minutes Micky Leighton and Tony talked through the incident over tea and biscuits. At the end of the evening Tony was happy with Leighton's honesty; however, the young starlet was left looking sorry for himself but clear in his own mind that the whole problem was over and done with.

Chapter 52

'How does it feel to be half way through your first season as a manager in the football league with the club in joint second position?' enquired Grant Evans during his weekly pre-match interview with Tony Davidson. 'It obviously feels good, Grant. To be perfectly honest I knew if I could get the right type of players to the club, a good team spirit and more essentially a few wins under our belt then we would keep going from strength to strength,' replied Tony in good humour.

'What are the most important things you've learned during the past four months?' asked the pressman.

'Ah…' murmured Tony. 'I don't know where to start for an answer. Let me think… Ah, yes the most crucial item I've learnt is that the Sharrington Board of Directors are very brave men indeed who deserve every success, purely and simply after the great risk they took when appointing me as the club's manager. They have given me every confidence and I just hope they will be rewarded. Secondly, I've made mistakes on transfers but fortunately the club hasn't suffered by any of them. I've also learned how difficult motivating players is, but once again we are not doing so bad are we?' replied Tony humbly.

'I understand you will complete the signatures of White, Cracknell and Bates on professional terms within the next week or so, is that correct?' checked Evans sucking his pencil.

'Well, I can definitely say that I've spoken to each player concerned and offered terms, and while I'm happy to say White and Cracknell will sign on 14th November, Bates, the goalkeeper, wishes to finish his apprenticeship with his current employer but should sign for us for the beginning of next season, depending upon his examination results,' answered Tony.

'Are there any injuries or team changes for the home game against Mannish today?' concluded Evans.

'No, the team will be the same as last Saturday at Lepperton. Micky Thomas is fit again but I've decided to keep Steven Holland at No. 6. Alan Hawkins should be fit for next Saturday's game and Aldway. Other than that we've no problems.'

'Finally, Tony, how do you rate Sharrington's chances today against Mannish Town?'

'I am optimistic, obviously, Grant. The lads have being playing extremely well just recently and our confidence is improving with every game. Also Mannish Town have suffered three defeats in their last three games and two, of course, in the league were well and truly convincing as well, by 1-3 at Harloft and 3-5 at Treecliffe. However, having said that, we will have to be on our guard not to let anything slip. After all they have drawn eight of their first fourteen matches and no doubt they would be happy to get the same result as in the opening game of the season,' analysed Tony in his usual confident manner.

At 3.00 Alf Henning kicked off on a bright but cold day. There was a sharp wind and the crowd was down from the previous home game. It had been recorded at 8,950. There were only a few supporters from Mannish. In the opening fifteen minutes Sharrington were attacking constantly and there were near misses by Baynes, Henning and left full-back Allan Smith. Mannish Town were extremely lucky to keep the score at 0-0. In the seventeenth minute the visitors' centre-forward and joint leading scorer, Bennison, beat Stephen Holland in the air only to see young Bates palm the ball to safety. That attack saw a change in play. Mannish Town slowly and deliberately played their way back into attack and Graham Bond had to be sharp to clear off the line from Toddy, the white-shirted No. 8. On the half hour Bates had to run from his line to kick a loose ball into touch and two minutes later Shilton the No. 10 for Mannish shot wide when it looked easier to score.

When the game looked to be slipping away from Sharrington the talented Neil Baynes turned the game for the home team. Graham Hart received a ball from Captain Bond before jinking down the right wing, passing three challenging defenders. At the edge of the 18-yard box he passed the ball to Baynes who masterfully drew the defender, Chatterton, out of position before firing the spinning ball under the sprawling body of keeper, Noskins. The ball bobbled awkwardly over the line despite the efforts of Captain Alexby to clear it. At half-time Sharrington were luckily 1-0 in the lead.

Sharrington were quick to try and increase their slender lead in the second half but constant attacks were proving fruitless. Mannish Town were defending bravely and, similar to the first half, they soaked up early pressure before establishing a period of attacks themselves. After 70 minutes Shilton appeared to be brought down by Allan Smith but the referee waved play on. Two minutes later right-winger Givens saw his shot from the edge of the penalty area strike the cross bar and headed clear by Tommy French to safety. Sharrington were failing to keep possession and Baynes, Leighton and White were forcibly being beaten to the ball by the white-shirted visitors. Tempers were beginning to fray and

Henning, French (of Sharrington) and Chatterton (of Mannish) were booked after some heated exchanges.

With ten minutes remaining the visitors equalised. A move involving centre-half Passon, No. 8 Toddy and No. 11 Staff, ended with the winger's cross being headed in at the near post by No. 10 Shilton, who was unmarked. This goal gave the Mannish team an incentive to attack even more but the Sharrington team, who were well marshalled by Captain Graham Bond, held on and in fact might have secured a winning goal when a break from defence by Holland had a 35-yard shot graze the outside of the far post with Noskins easily beaten by the pace of the ball.

The game ended 1-1 but not before Baynes was booked for dissent in the last minute. Mannish had earned their ninth draw of the season but Sharrington had not been as convincing as in recent weeks.

Chapter 53

On the following Saturday, after a relatively quiet week at the club, Tony Davidson had a full squad of players to pick from for the away league game at Aldway. By the time the coach left Sharrington at 10 a.m. Tony had not finally decided what team to select. During the first part of the journey Tony was locked in conversation with Barrie Trippett on the front seat of the coach. The two travelling directors Eddie Flannigan and Steve King were playing cards with Tommy French and Alf Henning. Another card game, on the opposite table, involved Allan Smith, Graham Hart, Sammy Chaddock and Mike Thomas.

Graham Bond was sat chatting to Stephen Holland, Paul Brooke was helping Alan Hawkins and Simon Docker with a crossword puzzle, Neil Baynes was making a point about a new motor car he had just purchased to the attentive listeners Micky Leighton and Tony White while Paul Cracknell was in conversation with Grant Evans and Alan Bates.

After a stop for a meal at 12.30 p.m. the coach continued on its journey to Aldway. During this leg of the trip Tony finally reached a decision on the team selection, with the help of Barrie. It had seemed such a long time since Tony could select a team from a full squad. He was not completely happy with his team's performance against Mannish Town and felt his forwards lacked aggression. He had noticed a general half-heartedness over recent weeks amongst Leighton, Henning, White and Chaddock to take on and beat defenders. He was a little worried that one or two players were becoming complacent and he explained to Barrie how he thought one or two changes at this stage might give these players the pep up they needed. He had stressed to all his players during the week's training sessions how the team had lacked a desire to challenge and win the ball and he proved this point by examples from the games at Lepperton and with Mannish. Tony was convinced Alf Henning had lost his scoring touch and he wondered whether this was to do with the fact that he was the only centre-forward at the club and had played twenty continuous games since joining the club without feeling pressure from anyone to compete for that position. Barrie agreed with Tony's opinion and made the comment that he felt the same applied to Sammy Chaddock.

About five miles from the Aldway ground Tony rose to his feet and stood at the centre of the coach after assembling the players at the rear of the bus.

'If I can have your attention, lads, I want to announce the team for today's game. I've decided on some changes on the basis that I feel, as I have explained to certain individuals during training this week, that two or three of you are a bit stale and look as though you have lost the basic appetite for the game. Therefore, with that in mind, I have selected the following team.' Tony looked straight ahead as he continued. 'In goal I've decided to bring Alan Hawkins back now that he is fully fit again. No. 2 Graham Bond, No. 3 Allan Smith, No. 4 Micky Leighton, No. 5 Tommy French, No. 6 Stephen Holland, No. 7 Graham Hart, No. 8 Neil Baynes, No. 9, well I've decided to rest you today, Alf.' The centre-forward nodded slowly as though he anticipated the manager's decision. 'Therefore, I want you, Paul, to play in that position today.'

Paul Cracknell seemed delighted at being selected as centre-forward.

'No. 10 will be Simon Docker and No. 11 Tony White. I've decided to rest you also, Sammy.'

The quietly spoken Sammy Chaddock looked disappointed but accepted Tony's selection in a professional manner, like Alf Henning had done.

'And finally today's substitute will be Paul Brooke.' The latest signing gave a broad smile at being in the team, albeit substitute.

Tactics for the game were discussed for the remainder of the journey at the rear of the coach whilst Eddie Flannigan, Steve King and Grant Evans quietly talked of Tony's decision to drop Henning and Chaddock.

'That's a surprise' said Eddie in an amazed tone. 'Yes, it's a shock to me, too,' announced Grant Evans, who was quickly jotting the team selection down in his note pad. 'He never ceases to amaze me. I just hope he won't regret his decision at quarter to five tonight,' whispered Eddie. 'All I can say is he must have had a jolly good reason to drop both these players. After all he has not made too many mistakes in his team selection over the season and, who knows, perhaps when he recalls Henning and Chaddock to the team they may hit the back of the net a lot more than they have been doing recently,' reflected Steve King adjusting the knot of his tie.

The Aldway ground was compact in every sense of the word. The playing area was surrounded by a four-foot concrete wall. The stand, above the dressing rooms, was a solid brick construction, old-fashioned and painted in the club colours of blue and yellow. There was a rickety shed-like construction opposite the stand and behind either goal was a small uncovered area with old railway sleepers for steps. In each corner of the ground were tiny floodlight structures of no greater height than 40 feet, with only 10 lights on each frame. Graham Bond remarked that it was like playing in a matchbox but usually Sharrington did well on this ground.

Aldway, after drawing 2-2 at Sharrington in the second game of the season, had slumped to fourth from bottom with a total of 12 points from 15 games. The team had played badly and thrown points away regularly in the closing minutes of many games. They had been knocked out of the F.A. Cup and League Cup in the first round and their star strikers, Allison and Jacques, were seeking transfers.

As the teams took to the pitch at 2.55 p.m. the dark heavy black clouds covered the sky. The floodlights were switched on and the pitch was emblazoned in a bright light. The crowd was very sparse and registered at 3,020. There was no atmosphere in the ground and during the game the players' voices echoed around the stand and the referee's whistle was so shrill it was deafening to the spectators.

The Sharrington defence were untroubled during the first half and Hawkins only had to make one full length save from a rare Aldway attack. Cracknell, Docker and White were keen to be involved in the match but the run of the ball wasn't in their favour. The first half was, in the main, Sharrington in possession of the greasy, white ball and Aldway's defence were at sixes and sevens constantly. At half-time, as the rain began to fall heavily, the score remained goalless.

At half-time in the gloomy and small visitors' changing room, Tony confronted his players with a look of bewilderment on his face. He waited until every player had sat down with a cup of tea before speaking. 'I'm mystified lads, truly mystified. I just can't understand why we suddenly changed tactics midway through the first half. It was so easy for us. We were playing the short ball, giving and going for the return pass with excellent chances falling our way. O.K. we were not converting the chances but Aldway were having trouble coping with our style of play. Then suddenly –' said Tony cautiously, '– we changed to playing long balls, the end result of which proved a difficulty with control and, if anything let Aldway off the hook. Why, oh why, I just don't know. Now, in the second half keep it short again and front men: keep moving off the ball and creating space. We should make easy meat of teams like Aldway who are clearly having all sorts of problems at the moment. Come on, lads, I want two points today not one, you are much the better team. Let's take our chances. Now finish your drinks and get out there and wrap it up.

From the re-start Sharrington played patiently at the back and the forwards were working sharp. The ball was skidding on the wet surface and proving difficult to control. Aldway were still lax in defence and a mistake by centre-half Ballantyne let in Paul Cracknell. The young centre-forward kept his head as he neared goal before side-footing the ball to Graham Hart who, also unmarked, drove an acute angled shot wide of the bemused Shipp, in the Aldway goal. It was 1-0 to Sharrington.

Aldway made a brief recovery but the Sharrington defence kept firm. After 75 minutes a short ball by Bond to Leighton saw the No. 4 in space. He ran at speed towards the back-pedalling home defence before accurately passing to Simon Docker who was on the edge of the area. The No. 10 turned like quicksilver, surprising his marker, Gregory, and in one continuous movement stabbed the ball into the corner of the net. It was an excellently well-worked goal with Docker showing more individual skill than Tony had ever seen him demonstrate before. The whole team mobbed Docker to congratulate his skilful goal.

With Sharrington 2-0 in the lead, huge masses of the crowd walked from the ground knowing their team had been well and truly defeated. Unfortunately for them and to the great delight of the remaining supporters, the Aldway star striker Allison scored a superb goal, right out of the blue, six minutes from time. It was a remarkable goal, a solo-effort of great skill. He collected a loose ball in the centre circle, dribbled nattily past Leighton and a lunging Tommy French before striking the ball with the outside of his right foot from just outside the penalty area, bending it between the advancing Bond and the crouching Hawkins, and inside the goalkeeper's right hand post. Without a doubt it was the best goal Tony and Barrie had witnessed that season.

Sharrington held on to the 2-1 lead in the remaining minutes despite late revitalised pressure from the inspired Aldway forward line. At the full time whistle it was two more valuable points for Sharrington and, on the reflection of the game, the result in their favour was justified. Tony was pleased with the performance of his team and yet extremely disappointed with the Aldway side. He was of the opinion that if Henning and Chaddock had played, the score might have been, more convincing but in the end he was happy with the way Cracknell and White had stuck to their task. He knew his defence was settling down into a solid unit but the experiment today had widened the scope of his future selection for a forward line.

Chapter 54

In the offices on the following Monday morning, Secretary Sid Parkin, dressed in his usual shoddy sports jacket and grey trousers turned to Peggy Hollingsworth as he addressed her: 'Fancy the Manager dropping Chaddock from the team for the first time this season and just a few days before his wedding on Wednesday.'

'Yes, it must have come as a surprise to him but as we have discovered the new manager is a strict professional and makes his decisions to benefit the club, not individuals,' replied Peggy as she made an entry into the petty cash book.

'That's as may be but I wouldn't have thought Chaddock will relish the thought of marrying at a time when he is out of favour with the boss. After all, Peg, Chaddock is only one of six of the original players left and I think Davidson will get rid of all those players slowly but surely. Sammy must think his numbers up,' remarked Sid forcibly.

'We don't know what the Manager's plans are. He seems to be happy with the current squad according to newspapers articles,' said Peggy flippantly.

'Well, I think he will get rid of everyone who was attached to the club, when he joined, by the end of the season,' stressed Sid miserably. 'It'll happen you just mark my words.' Peggy put down her pen and turned sharply towards Sid.

'You know, Sid, I don't know why you don't look for another job. Every day you moan about Mr. Davidson, so much so, that I am sick of listening to you. He is getting the best results this club has experienced for many years and in my opinion he's a gentleman who is successfully achieving what he set out to do and I enjoy working for him,' shouted Peg.

'Keep your voice down, Peg! You know what I think so we can only wait and see what happens. As for working here, the workload seems to get more every day. and once this lottery gets underway next week the administrative side of the job we do will double,' mumbled Sid breathlessly.

'Humbug, Sid, you're nothing but a shirker and if you carry on with this depressing mood day after day I am going to find another job,' shrieked Peggy as she raced from the office slamming the door behind her.

Sid shook his head slowly from side to side before lighting a non-tipped cigarette and rested his feet on the metal desk in front of the filing cabinet.

'Nothing to do, Sid?' asked Tony as he breezed into the Secretary's office.

Sid quickly removed his feet from the desk and stubbed out his cigarette, once he realised his non-activity had been witnessed by the manager. 'No, there's plenty to do as always I, I… I was just having a break for a couple of minutes,' mumbled Sid.

Tony wasn't impressed. 'It seems to me, Sid, you are taking too many of these two minutes breaks during the day. I am also getting a little bit tired of the heated arguments between you and Peggy as well. Can you please ensure that the rows stop at once and the work rate increases? I must say that I am not over-impressed with your efficiency, Sid. I don't appear to have your wholehearted support on work matters and unless I see an improvement in the near future I suggest we lay our cards on the table, don't you,' said Tony fiercely.

Sid was dumbfounded. Here was his opportunity to discuss his position at the club with Tony but he could only sit motionless with his mouth open. He eventually nodded slowly before turning to his work.

'By the way, Sid, the lads are having the day off today and I am leaving about 2 o' clock with Barrie for the game at Crest Town tonight, so you will be in charge, OK,' stressed Tony.

'Yes, that's all right. Who are they playing?' murmured Sid, still looking at his work.

'That is just what I've been trying to get through to you, Sid. You've no idea, have you? No interest in what's happening in our profession at all,' shouted Tony. Sid looked up from his work in disbelief. 'It's in there man,' exclaimed the Manager throwing the daily paper at the dishevelled secretary 'The League Cup 3rd round 2nd leg against Woodville, who are our F.A. Cup opponents a week on Saturday, if you had forgotten that as well'. Tony slammed the office door as he made his exit. Sid felt embarrassed and annoyed.

'What was that all about?' enquired Peggy as she returned to the office.

'Oh, it was just me and the boss clearing the air,' said Sid sullenly.

'I don't know about both of you clearing the air, I could only hear Mr. Davidson's voice as I was walking down the corridor,' exclaimed Peggy.

'Oh, shut up woman, and get on with your work. We've plenty to do and as we are the only two putting in a full day's work today we are likely to be extremely busy,' shouted Sid, lighting another cigarette.

'I think Mr. Davidson has had a go at you, hasn't he? Not before time that's all I can say. Not before time,' repeated Peggy with a wry smile.

'Look, Peg, what we discussed is confidential and not for your ears. Here, can you deal with these?' said the embarrassed Secretary passing a basket of forms to her for typing. Peg didn't answer. She turned away from him and quietly laughed to herself, knowing Sid had had a dressing down from Mr. Davidson.

On the following Wednesday at 2.30 p.m. Tony, Barrie, the chairman, the directors, and all the playing staff from the club attended the wedding of winger Sammy Chaddock to Shirley Bell. After a small reception, the newly weds departed to spend a three day honeymoon on the south coast, before Chaddock returned to join the team for the journey to Holydice-on-Sea and the club's seventeenth league game. "Action man" had a good send off from his colleagues and didn't let any disappointment in being dropped the previous Saturday spoil the day.

After the wedding reception, Tony drove to Sprannon Albion's ground following an invitation from the First Division club to watch their 2nd leg 3rd round League Cup game against current Second Division leaders Ravenhead Athletic. Not only was the game finely balanced owing to Ravenhead's 2-0 lead from the first leg but the visiting team featured the much improving Greg Hanby, who was Tony's first sale from Sharrington. The attendance was recorded at 37,000 and although Sprannon scored an early goal to reduce the aggregate score the well-organised Ravenhead equalised just before half-time and ran out shock winners during the second half by 3-1 and 5-1 on aggregate. Tony enjoyed the game and was very impressed with the performance of Hanby who scored the third goal from 30 yards. Tony felt Hanby had benefited from joining the Second Division side but he did not resent transferring him without giving the centre-forward more time to prove himself with Sharrington. What he did realise was that the Ravenhead team were a more polished side than Woodville, of the same division, who Tony had seen fall 2-1 to Crest Town two days earlier. He had noticed one or two weaknesses in the Woodville team although he still rated them as an excellent outfit and a side who would be difficult for Sharrington to beat. Woodville, who had earlier beaten Crest Town 2-0 in the first leg at home, would be favourites to beat Fourth Division Sharrington in the 3rd round of the F.A. Cup.

Chapter 55

'This is going to be another difficult game for us today, lads, particularly as Holydice have improved remarkably since we beat them at home over 3 months ago,' remarked Tony as he spoke to his team in the dressing room at the Dice Ground. 'They have only lost once in the last eight games in the league and have only six points less than us at the moment. Again, lads, it is vital we do the right things here today. The pressure will stay with us now we are in the top three and it is essential we play as a team to get a good result.' Tony sat down on a bench as the players finished changing into the familiar red shirts, black shorts and red socks. 'If we can soak up any early pressure but be prepared to attack if Holydice start a defensive game, thereby giving them the problems, we can then only take any chances which fall our way. All the best, lads, and don't forget work for each other, don't be too selfish and play the ball out wide when attacking, giving support where necessary. Likewise, forwards get behind the ball and help out when we are defending,' stressed Tony once he had got every player's attention.

There was an average crowd of 5,250 for this game and at 3 o'clock the wind was fresh to strong with a cold chill to it. The clouds surrounding the peculiar little ground were dark and the floodlights were on full, illuminating the well-grassed pitch. Behind the spion kop was the rough sea, which gave an unusual setting for a football match.

The Holydice team in their bright yellow kit kicked off towards the sea end and were quickly into stride with some brisk and accurate attacks. The Sharrington defence were lucky to keep the score at 0-0 in the first 15 minutes. The home team's three front men: Vinter, Rastle and Wayne were linking well and causing the Sharrington defence many problems. After 18 minutes a run by Moore on the right wing ended with Stephen Holland mistiming his tackle and being adjudged by the referee to have brought down the winger in the penalty box. From the resultant penalty Vinter crashed the ball wide of Hawkins to make the score 1-0 to the home team.

Unfortunately for the seasiders, they were unable to press home the advantage from the restart. The Sharrington team were blending well together and Alf Henning, the only change from the game at Aldway, was beginning to cause the tough-tackling home defence many problems. As the first half neared its end Tony was happy with the way his team had weathered the storm and played their way back into the driving seat. The team were pressing for an equaliser with some tidy football as the referee brought the first half to an end.

'It's good to watch, lads. There's plenty of character in your play today. Slowly but surely you are wearing their defence down and, Alf, I think that rest last week did you the world of good,' said Tony looking surprisingly pleased with himself to say Sharrington were trailing 1-0. The striker nodded before wiping the beads of sweat from his forehead.

'Their defence is just as stubborn as it was in our home game,' stressed Graham Bond before drinking from an enamel cup full of tea.

'The way I see it is for us to run at the defence and play short one-twos on the edge of the area,' commented Tony still smiling.

'Yes, the long ball from the wing is being cut out every time,' remarked Neil Baynes retying his left bootlace.

'I agree, Neil. I also think we should try some long-range shots and hope for a goal that way, or at least a loose ball for Alf and Simon to pounce upon,' shouted Barrie above the growing dressing room conversations.

'Quiet a moment, lads. Quiet' said Tony. 'I've no complaints. You're all playing well and I am sure the goals will come. Just keep the pressure on and challenge hard. Keep going right to the full-time whistle and I am certain we will bring something away from this game'.

Straight from the start of the second half a low cross-cum-shot by Graham Hart struck the home team centre-half, Hyton, on the hand, but the referee waved play on. After seven further minutes of Sharrington pressure, Docker beat two men on the left, passed to White, overlapping on the edge of the area, who crossed the ball into the path of Neil Baynes. The No 8 back-heeled the ball into the direction of Alf Henning at the edge of the penalty area, right in front of goal. The centre-forward simply swung his left boot at the bobbling ball and saw Ray Filling, the goalkeeper, jump to his right and palm the ball into the net. Sharrington had equalised.

Sharrington were on top. Their play was skilful and superior to Holydice. They were building steadily from defence, through their wing-halves and controlling the attacks accurately and quickly. Holydice were now finding it difficult to put their visitors under pressure.

After 72 minutes, however, a long ball by full-back Cross sent inside left Wayne challenging for possession with Tommy French. The centre-half was clearly losing out to the battling Wayne and when the latter pushed the ball in and seemingly out of reach Hawkins ventured from his goal. At a point just inside the penalty area the three men fell in a heap and the ball bobbled slowly passed the goal. The crowd jeered for a penalty and didn't have to wait long before the referee pointed to the penalty spot. Hawkins, Bond, French and Smith all ran to the referee but his actions to the remonstrating players clearly showed the two Sharrington men had sandwiched Wayne. To the Sharrington players' credit they did not argue with the referee's decision. Once again Vinter smashed the ball wide of Hawkins to make the score 2-1 to Holydice-on-Sea.

It was an unfortunate incident but Sharrington were still building carefully and causing problems by daring attacks from left, centre and right of the goal. Eventually a precision pass by Neil Baynes found Graham Hart on the right wing. The youngster slipped like quicksilver past the challenging Cross before racing pointedly to the near post. He drew two defenders and the goalkeeper to the nearside before squaring the ball unselfishly into the path of Alf Henning who had the easiest of chances to side foot the ball over the line. The score 2-2 remained for the last eight minutes and both teams were happy with the point but, without doubt, Sharrington were the more skilful team on the day.

After the game Tony was in discussion with Brian Maxwell, the Holydice Manager, and was completely taken aback when he was asked if an offer of £30,000 for Alan Hawkins or £15,000 for Tony White would tempt him. Tony was adamant that no players were for sale but it made him realise his young team were attracting the attention of other managers.

Chapter 56

At the start of the following week things were looking healthy at the club. Sharrington, after the 2-2 draw at Holydice, were second place in the league, one point behind Seamingway and on level points, but with a better goal difference than near neighbours Treecliffe.

It was also the commencement of the "Gold Spot Promotions" Lottery and judging from the response from people willing to sell tickets it was anticipated, if the enthusiasm was maintained, that the club could expect the estimated maximum profit of £600 per week. The lottery had been well published and more than a dozen local firms and businesses had supported the campaign. The directors of Sharrington Football Club were delighted with the state of affairs.

Tony, Barrie and the players were also busy preparing for the 3rd round F.A. Cup game at Second Division Woodville. The training was hard, as usual, but Barrie ensured it involved plenty of variety. Tony had suggested to Barrie the correct system to adopt and what practice to restrict the week's training to, on the basis of witnessing Woodville's style of play during the previous week. While Barry concentrated on the training sessions and treating minor injuries, Tony was busy in the office dealing with an abundance of paperwork on club matters, and Sid, along with Peggy, were attending mainly to requests for tickets for the game at Woodville.

The Woodville ground held a capacity of 35,000 and although there was no danger this amount of spectators would attend the game; it was clear from the Secretary's records that the Sharrington team would have a following of in excess of 1,500 people. The local bus company had had to hire an extra number of coaches to meet the demand. The town of Woodville was 200 miles from Sharrington in a southeasterly direction. There was no major railway line on this route. Therefore, all supporters would have to travel by road. Many people would of course, travel by car but a total of fifteen coaches would make the trip. The excitement of Sharrington's current league position plus the possibility of a shock win at Woodville certainly had the town talking in true cup-fever style. The press coverage was impressive, both locally and nationwide. The scene was set for a great cup game.

Tony received a request from Walter Marriott, the manager of Hooper Brook Rovers. He had asked if he should arrange the accommodation for an overnight stay for the Sharrington team after the game, particularly as Hooper Brook were only 20 miles from Woodville, but Tony declined, saying they were turning home straight afterwards. However, he sent two complementary tickets with his reply to appease the good-natured manager.

The only other Fourth Division teams left in the F.A. Cup were leaders Seamingway (away to Hollowbrook – amateurs) Treecliffe (home to Mirth Cross – 3rd Division), Braman (home to Hambridge – 2nd division), Dabrook (away to Crest Town – 2nd Division) and finally, Crookaby (home to Evercroft – 3rd Division). However, the Sharrington game at Woodville was creating the most excitement of all, in football circles.

On the day before the game Tony, quite surprisingly, announced his team, after the final training session. It was:

1.	Alan Hawkins
2.	Graham Bond (captain)
3.	Allan Smith
4.	Micky Leighton
5.	Tommy French
6.	Mike Thomas
7.	Graham Hart
8.	Neil Baynes
9.	Alf Henning
10.	Simon Docker
11.	Sammy Chaddock
12.	Tony White

Tony had decided to rest Stephen Holland and bring in Mike Thomas to give the defence more aggression. Thomas was a tigerish player and ideal for upsetting opponents who relied on time on the ball. Tony thought Thomas' qualities would be better suited on the day, rather than the calm, casual style of Holland. Tony also opted to bring back Sammy Chaddock to link up with Simon Docker on the left hand side but he covered himself by making young Tony White substitute, just in case the partnership failed to work. White could play in either position but also he would be an ideal player to bring on in any role should this be necessary through either injury or purely for tactical reasons. This meant that new signing Paul Brooke was not to play for Sharrington again. The young player was disheartened but reassured by Tony that he had not been forgotten. He convinced Brooke and both Cracknell and Holland, the other players not involved in the cup match, that they were all vital and essential players for the future of the club. Tony knew his words were little comfort for these young players, particularly when they were all eager to prove their worth out on the pitch. He was anxious that Brooke had not been selected since signing from Leston Utd, where he was performing excellently in every game, but both full-backs were doing so well he honestly didn't feel he could drop either of the them to give Brooke a game. This problem was Tony's main concern at the time of team selection and he hoped the new player would be patient for a little longer.

At 3 p.m. on the Friday afternoon the club bus set off for a hotel just outside Woodville in the village of Cutterholme. The party comprised of all the playing staff, the chairman and the directors, the club doctor, Grant Evans, and an associate, Ben Fellows, from the *Sharrington Echo*, Barrie and Tony. After the three and a half hour journey travelling through a rain storm, two wrong turnings and a close shave with an articulated lorry, the whole party were delighted to step into the Victorian-styled hotel with its quaint oak beams which caused everyone to enter with their heads ducked to one side. Once the evening meal was completed the players were packed off to their rooms at 9.30pm.

'Are you nervous?' enquired Graham Bond's roommate, Alan Hawkins.

'No, I am not, Alan. Not yet anyway,' answered the captain as he unpacked his suitcase.

'I bet we will be nervous in 12 hours time,' mused Alan Hawkins. 'Aye, I suppose we all will be, but it's a good sign, don't you think?' 'Mmm, perhaps it is. I just hope we can perform well tomorrow against Woodville,' stressed the goalkeeper.

'It's certainly our biggest test this season and, as the boss says, it'll give us some idea of just how well we are playing,' commented Bond before washing his face in the small washbasin.

'It's funny really, isn't it, Graham, how the boss approaches each game,' laughed Alan Hawkins jumping into his single bed.

'How do you mean?' questioned Graham Bond, spraying the room with water.

'Well, every week is different. Sometimes he builds us up as though our playing careers depended upon it, then other weeks his approach is almost casual and lax,' said Hawkins, almost bashfully.

'Yes, I know what you mean. It's just his way I suppose. Anyway, whatever it is, his planning, preparations, team talks, training sessions and recommendations all seem to be working for the success of the club. It's the man's personality and character isn't it? He is… well he's just good at managing. I suppose some people are born leaders, others aren't. It just so happens he certainly is, without a doubt,' stressed the captain as he dried his face with a towel.

'I hope we play well tomorrow and prove to everyone that the confidence he puts in us is warranted,' mused Hawkins.

'I am confident we will play well, and, for the first time since I joined the club, there is an excellent team spirit and a good 100% approach to each game. The players he's brought to the club have given the right blend to the team. There's no doubt that certain players weren't pulling their weight at the start of the season, and just had to go if the club was to survive another season. And I'll tell you this, Alan, if Davidson hadn't have had the guts to act as he did then I wouldn't have bet against him being sacked by Christmas. Credit to the man. He knows what he's doing all right, and if he continues to do so, I honestly can't see any reason for him not taking this club to the top, and I mean the First Division, not just the Fourth Division championship. He has the club at heart and if our directors continue to let him run the playing side of the club then I am sure he won't rest until he sees Sharrington with the League Division One championship,' stressed Graham Bond.

'Yes, he certainly gives that impression. I am just wondering why he has played down tomorrow's game as though it's only a friendly game. Every quote in the newspapers was very non-committal. I would have thought he'd build up the game more than he has done and put the pressure on Woodville. Wouldn't you?' asked Alan Hawkins.

'Everything he does is carefully planned to the last detail. I agree that he has been particularly quiet on his pre-match comments. Anyhow, I am sure we will put up a good performance. As always Alan, the games are decided on the pitch on the day, and not beforehand,' urged Graham Bond sliding into his bed.

Eventually, after discussing further thoughts about their manager, the lights were put out and the two players fell asleep.

'Cup day special! Cup day special!' shouted a Woodville official outside the ground as the spectators mingled around twenty minutes prior to the start of the game. 'All the information on today's teams.' He continued whilst selling copies to clutching hands.

'Looks like a good crowd today, men,' stated Bob Bennett.

'Yes, it looks like a big ground too,' answered Frank Sneddon taking the cigarette from the corner of his mouth.

'I've seen enough of our supporters to fill it though,' joked Eddie

Fisher.

'Are you still confident, Eddie?' questioned Frank. There was a brief pause as the men found the right queue. 'I am not sure, to be honest. The surroundings put me off a bit. I suppose it depends how our lads adjust early on,' murmured Eddie adjusting his red and black scarf.

'I am feeling nervous myself, so I hate to think how the players are reacting to the thought of the game,' shouted Bob.

'You haven't got a chance, mate,' quipped a Woodville supporter immediately in front of Bob in the queue. 'Don't be so sure my friend. It's a funny game football. We are playing well at the moment and just might surprise your team today,' said Frank seriously.

'Can't see it, somehow. We are a good side too and two divisions higher than you. It is important,' responded the Woodville fan.

'Not in cup matches, buddy. Not in cup matches,' repeated Bob confidently.

'I can't see our lads losing today, regardless,' chirped the blue-scarfed supporter.

'Well, I can, buddy. I can,' said Bob, but this time not so confidently. As he said that the home supporter disappeared through the turnstile and was lost from sight.

The three men found their seats quickly and sat nervously waiting for the game to start. The ground was modern in every way. The cantilever stand was brand new and very spacious. It ran the length of the pitch. Opposite was another stand, which was already full to capacity. Behind each goal was covered terracing, also well populated. There were numerous floodlights scattered around the ground, all of which were switched on to penetrate the gloomy and misty weather conditions. The crowd was recorded at 21,000. The three men remarked on the last cup game Sharrington played in front of a large crowd but dismissed the same outcome today. The home team were first onto the pitch to a tremendous reception. They were kitted in all blue and looked a fit and confident team. They were currently positioned third in Division Two and had reached the fourth round of the League Cup. They were drawn to meet Ashton from the First Division.

Sharrington followed the home team down the tunnel, which was positioned in the centre of the cantilever stand. When compared to the home team, the Sharrington players appeared less confident, but Graham Bond, Neil Baynes and Alf Henning were quick to rally round to keep the other players on their toes. The tension around the ground was building to a crescendo. The kick-off could not come soon enough.

Alan Norris, the Woodville Captain, won the toss and chose to stay as they were. Just as Alf Henning was about to kick-off, Tony Davidson ran down the tunnel and quickly bobbed into the dugout.

Woodville were soon in possession and passing the white ball remarkably accurately amongst the forward line. It was one-touch football. After six fast passes the ball rested at Steve Wallace's feet and before he could turn his marker, young Mike Thomas kicked wildly at the ball, but missed and caught the forward's left ankle. He fell and rolled in agony. Mike Thomas pleaded with the referee that he had gone for the ball but the official immediately showed him the yellow card and gave him a stern talking to. The crowd was incensed. After a brief stoppage for treatment the resultant free kick was glanced against the crossbar by centre-forward Ray Palmer. The loose ball was cleared desperately by Smith. The next attack brought another booking for a visiting defender. Micky Leighton upended No 10 John Whiting as he was about to shoot at goal. Again the free kick caused concern in the Sharrington defence. Whiting lunged at the centre and brought an excellent save from Hawkins. The ball was forced from the goalkeeper's hand and a scuffle broke out with several players. After what seemed an eternity the ball was booted downfield by Tommy French but the referee had blown for a free kick to Sharrington.

Wave after wave of Woodville attacks tested the Fourth Division defence but constant fouling, niggling and doggedness kept the score at 0-0 after 30 minutes. The play became rougher and rougher, so much so that both captains were warned to keep the game clean by the strict referee. Occasionally the skill of Baynes penetrated the Woodville defence and there were good efforts from Chaddock, Henning and Docker which caused the blue shirted side to concentrate more on their defence. During this time Woodville had two defenders booked for fouling and dissent. Just as the game was evening itself out, Woodville took control again with their excellent fluent passing. A right wing corner was headed onto the upright by Chalmers the home team's centre-half and two minutes later Palmer fired an accurate volley under the bar, but somehow Alan Hawkins threw himself into the path of the ball and scooped it over and out of play. The following corner resulted in a clearance by French which sent Hart racing infield with a three against two situation in favour of Sharrington. The young winger escaped the tight marking Ward before touching the ball to Chaddock who carefully crossed to the unmarked Alf Henning racing into the penalty area. The experienced centre-forward took the ball in his stride, dummied the goalkeeper and struck the ball firmly with his right boot into the empty net. The Sharrington players went delirious. The referee, however, saw the linesman standing with his pink flag raised above his head. After consultation it was ruled that Henning had been judged to be offside. The much-travelled veteran argued with the referee that the ball had been passed back to him by Chaddock and couldn't therefore have been offside but his efforts cut no ice. The goal was disallowed. The score remained goalless at half-time.

'Good work, lads! It's been hard for you but well worth the effort. I know the crowd don't like some of our tackling but as far as I am concerned it's an excellent fighting spirit. 110% that's what you've given me in the first half! We've defended well again and attacked quickly and sensibly. It's an excellent all-round performance. Tremendous,' enthused Tony. 'Just keep it the same way this half. Don't let their crowd or players bother you. They are not used to seeing teams gritting their teeth before challenging for the ball. We are working well and have every chance of getting our name into the hat for the next round.'

The players were refused the chance to freshen up. They were asked just to take a sip of tea and start the second half as they left off. They all seemed surprised at Tony's request of not allowing them to wash their faces or comb their hair but they jumped up and filed back out onto the pitch just as the referee's bell rang out.

For the first fifteen minutes of the restart it was end to end, with Woodville just having the edge. As the game progressed the rain began to fall and slanted into the defending Sharrington players' faces. Players were slipping and sliding on the greasy turf but the dramatic goalmouth incidents continued. After 63 minutes Palmer brought a great save from Hawkins. Three minutes later, captain Norris fired over the bar from only eight yards out. Two minutes later an appeal for a penalty, after Whiting was seemingly held back by Thomas, was turned down. At the other end Henning hit a post after 69 minutes and Leighton had a shot turned around the other post by the acrobatic Sheppard in goal. The crowd was spellbound with all the goalmouth incidents, but after 76 minutes the home supporters were rewarded with a goal. The move down the Woodville right wing saw a quick pass to Norris who kept the ball moving forward first time by glancing it to No 8 Steve Wallace. Before his tight marker, Thomas, could snuff him out again, as he had done all during the game, the blond-haired starlet hit the ball on the turn which surprised Alan Hawkins leaving him helpless as the ball shot past his head and bulged out the netting. It was 1-0 to Woodville.

Sharrington were shattered. The goal lifted the Second Division side just when things were beginning to go against them. Woodville were revitalised by the shock goal and Wallace was the hero. As the rain poured down, the Woodville forwards shot from all angles and distances but Hawkins saved them all without fault. Tony Davidson brought on Tony White in place of the rapidly-tiring Simon Docker with eight minutes remaining. By this time the experienced Second Division defenders had shackled the disheartened Sharrington forwards and on many occasions rolled a long ball back to keeper Sheppard to avoid any possible late danger. Sharrington stuck to their task but the time was ticking away all too quickly for them to save the game.

Just before the rain-soaked referee blew the whistle for full time, a left wing cross by Chaddock skidded dangerously through the Woodville goalmouth but despite lunges and leaps by Sharrington players to deflect the ball into the net it ran through untouched and out for a goalkick. As soon as Sheppard took the long kick the shrill of the whistle brought the game to an end. The favourites had won through, but they had had to work for it. They would remember Sharrington, who after a scrappy start had matched their victorious opponents in every department but one, a valid goal. The Sharrington team had given of their best and would be remembered by the Woodville club and supporters, for their grittiness and style.

Chapter 57

"WALLACE'S WINNER" "WOODVILLE WIN CLIFFHANGERS" "ROCK HARD SHARRINGTON PIPPED AT THE POST" "STIRRING CUP TIE GOES TO FORM" "REFEREE'S DECISION OUSTS PLUCKY SHARRINGTON" "WHAT A FINAL THIS GAME WOULD HAVE BEEN" – were some of the newspapers' headlines on the following Sunday morning. Sharrington had certainly come out of the game with nothing but praise for the way in which they had stuck to their task at Woodville. The disallowed Henning goal just before half-time was the major talking point, not only in the newspaper reports but in the town of Sharrington also. The Fourth Division team's supporters were convinced that Henning's goal was a good one and felt the decision of offside was harsh to say the least. The match reporters were also critical of the referee's decision but were quick to point out that the linesman was up with play and had raised his flag before Henning slotted the ball into the net.

All in all, Sharrington had been beaten and were now out of the F.A. Cup for another season. The club could now concentrate solely on the Fourth Division and aim for promotion.

Tony Davidson woke early on Sunday morning and was happy to prepare breakfast for himself and his wife, Penny, before returning to bed to read an assortment of newspapers. He was satisfied with his team's efforts and delighted to read that the match reporters were impressed with Sharrington's overall play. He spent a leisurely day at home and tried to put Sharrington's cup game out of his mind. During late afternoon, however, the telephone rang and Penny answered it, hoping she could give her husband at least a day's rest from football.

'Is Mr Davidson there?' enquired an eager male voice. 'Well, he's busy at the moment,' said Penny as she winked at Tony, who was lying on the leather settee watching a film on television. 'It's very important. Can I speak to him, please,' demanded the caller. 'Who is it speaking?' asked Penny, knowing that the urgency of the voice suggested her husband should talk to the caller straight away 'It's Ben Norton, I am a neighbour of Jack Elliott, the Sharrington chairman,' stressed the voice quickly but precisely.

'Just one moment, Mr Norton,' replied Penny before covering the mouthpiece of the telephone and informing her husband who the caller was. Tony appeared mystified but rose to his feet to speak to Mr Norton.

'Tony Davidson here'. 'Oh, Mr Davidson, I am sorry to trouble you but I thought you should be informed that Mr Jack Elliott has just been rushed to Sharrington General Hospital following a heart attack,' said the anxious voice.

'What… oh no… when?' panicked Tony. 'About twenty minutes ago, that's all,' replied Mr Norton. 'Well, I'll go down right away. Tell me, how was he?' enquired Tony. 'He was just unconscious when the ambulance took him away,' remarked Mr Norton.

'Oh…. well, thanks for phoning. I'll get their immediately,' said Tony replacing the receiver hurriedly.

'What on earth's the matter?' shrieked Penny. 'Jack's had a heart attack. They've taken him to the General. I must get down there straight away Look, love, can you phone all the directors and Sid and Barrie please and let them know. I'll phone from the hospital as soon as I can,' stressed Tony as he tried to regain his composure.

'Oh no, poor old Jack. That's terrible. Hurry love, please! I'll phone everyone,' urged Penny.

Tony quickly laced up his shoes, grabbed his car coat and had driven out of the drive no more than two minutes after putting down the phone. Penny quickly made the phone calls, starting with Eddie Flannigan. Tony drove as fast as he possibly could to the hospital. He was in so much of a hurry that he forgot to fasten his safety belt and, on two occasions, increased his speed to beat the changing traffic lights. Fortunately the roads were quiet, as was normal on a Sunday, therefore the journey was soon over. The distance of seven miles from Tony's home had taken just under fifteen minutes to complete. Tony parked his car haphazardly outside the main hospital entrance and rushed towards the reception desk in the foyer. A young nurse behind the desk looked up in surprise as Tony stormed in through the doorway.

'Can I help you, sir?' asked the nurse politely. 'Yes, oh, yes. I understand a Mr Jack Elliott has been admitted about half an hour ago.'

'He's had a heart attack,' replied Tony as he looked around him as though to get his bearings.

'That's right. He's on Ward D, but I am afraid no visitors are allowed to see him,' said the dark-haired girl officially.

'Is he all right?' demanded Tony.

'I understand he was unconscious but I cannot add anything further, at this stage,' commented the nurse.

'Can I see the doctor? Is Mrs Elliott here? Which way is the ward?' asked Tony quickly.

'If you sit over there for a moment, I will try and get in touch with the doctor and find out the position for you,' explained the nurse as she picked up the telephone receiver.

'Yes, thank you,' said Tony after realising that his presence at Jack Elliott's bed would be futile. Tony sat down wondering if his wife had contacted the directors. Suddenly his attention was drawn to the nurse's telephone conversation.

'Excuse me, sir, what is your name?'

'Err, Err, Tony Davidson,' he replied hesitantly, as though disturbed from a trance. The nurse informed the person on the other end of the phone. She continued her conversation. Tony wondered whether he should telephone Eddie Flannagan personally, but knew he would have no news to give him.

'Mr Davidson, the doctor would like a word with you. Can you go to Room 221 on Ward D, please? Its on the fourth floor.' Tony didn't need asking twice. He followed the signs to Ward D at a brisk pace. The doctor was waiting outside the door to room 221 and signalled Tony to him. Tony entered the room to find Mrs Elliott deeply distressed. Tony comforted her as the doctor spoke.

'Mr Elliott is still unconscious but he has suffered a massive coronary and remains in a critical condition. We are doing everything possible, Mr Davidson. It will be a question of whether he will respond to the emergency treatment. The next twenty-four hours will be crucial.'

Mrs Elliott sobbed uncontrollably onto Tony's shoulder while he stared aimlessly into mid-air. Shortly afterwards the doctor informed both Steve King and Eddie Flannagan of the news. The doctor left the room to attend to Jack Elliott while the visitors sat motionless, waiting in hope.

At 8.30 p.m. in the evening, Bill Boothroyd arrived at the hospital. He had been out of town visiting friends and only heard of the shock news on his return. He too was speechless but unlike the other visitors he fidgeted constantly. His nervous habits became so annoying to the others that Eddie Flannagan took him for a walk on the pretence that he wanted a quiet word and a smoke. Whilst the two men were out of the room, Doctor Sweizner returned to say there was no change in Mr Elliott's condition and suggested the visitors went home for the night. Mrs Elliott, by this time, had stopped weeping and agreed to go home with her son. The doctor promised to telephone all concerned should there be any developments to report.

The visiting party returned to their respective homes after agreeing to keep each other informed of news they received during the following day. The shock news saddened the whole of Sharrington. Jack Elliott was a much-respected man, not only in the football fraternity, but in both the business world and local councils. Everyone wished for his speedy recovery but the night passed painstakingly slow for his family and friends. At 7.30am on Monday morning the hospital reported that Jack Elliott was still unconscious but his condition had improved slightly during the night.

Chapter 58

'Right, lads, I want to start this week's training with a ten mile run. I know it's probably the last thing you expected to do on this bright Monday morning but I can assure you the rest of the week will be spent on ball skills,' shouted Barrie Trippett to the full squad of players gathered around him on the pitch. 'I know last Saturday's match was hard but if we can start off with a bit of stamina training I'm sure you'll get the benefit for next Saturday's match'.

'Are we running round the pitch, Barrie' enquired Micky Thomas.

'No, I think you'll find that a bit boring. I had in mind a street run to Chaple End, down through the woods, along Canterbrook Road, up and over by Briargate and back up to Chaple End and return here. I would say that's about ten miles, wouldn't you?' sneered Barrie.

'Why on the public roads, Barrie. It's so embarrassing' asked Alan Smith.

'Exactly, Smithy, it's for that reason alone. It makes sure you do your best by giving it all you've got. That way you don't make yourselves look like mugs to the man in the street. I don't want any world records, just get it done and out of the way. Now you all know the way don't you?' said Barrie cheekily.

Some players nodded. Some joked about old injuries coming on overnight. Others purposefully made excuses that they had forgotten Barrie's directions. Eventually Graham Bond led the players out of the ground and into the main street in the direction of Chaple End. Barrie brought up the rear, taking it nice and steady and joked that if he beat any of them back they would have to do the run again tomorrow.

The run went smoothly with no problems reported on returning to the ground. Graham Hart had fallen down in the stream during the run in the woods but apart from being covered from head to foot in mud, he was all right. The players bathed and showered, after a massage, before going home. Barrie cleared up the changing room with the help of Steve Holland and Simon Docker. It was club policy that, as there wasn't a member of ground staff, a rota was drawn up for two players each day to give assistance to Barrie. Tony personally felt this somewhat menial task helped to create a better spirit within the team. With certain players there was an initial refusal to do this work but after constant ribbing from other players, the shirkers soon came round to the idea, albeit reluctantly, that it was in the best interests of the club. As soon as the three men had finished their chores, Tony entered the dressing room.

'How's it gone today, Barrie?'

'Oh, very well. They all did the run. Apart from them feeling tired there was no problems,' replied Barrie cheerfully. 'By the way, what's the latest on Jack?' asked Barrie in more melancholy mood.

'There's no change at all, the last I heard the doctor said if he survived the 24 hours after the attack his chances would improve. We can only wait and see. I hope he pulls through,' reflected Tony.

'Yes, me too. The players were most concerned and they all asked if you would let them know if there was anything they could do to help,' stressed Barrie.

'Good, but I think the only way they can be of any assistance is to keep the club at the top of this division. I'm sure that as soon as Jack regains consciousness he will ask whether the lads are still winning and sticking to the task of getting promotion,' urged Tony.

'We all hope to do that,' said Stephen Holland as he coiled up the water hose and placed it in the storeroom.

'Aye, I wouldn't like to be in Dabrook's boots on Saturday. They'll take the brunt of it. They won't know what's hit them,' joked Simon Docker. 'That's the spirit. Let's keep the flag flying. Old Jack would want it that way,' remarked Eddie Connolly as he entered the dressing room with an arm full of clean towels. 'Now then, Barrie, where do you want these? I haven't got all day to carry out errands for Mrs. B, I've got some drainage work to attend to'.

They all laughed and left Eddie to get on with his work.

'Take him on, Sammy, go on lad, you've got him beat… that's it… well done, now cut in and drive in to the far post… yes, excellent effort, much better, Sammy,' shouted Tony from the touchline during the following day's practice match. 'Now, lads, gather round… it's been a good work out today. At last I can see signs of us beginning to understand each other's style of play. I can't say how impressed I am with the defence. We are getting to grips with the basics. Safety first is the policy. You are all reading the game so well. You seem to know each of your jobs. It looks impressive, it really does.' Tony paused momentarily before continuing. 'Micky, Neil, Simon and Tony you are interchanging roles very well. I'd like to see a bit more aggression, though, from you all. You are shouting for the ball and look eager to have possession. Keep it going lads. Sammy, I don't know if its marriage or due to being dropped recently but it's a pleasure to see you taking on the full-backs and causing them so many problems. That's what I want from you. Graham's been doing it on the other wing and if we can attack like that down both wings it will give our other forwards such an easier job, not to mention the problems for the opposition's defence'. Tony scratched the side of his head before pulling the woollen bobble hat further onto his head. 'It's been a good session today, lads. Well done. Go and shower off and I'll see you tomorrow morning'.

The players made their way to the players' entrance before disappearing under the stand. Tony and Barrie collected the balls and other equipment before leaving the pitch. 'It's good to hear that Jack's regained consciousness,' said Barrie.

'So it is, Barrie. He is recovering very well, apparently, but the doctor told Mrs. Elliott that he would have to have a complete rest for the next two to three months'.

'I bet the other directors were relieved?' enquired Barrie, juggling one of the practice balls on his knee.

'They were delighted. Absolutely delighted with his good recovery.'

'When did he regain consciousness, Tony?' asked Barrie as the ball shot forward off the end of his toe and bounced in the direction of the players' entrance.

'About 8 p.m. last night, apparently. We were all getting a little bit worried when he hadn't recovered within the 24 hours after he had his heart attack. Anyway, he will have to take it easy, but we will have to manage without him for some time; although, his absence will be a loss to the club,' replied Tony as he pulled a flag out of the ground.

The two men went towards the storeroom underneath the stand.

'That was an interesting game, apparently, at Storr Town last night in the 3rd round League Cup replay against Low Grove'.

'Yes, I heard so on the news last night. Didn't both teams go into extra time after scoring two penalties each?'

'That's right and Storr Town got the winner in the last minute, direct from a corner kick according to this morning's newspaper'.

'Well, that won't have helped Low Grove's confidence. I see that the First Division outfit Parringway clinched it over Ranchley after extra time as well.'

'Yes, 2-0 and now they have got probably the easiest draw in the 4th round against Third Division Summerstone'.

The equipment was put into the storeroom and the two men made their way up to the Manager's Office.

'The first week's tickets went well in the lottery. Don't know the winners yet though,' stated Tony as he sorted through his paperwork.

'I bought my wife £2.00's worth. I don't suppose she'll win though.

We've never been that lucky in raffles and draws of any kind'.

'If she did win the public might think it's fixed,' laughed Tony.

The telephone rang before Barrie could think of something to say. Tony answered it and after finishing with the call he told Barrie that the caller had been Mrs. Elliott to thank everyone for their concern and help.

'I wish him a speedy recovery. I also wish the team have a speedy recovery on Saturday. I'm sure a win over Dabrook will aid Jack's recovery,' added Barrie.

'I feel confident, particularly after today's work out. We are beginning to take shape. I also thought our performance at Woodville gave us some much needed confidence at this stage of the season,' said Tony thoughtfully.

'What team will you play?'

'Oh, I think we must keep the same side, barring injury of course. My only major concern is that young Paul Brooke has been with us now for 6 weeks without a chance to prove his worth. I will have to draft him into the team soon to keep him in trim and also to keep his interest in the club,' reflected Tony.

Chapter 59

'OK, lads, let me have your final attention before you go out,' stressed Tony in the dressing room at 2.00 p.m. prior to the home league game against Dabrook. 'It's been a topsy-turvy week at the club. We had a good performance against Woodville, a tragic piece of news involving the club chairman and an excellent week's training. We have forgotten about the FA Cup and League Cup for another season. We are only concerned with League Division Four. We are playing for the town of Sharrington, the club and for Jack Elliott today and for the rest of the season. We are second from the top as we stand now and with a chance to start to break away from the likes of Harloft, Treecliffe, Ellistart, Low Grove and today's opponents. We've got some hard matches coming up over Christmas time and the early part of the New Year so we've got to take full points today.' Tony started to walk around the dressing room as he talked about Dabrook. 'We drew 0-0 up there earlier on this season in a poor and uninteresting match but make no mistake about it, they are here today for 2 points. They've taken 7 points out of the last 10 with some surprisingly good results. They are only 2 points behind us now and, like us, they only lost 1-0 last week to a Second Division club, Crest Town, away from home in the 3rd round of the FA Cup. They will be fighting hard today but if we play as planned during training we should be opening up the gap between us to 4 points.' The referee's bell rang in the dressing room. 'That's it, lads. Get to it. You all know your jobs. Give the crowd a positive performance and two or three goals to cheer. Best of luck, lads'.

Barrie echoed Tony's wishes as the players lumbered out of the door and down the tunnel.

It was another miserable afternoon. The grey clouds seemed to stretch forever and rain was just beginning to fall, as Dabrook, in their all white strip, kicked off. The crowd was registered at 7,653.

Within two minutes the visitors' centre-half Bannister had committed two fouls on Alf Henning and been booked by the referee. At the other end of the pitch Tommy French had upended his namesake French, the Dabrook centre-forward, just yards outside the penalty area. The free kick was wasted.

Leighton and Baynes were linking well together and after a perfect through ball by the former, Sammy Chaddock skilfully twisted and turned on the greasy surface before centring to Alf Henning who headed perfectly past the keeper, Montrose, only to have the ball nudged round the post by the retreating left full-back Thickett.

It was an interesting dual as the rain came down heavier, but the goalless score sheet was changed after 34 minutes when Bannister got caught in two minds and in his mix-up Leighton robbed him of the ball and startled Montrose with a shot out of the blue. It was 1-0 to Sharrington.

For the remainder of the first half, Dabrook were punished by the earnest and skilful home team play. Before the visitors could settle after the restart, Hart jinked his way into the massed defence and his shot-cum-cross hit the far post and went over the line. Only 1 minute later on, Baynes combined well with Docker and Henning to score easily while the Dabrook defence appealed for an infringement against Henning. At half-time, Sharrington led 3-0.

Whatever was said by Hemmingway, the Dabrook Manager, at half-time, it certainly caused his side to get right back into the game. Sharrington seemed to take life a little bit too easy at the start of the second half and the visitors took full advantage.

A quick throw-in by the captain Bridge sent right-winger Salmon streaking past Allan Smith. His cross was inch perfect and No. 10 and leading goalscorer Heaton headed firmly into the corner of the net to leave Alan Hawkins rooted to the spot.

Dabrook pressed forward time and again but Sharrington's defence were beginning to weather the storm effectively and Tony and Barrie felt their team had taken the worst Dabrook could throw at them when to everyone in the ground's surprise, Micky Thomas, who had had a splendid game, casually struck a back pass to Alan Hawkins but Charlie French had anticipated it a split second earlier and raced onto the ball to deflect it into the goal. Dabrook had pulled back to 3-2 with the help of Thomas and quick thinking of striker French.

Graham Bond roasted Thomas and deservedly so, and, as there was only 11 minutes of play left, the wing half's carefree attitude had put Dabrook in with a chance of getting back on level terms after being 3-0 down.

Before Sharrington's defence could experience the Dabrook onslaught the old campaigner, Alf Henning, saved the day. Only 3 minutes after Dabrook's second goal he fought for a loose ball on the right wing, beat off two wild challengers, bravely chased what seemed a lost cause, won the ball back again and charged towards the Dabrook goal with his head down. All the while the excitement was building up around the home supporters when, as Alf Henning got to the edge of the penalty area directly in front of goal, he briefly looked up, swung his right boot and the greasy ball flashed into the net to give the match to Sharrington 4-2.

Chapter 60

'I wish to report that Jack Elliott is convalescing at his home and Mrs. Elliott informed me that he was absolutely delighted with the victory over Dabrook on Saturday,' stressed Eddie Flannagan, beaming with delight. 'She felt the 4-2 scoreline in Sharrington's favour was just the tonic Jack needed after his recent ordeal'.

'Will the doctors say when he can return to our meetings again?' enquired Peggy Hollingsworth. She was the only member in the meeting who had not had the opportunity to visit the club chairman.

'No, Peggy, he won't. Personally I don't think we will see Jack back this season but I am sure we can hold the fort between us ready for his return next season,' replied Eddie rather solemnly.

'I agree, Eddie, we cannot push Jack out prematurely. It is up to him to decide on whether he feels he must step down or not,' countered Steve King.

'True. In fact Jack has indicated that we three directors are to guide the ship until further notice,' stated Eddie, who had taken it upon himself to sit in Jack's chair and assume the role of relief Chairman. 'If you could minute that, Peg, I think we should now move on. No one raised any objections to Eddie but as he had the strongest personality of the group it was as though everyone had automatically assumed Eddie would take charge.

The meeting continued for 2 hours and discussions were raised on the weekly lottery, arrangements on staffing, the turnstiles for the forthcoming home game against Harloft on 27th December, travelling arrangements to Low Grove on 24th December and to Harloft on Boxing Day, the accounts, bonuses, expenses and finally on the manager's report covering the state of affairs in the 4th Division.

It was agreed to travel back from the Low Grove game as soon as possible so that the players could spend Christmas Eve and Christmas Day with their families. The team would travel to Harloft on Boxing Day morning at 12.00am after a short work out at the Sharrington ground.

Tony requested the Board's permission for the team to be kept together in a hotel near Harloft after the game but although Steve King thought this to be a good idea, both Eddie Flannagan and Bill Boothroyd considered it to be too expensive at Christmas time and, in addition, as it was only 68 miles to Harloft, they felt the players should return to their families. Tony argued about the decision but to no avail. He made the point that the players were paid as professionals and should expect to be away from home in these circumstances and also that it would give them all a break from any pressure. However, his appeal was quashed and it was minuted that the cost of the proposed exercise was prohibitive and unnecessary.

The meeting ended with the three Directors highly satisfied about the club's league position. Sharrington were joint top with Seamingway and Treecliffe. Sharrington's next opponents, Prent Park, were next to bottom and Low Grove and Harloft, the following two fixtures, were sixth and fourth respectively.

On the following day prior to training, Tony informed all the players that the board had agreed a bonus scheme on the following terms. He read from a piece of tattered white paper: 'It is agreed by the Sharrington board of directors, following requests by a representative of the players, that as an additional incentive a sum of £100 will be paid to each player (professional or part-time) once per calendar month if the club can maintain a position in the top three places in the Fourth Division on a pro-rata basis with the other teams in the same division as at the last league game in that calendar month. The league position will run concurrently and if the club register a position out of the top three places for any one week within that month, the bonus scheme will be started afresh from the next time the club return to a top three place. The board of directors will decide when the payment will be made.' Tony pushed the piece of paper back into his pocket. 'It may sound complicated lads but basically it is more of a consistency bonus than a straight regular bonus. The board frowned a little on your suggestion of a £30 bonus if you maintained a place in the top three every week. I appreciate that their offer appears somewhat stingy but it is a new venture for the club and these things take time to establish. Who knows, if you maintain your regular form and the money situation eases within the club, the board may re-schedule it for a bonus every fortnight or perhaps every week. But, and I stress this with a sigh of relief, the board to my surprise and certainly in my mind a totally unexpected gesture have agreed for the sum of £100 to be paid to each member of the squad as from the 1st of this month for your remarkable team displays and for maintaining a top three place during November. I don't think they can be fairer than that, lads, at this stage, do you?' asked Tony light-heartedly.

There was delight and surprise amongst the players. Graham Bond was the first to speak. 'I was a bit concerned with their offer. It seemed a bit of a cheek to me, particularly when for the first time since I can remember we have given this club a good reputation but I think the backdated offer is generous and I will accept their proposals'.

'Just a minute, Graham,' shouted Alf Henning over the general hubbub in the dressing room. 'I know money's tight, Tony, and the chairman has suffered a serious illness. I also know there's a long way to go this season but I feel we have put in an awful amount of hard work and effort to keep this club up in the top of this division'. Tony had never seen Alf speaking so confidently. He was wondering what the veteran centre-forward was leading up to. 'As I understand it, if we are, say, in the top three places for three weeks and then fall to fourth place, although this might not mean we should have lost that game, then we would lose out on any bonus at all for that month. Is that correct?' enquired the diligent Alf Henning.

'Yes, Alf, I'm afraid that is correct,' Tony could not find any more words because he saw this as a déjà vu situation from his discussion with the board only the night before.

'Well, I think that's a bit much to swallow. I don't think they fully appreciate just what we are doing for this town,' ranted Alf adamantly.

'I'd go along with what you say Alf but, knowing this club as I do, I think we should accept what they have offered now and go back to them for reconsideration in a couple of months if the bonus scheme is not working and if we have not been in the top three due to no fault of ours,' came the quick statement from Allan Smith.

'I think they've got a bit of a nerve to keep us chasing after the carrot like that but I would have much preferred a weekly bonus scheme,' commented Tommy French from the back.

'It's pathetic isn't it really, boss,' said Neil Baynes. 'I would think you are as disappointed as the majority of us but I've known more stingier Boards and as Graham and Alan have said we will have to accept it but look at it again if it's not coming out in our favour'.

'I am just glad to be picking up £100 extra for enjoying myself really,' stated Graham Hart bluntly.

'Me too,' chirped Tony White.

'And me,' said Steve Holland.

The older pros laughed in good humour and Sammy Chaddock tapped Tony White and Graham Hart on the backs summarising the more experienced players feelings. 'You'll learn, lads, you'll learn'.

Tony Davidson smiled and put both his hands up in front of him as if to say I've tried lads and I understand your reluctance but we'll see. 'Can I take it we will accept the board's offer for the time being then?'

There was a general consensus of opinion before a "yes" was given by the whole playing staff.

'Good. I'm pleased you've accepted, but I promise I will make it known to the board that the whole system of this bonus should be looked at again shortly. Right, lads,' said Tony after a pause. 'It's back to work, noses to the grindstone, let's get ready and do some training. After all, we are getting paid for our work.' He clapped his hands together and the players started to get changed.

Chapter 61

The rest of the week passed smoothly and the home game against Prent Park was recorded as a formality. 8,750 people had paid to witness Sharrington outclass and demoralise the lowly Eastern club by 4-0. The game finished just as it had started, with Sharrington attacking strongly and quickly and creating so many scoring opportunities that one sports writer counted as many as twenty clear-cut chances.

Prent Park had had a poor season. They had only won one game (at home to Rallingborough 2-0), drawn four games away and lost by 6-0 to Seamingway (away) and 4-1 (at home) to Dabrook. Sharrington had beaten them 2-0 at Prent Park and had now completed the double over them.

Admittedly they had had a season with more than their share of injuries but on the day they never looked like scoring against the progressive Sharrington team.

Tony Davidson had named an unchanged team. He had motivated his team to perform as well as ever and got their minds off the bonus scheme. He changed the substitute from White to Brooke with a view of giving his latest signing a game. The young full-back's chance came after 65 minutes, when Sharrington were leading by 3-0, albeit out of position. Graham Hart had been hurt in an awkward-looking tackle but though he had told Barrie Trippett he was keen to carry on, Tony asked Graham Hart to come off. Paul Brooke leapt at his chance to play again in front of a crowd. He was as quick as Tony remembered him at Leston and he showed some nice touches as a right-winger. It was an easy introduction for him into the Sharrington team.

Baynes had scored twice in the first half in the 11th and 31st minute. He was by far the most skilful player in the two teams. His first goal was a simple tap-in from a poor clearance by the visitors but his second goal was scored from 30 yards. He received a pass from Graham Bond, jinked past two Prent Park players and as a complete surprise to everyone including the flat-footed goalkeeper, Gannon, hit the ball on the run with his right foot. The ball never left the ground and hit the metal stanchion in the back of the netting.

The two goals in the second half were scored by Micky Leighton after 56 minutes from another bad clearance out of the visitors' defence after a corner by Graham Hart and the final goal came almost on the stroke of time by Sammy Chaddock who slithered his way round three defenders before jabbing the ball underneath the diving body of Gannon. Ironically, it was only Sammy Chaddock's second league goal. His first was scored at Prent Park.

In between the two second half goals were blatant misses by Alf Henning, Neil Baynes, Simon Docker, Sammy Chaddock and Micky Thomas who dribbled his way through the heart of the defence and with only the advancing goalkeeper to beat he fluffed his shot to hoots of derision by the home supporters.

After the game Tony was hounded by the newspaper men for his comments. 'It was easy for us today. 4-0 is a convincing margin and I know we missed many more chances but I'm delighted to be keeping up our challenge at the top of the league. We have now gone 9 matches without defeat and if I can say 11 matches after our game at Harloft Town on Boxing Day, I think we will take some stopping.'

'Have you heard that the other top three clubs have also won today?' asked one bald-headed journalist.

'Yes, I'd heard the results but they don't worry me unduly. I was, however, pleased to see that Seamingway chose to get back onto the winning way by thrashing our next week's opponents, Low Grove, 4-1. I'm obviously concerned about Treecliffe's good form but it will be interesting to see if Sam Dyson will be tempted by that very generous offer made by Crest United of £100,000 for Bob Villers. If they accept it, I would think it will have a considerable effect on the team's consistent performances'.

'Would you sell your star centre-forward for that amount at this stage of the season?' asked a goofy, eloquent journalist.

'I cannot relate the policy of this club and Treecliffe. In the same position as we are in now, I wouldn't wish to part with my leading scorer. Now they are out of the League Cup this may shed a different light on the matter,' replied Tony thoughtfully.

'How about the two Christmas games against Harloft Town?' questioned the bald-headed man.

'To be perfectly honest, these games will be our toughest test yet. In our favour they entertain Treecliffe next Saturday, which won't be an easy game for them. They are unbeaten at home but they've dropped three or four points to some lowly clubs. If we play as we can I am sure we will give them a good game,' smiled Tony.

'The two games after Christmas won't be easy for you either will they?' enquired Grant Evans.

'Oh, that's a long way off yet, Grant. Let's see how we fair over Christmas before I answer that one'.

'Is it true that you have had an offer from a top First Division club for Graham Hart?' asked Grant Evans quick to change the subject.

'That's news to me, Grant. I've not heard or seen anything'.

'I was to ask you that question. We had heard it was Cotterton,' raised the articulate reporter.

'No, I've not heard that, sorry' said Tony. 'Can we call it a day now, gents. I wish to see the team before they leave'.

'Just one more question, Tony. Do you regret selling Greg Hanby to Ravenhead now that he's a top scorer with 14 goals?' said the sly, bald-headed journalist.

Tony looked him in the eyes before turning away to leave the question unanswered. He checked after only a few paces before turning back and looking at the bald-headed man. 'All I will say is that everything this club has achieved this season started from his transfer'. He paused momentarily. 'And that's not too bad is it!'

Chapter 62

'MANAGER DENIES RUMOUR' 'GRAHAM HART TO COTTERTON BY XMAS' 'DAVIDSON SILENT OVER HART DEAL' '£60,000 OFFER FOR WINGER HART'

'Where on earth do they get their stories from?' asked Tony as he looked through the following Monday's newspapers.

'Beats me, Tony. I think they invent them on occasion,s' replied Barrie Trippett as he flicked from one paper to another.

'Grant Evans asked me if I knew anything about it after the match on Saturday. That goofy reporter from the *Sketch* said something about it as well. I've a good mind to ask Grant where the stories come from because I certainly haven't heard a thing from anyone and that includes Cotterton'.

'As they say, Tony, there's no smoke without fire so I'd sit tight and see what happens'.

'Well, if Cotterton think I'm willing to part with Graham Hart they've got another think coming,' stressed Tony.

'What if an offer is forthcoming for £60,000, as reported, don't you think the directors may pressure you to sell?' reasoned Barrie.

'It's certainly worrying, Barrie, and without an active Jack Elliott I feel particularly vulnerable at the moment. Graham's certainly been playing very well and he is a good natural winger with great talent. I suppose it's only to be expected for the top clubs to be showing interest but he's only played about 20 games and on that limited experience it would come as a huge shock if someone offered £60,000. I can see the practicality of his transfer for that sort of fee but I don't want to lose him. He's so important to us,' said Tony gritting his teeth and slapping the palm of his right hand on his desk top

'Let's just wait, Tony. It's no use getting uptight on a rumour,' stated Barrie.

'Aye, suppose you're right. Let's organise this week's training sessions.'

The manager and trainer discussed the week's schedule of events in detail.

The week passed quickly and the atmosphere in the club was good, with Sharrington holding the second spot in the league, only 1 point behind leaders Seamingway. By Friday evening everything was set for the journey to Low Grove in the important league game on Saturday, which was Christmas Eve. But on the Saturday morning when Tony arrived at the ground at 8.00am, all the players were present barring Micky Leighton.

'Where is he? He knew we were to set off at 8.30am. It's a long journey. It'll take us at least 5 hours. Has he phoned in, Sid?' asked Tony. 'Not yet, Tony. I've been in the office since 7.30 a.m,' replied Sid wrapping his scarf round his neck.

It was a bright and cold morning with a touch of ground frost. The car windscreens parked in the surrounding streets were white and as people were talking the heat of their breath escaped into the atmosphere.

'Phone Mrs. Maxwell, Sid,' shouted Tony pacing up and down outside the main building.

Sid immediately phoned and within two minutes shouted out through the office window to Tony and the players who were waiting for the team coach. 'He's overlaid, boss. Mrs. M. said she had difficulty getting him out of bed. He's just setting off now'.

'Well, he's got fifteen minutes to make it? Where's the coach? It should be here by now. I've got some freezing players out here,' shouted Tony.

Just as he finished speaking, the team coach pulled round the corner and into view. 'Sorry I'm late, Tony, but I had a bit of a problem with the heater. Thought I'd better get it fixed before a long journey on a day like this,' said Sid Johnstone rubbing his hands. 'It's okay now'.

'That's good, Sid. I agree we will need it today. It's very cold. We are still waiting for Micky Leighton, in any event,' replied Tony, looking somewhat apprehensive.

'We can give him twenty minutes or so. It's motorway all the way,' stated Sid who was assisting the players with the skip and balls.

Tony didn't answer. Everyone sensed an uneasiness in the manager. He was edgy and more serious than normal. The players had noticed the change in him from about the time Jack Elliott fell ill, but they put it down to the pressures of management.

Barrie Trippett had also noticed the change in Tony's manner. He seemed quieter and snappy over certain matters which Barrie thought wouldn't have bothered him at the earlier stage of the season. He wondered if there was a private problem at home which was bothering Tony.

The players mounted the bus complaining about the cold weather. Barrie Trippett sat with Steve King who was the only travelling director. Grant Evans was writing something in his notepad. Tony was still pacing up and down looking at his watch every ten or fifteen seconds. It was now 8.40 and there was no sign of Micky Leighton.

Sid Parkin asked if he should phone Mrs. Maxwell again. 'No, she said he was on his way and that was 8.15. It shouldn't take him fifteen minutes to get here never mind twenty-five,' stormed Tony. Sid had always had a reaction like that from Tony. He hadn't noticed any change in his manner over the recent weeks. He began to think that nothing he did ever pleased him. Tony paced a little longer before walking towards Sid Parkin who was at the office window about 50 yards from the team coach. After a brief chat Tony walked sternly back to the coach and got on board. 'Right Sid, take her away.'

'Aren't you going to give him a few more minutes, Tony?' asked Sid Johnstone and Barrie Trippett.

'Nope. He knows the rules. It's 8.45 now. He's fifteen minutes late. He will suffer the consequences. Drive on, Sid,' said Tony forcefully.

The noise of talking amongst the players stopped and Tony White, Tommy French, Alan Hawkins who were sitting on the back seat all turned around to look out of the rear window to see if Micky Leighton pulled up in his car as the coach slowly moved off. By the time the ground went out of view Micky Leighton had not arrived. Everybody felt that it was going to be a very long and quiet journey, not to mention the upheaval this incident would cause in the club.

At nine o'clock Micky Leighton drove into the club car park. Sid Parkin ran towards him.

'They've gone, Micky. Tony wouldn't wait any longer. They left at quarter to nine. If you rush you might catch them up. They will be going towards the motorway,' said Sid breathlessly.

'Oh, surely they could have waited a bit longer. I didn't feel too well this morning. That's why I am late,' replied Micky Leighton as he got out of the car. 'What did the boss say?'

'Well he said for me to tell you to report to his office on Monday morning at 8.30am and…' Sid paused '… he did say for you not to follow them or get to Low Grove on your own, but I can say that you drove on before I had a chance to tell you.'

'Thanks, Sid, but is it worth it? He'll clobber me for this. He won't believe I was ill, will he?' said Leighton slowly.

'If Mrs. M. had phoned earlier he might have hung on.'

'Well, I told her I would be up in time but I must have dropped back off to sleep again.'

'Ah well, come and have a coffee with me. I'll phone Tony at Low Grove and explain things but as you say, for what it's worth…'

'You reckon he'll suspend me, Sid?'

'Knowing him as I do it wouldn't surprise me. It was just the Christmas present he didn't want. I'd hate to be in your shoes if they slip up today. In fact I've got a funny feeling that life is not going to be too good for us all now from here on,' said Sid Parkin dismally.

'How do you mean, Sid?'

'I don't know exactly, Micky. I think the job is getting to him and if we don't stay on the course for promotion his ego will deflate, you mark my words,' said Sid profoundly.

Micky Leighton sat down in the corner of the office. He didn't know what to say but he thought he had blown his chances and would suffer the consequences.

Chapter 63

The Sharrington team coach arrived at the Low Grove ground at 1.45 p.m. after a 45 minutes stop on the journey. Tony received a phone call from Sid Parkin explaining the story behind Mick Leighton's lateness; however, the tall, fair-haired manager was abrupt with Sid but finally thanked him for making the phone call.

The skies were grey and the wind was strong and bitterly cold. The ground was small and homely and a reasonable crowd was gathering in front of the main entrance as the Sharrington players made their way onto the pitch to test the ground conditions. It was firm in the middle but soft down the wings. The players decided on a long-studded boot as it was thought the hard patches would loosen up as the game progressed.

Tony named Paul Brooke in place of Mick Leighton and decided to make Stephen Holland substitute. The rest of the team was as the week before against Prent Park.

Low Grove were four points behind Sharrington. They were undefeated at home with five wins and three draws in the league and also undefeated in the 3 games they played in the League Cup matches at home, although they were now out of that competition.

Their away form was spasmodic but they had been the only team to beat Sharrington at home this season. They had suffered two or three crucial injuries to their defenders but everyone considered it to be a hard game at Low Grove.

Tony was quiet before the kick-off. He told the team to play the three front men hard, and for Alf, Graham and Neil to play on the home team's young No. 3 from the start.

The crowd of 6,950, which, after the Low Grove hammering of 4-1 at leaders Seamingway only the week before, was considered a good crowd. It was also Christmas Eve, which was known to be low for football crowds, as most people would be doing their last bits of Christmas shopping.

Sharrington were sharp and more involved in the early stages of the first half. Paul Brooke was playing in an unfamiliar position, not the one he was used to, but he was performing very well, although on occasions he was drifting too far up field and leaving his other defenders with an extra man to mark. Tony and Graham Bond were on hand to shout him back before any trouble could come from his overlapping play.

Low Grove seemed to be saving themselves for Treecliffe who were their visitors on Boxing Day and then their hosts on the following day. They lacked a force to drive them upfield into the Sharrington penalty area. On the other hand, Sharrington were beginning to have more problems opening up the home team defence as the first half progressed. It was a dull first half overall and scoreless.

Tony and Barrie urged their team that if they scored only one goal they should win the game. They didn't feel Low Grove were confident at all and put it down to the thrashing the week before. Tony wanted his forwards to push the ball about a lot more and try some more long-range shots on target with the other forwards following up for goalkeeping errors. He seemed more relaxed than he did at the beginning of the game.

Low Grove were more enterprising at the start of the second half. Their manager, Paul Taylor, was now on the touchline and adding a considerable amount of vocal support. They were harder in the challenge and playing with more dedication. Sharrington were countering the home team attacks and the game became a more interesting battle.

On seventy-five minutes Low Grove were awarded a free kick on the right hand edge of the Sharrington penalty area just in front of goal. Before the visitors' wall was assembled Carter, the No. 4, touched the ball to his left and Williams, the No. 10, shot ferociously through the packed defence and the ball went past Alan Hawkins as clean as a whistle and into the bottom of the net to the goalkeeper's left hand. The Low Grove players mobbed Williams and the Sharrington players mobbed the referee. They were making out to him that he hadn't blown his whistle and demanded the free kick was re-taken. The referee pushed them out of the way and forced his way back to the middle of the pitch.

Unfortunately, Allan Smith and Tommy French pursued the issue too long and were both booked for dissent. Tony shouted for both players to retreat before the booking but either way they were so angry or were so incensed by the wrong decision that they never heard their manager from the touchline. Graham Bond had also made efforts to stop the two players arguing but to no avail.

Tony put his head in his hands as he sat on the small wooden bench and Barrie urged his team to settle down.

Just to make matters worse the heavens opened and the rain poured down. The surface became greasy and the players were soaked to the skin.

Neil Baynes, once again, proved his worth to the young Sharrington team by taking control of the situation. He slowed the game down, made good passes and encouraged the whole team. Low Grove still came forward in bursts and with only eight minutes remaining after

Sharrington had been pushing forward, the home team caught the visitors square and, as centre-forward Cartwright turned passed Tommy French and sped away from him at speed, the centre-half grabbed him around the waist and pulled him to the floor. The crowd jeered and Tommy French tried to claim he had slipped to the angry Cartwright but the referee ran up to French and produced a red card from his tunic pocket. Tommy French looked at the referee in amazement but after standing his ground for a few moments he turned away and walked to the players' tunnel with his head bowed.

Low Grove pushed men forward for the free kick but to Tony and Barrie's amazement the kick bounced off the Sharrington wall and spun high over the kicker's head to Sammy Chaddock who controlled the bouncing ball supremely and all in one moment he winged his way past the half way line and down the left hand wing. The right full-back, Sexton, tried to hold Chaddock at bay while his fellow defenders got back to help, but the crafty winger slipped the ball past him towards the edge of the penalty area. Sexton slipped and Chaddock was gone, sprinting after the ball. He momentarily looked up as he lunged at the ball just as it was about to run out of play and the left-footed cross veered away from the goalkeeper and Alf Henning ran up from the blind side, unmarked and met the ball firmly with his forehead and steered it into the back of the net. The net bulged out and covered the spectators immediately behind the goal with droplets of water

The Sharrington team were delirious and massed around Chaddock and Henning. Tony and Barrie were linking arms and jumping up and down on the touchline. Even Steve Holland and Tommy French returned momentarily to join in the delight.

Tony quickly brought Alf Henning back to centre-half and Sharrington held on to the final whistle for a 1-1 draw.

Chapter 64

It was an anxious Christmas Day for Tony Davidson. His wife, Penny, did not feel at ease with him. She had asked him on a number of occasions what was wrong but he had passed it off as nothing. They had Christmas lunch with Penny's parents, who lived in nearby Beckham. Tony had to leave at four o'clock to visit the ground to make arrangements for the following day's visit to Harloft Town who had defeated Treecliffe 2-0 to go level on points with Sharrington.

Tony finally decided by himself to suspend Micky Leighton for the two Christmas games. He had spoken to Leighton on the telephone and refused to accept his player's excuse. He said that he could not allow any of his players to be late and was insistent on punctuality at all costs, unless there was a valid and authentic reason for a delay. He was suspicious that Leighton may have been out late on the Friday evening and was possibly suffering from a hangover but without any evidence of this he could not prove it. He knew Leighton was an important player for the club but he could not allow that to come above discipline. He was reluctant to slap this ban on Leighton and knew it would not please the directors or spectators but he felt in his own mind that to ban him from playing was in preference to a fine on its own. Tony did however decide to include a token £30 fine on top of the two game ban.

Tony was also dissatisfied with the dissent shown by Smith and French and was in two minds whether to fine both players as well. He knew French would be automatically suspended by the league for Boxing Day's game at Harloft Town and decided to leave the decision on fines until Boxing Day itself. He had personally torn a strip off both players after the game at Low Grove. He completed his work and returned home at 6.30 p.m. Penny was quiet and ignored her husband's return by concentrating on the programme that was on T.V. Tony sat in the living room but was on edge. Finally after an hour of silence Penny got up, put the T.V. off and sat next to her husband and demanded that he spoke to her about whatever was bothering him. He wasn't forthcoming but after a brief heated argument between the two of them, when Penny accused Tony of spoiling her and her parents Christmas dinner, he would only say to her that the pressure of the job was bothering him. He wouldn't say any more but Penny knew it was more than that. It wasn't a happy Christmas Day for the Davidsons.

On the following morning Tony arrived at the ground at 7.30 a.m.

The journey to Harloft was 68 miles but he wanted to decide on the team and other matters in the quiet of his office. The players were to arrive for a short training session at 10.00 a.m. before setting off at mid-day by coach. Barrie joined Tony at 9.00 a.m. and was informed on his arrival that he had suspended Micky Leighton for the two Harloft games plus a fine of £30, and Smith and French £20 each for showing dissent. Barrie said he couldn't quite understand Tony's decision to ban Leighton when the player was so important and the two games were so crucial to Sharrington. The trainer also said he thought Tony was being too severe on Leighton, particularly when Tommy French would have to miss the match as well.

Tony looked up at Barrie, leant forward in his chair and said, 'I appreciate your concern, Barrie, but I've got to follow what I think is right and fair. I've thought about it long and hard and as I've said to the lads from the outset, discipline is important if we are to succeed.'

'What team are you putting out today then, Tony? Don't forget that young Graham Hart had another kick on that bad left ankle and it may be touch and go to risk him today.'

'I phoned Graham yesterday teatime and he said the swelling was down but it was still a bit sore. I told him we would see how he felt this morning before making a final decision. I have the following team for today's game,' said Tony looking at the note pad on his desk:

No. 1 Alan Hawkins
2 Graham Bond
3 Allan Smith
4 Paul Brooke
5 Stephen Holland
6 Micky Thomas
7 Graham Hart or Paul Cracknell
8 Neil Baynes
9 Alf Henning
10 Simon Docker
11 Sammy Chaddock
Sub Tony White

'I've told Micky Leighton to travel with us today.'
'How did he take it?' asked Barrie as he looked at the team.
'Oh, not as bad as I thought. He sounded as though he felt sorry for himself, but after I had given him the club policy again he apologised and hung up saying he would see me today before midday ready to travel to

Harloft.'

'What shall we do for training? A few sprints and exercises followed by a hot bath?'

'Yes, that should be all. Just a number of light things to loosen them up,' said Tony.

'By the way, have you heard any more on the Graham Hart and the Cotterton rumour?'

'No, thankfully, I haven't, and hopefully I won't. I don't really want to be faced with an offer at this stage of the season,' reflected Tony without looking at Barrie. The two men left Tony's office to go to the dressing room and await the arrival of the players.

Are you ready, Bob?' yelled Eddie Fisher.

'It's every other week. Why can't you be ready on time?' Frank Sneddon revved up his car.

After a few moments, Bob Bennett, the chubby Sharrington supporter, arrived and quickly got into the back seat of Frank's car.

'Sorry I'm late, fellows. Timekeeping's never been one of my strong points.'

'You can say that again,' said Frank blowing out a mouthful of tobacco smoke.

'Did you have a good Christmas anyway, chaps?' stated Bob trying to change the subject.

'Busy, very busy,' replied Frank. 'Me too, it's all eat, drink and sleep, isn't it?' chipped in Eddie. 'Yea, I've had my share of food and booze too. I nearly exploded last night,' said the tubby back-seated passenger. The two men in the front seat looked at each other and shook their head in disgust at Bob Bennett. Before they had time to comment Bob changed the subject again. 'Good result for us on Saturday, eh? I listened to it on the local radio and I thought that when Low Grove scored near the end that we'd had it. Apparently, according to all accounts Sammy Chaddock did well to cross the ball after running at the full-back.'

'I was relieved when I heard Alf had equalised for us. It was a good point for us, particularly when Treecliffe lost at Harloft,' said Eddie. 'Yes, we will have to do well to get a point today, in my opinion. They are a good side Harloft, so I've heard, and unbeaten at home so far,' commented Frank as he was driving through the town centre.

The car journey to Harloft continued and the three men discussed the Fourth Division in detail and also the general state of football in the country. During the journey the sports programme started on the car radio. There had been three or four morning kick-offs and the three men were eagerly awaiting the Warworth v Seamingway game result.

After the introduction to the programme the presenter said, 'and now I think we can give you all the early kick-offs: League Division One – Fillingway 2, Steeple Bay 2. League Division Two – Streeton 2, Trandon Rovers 4. League Division Four – Dabrook 1, Crookaby 0, and Warworth 2, Seamingway 0.'

'Hoorah, Hoorah,' shouted Bob. 'That's an unbelievable result,' yelled Eddie. 'Amazing, that's hard to believe,' laughed Frank. All three men were absolutely delighted with the Seamingway defeat. 'That's a great bonus for us, isn't it?' said Eddie. 'It's fantastic. A great result. It's certainly a surprise. Do you think they've got it right?' asked Bob from the rear seat. 'It will open the top of the league up and if we win today we will go clear at the top. Superb,' commented Eddie in total disbelief.

'I know Seamingway objected to making the 550 mile trip to Warworth on Christmas Day but I didn't think that they'd have lost to Warworth,' summarised Frank as he concentrated on his driving.

'Yes, it was silly to arrange such a fixture as that at Christmas time. I'm surprised the league didn't change it,' stated Bob.

'Me too but as compensation they cancelled the return match until 2 weeks tomorrow. It still amazes me why they should have to play the game in the morning or for that matter why couldn't they have re-arranged it for tomorrow afternoon,' reflected Eddie.

'It beats me for sure, but I think Warworth wanted to take full advantage of the League's error. But when you look at Warworth's recent form, that's four games on the trot that they've won. They are apparently adjusting to league football and on recent reports they are doing very well and Turner is having a good run as centre-forward. I wish them well, they've done us a good turn today, that's for sure,' said Bob languishing on the back seat. 'Only thing that bothers me is that we have to go up to Warworth for our last match of the season,' remarked Eddie.

'We thrashed them 5-2 at home, Eddie. We shouldn't have any problems with them. Anyway, hopefully we should have it settled before then,' said the chubby man.

'Nonsense! I think it will go right to the end of the season, now,' suggested Frank.

'Listen,' shouted Eddie. The sports presenter was speaking. Eddie put the volume up.

'Brian Williamson scored two goals in the first fifteen minutes against league leaders Seamingway this morning to give the newly promoted Warworth two more valuable points. Their highest crowd of the season saw the home team sustain a lot of second half pressure but held on to give them a tremendous victory. After the game the Seamingway manager Paul Royston re-affirmed his annoyance of having to travel so far on Christmas day although he did admit that his team had stayed in Mannish after Saturday's game.' 'Well isn't it amazing, I didn't known that. That would have reduced their journey by half,' stressed Bob. 'Maybe so, but I think it's a bit much to expect a team to be away from home on Christmas day,' remarked Eddie.

'Never mind that, lads. Shall we pull in here for some light refreshment,' asked Frank pointing towards a public house.

'Good idea, Frankie, I could manage one,' shouted Bob.

'I agree. Get parked up Frank,' confirmed Eddie, licking his lips. 'We can spare half an hour.'

Chapter 65

'Harloft, Harloft, Harloft, Harloft,' chanted the home supporters as their team took to the pitch.

There was a light drizzle and the wind was bitterly cold. The floodlights were switched on. The crowd was recorded at 8,200.

Harloft played in the Sharrington colours of red shirts, black shorts and red socks. Sharrington changed into their second strip of white shirts, black shorts and black socks. Harloft were unchanged from Saturday's 2-0 victory over Treecliffe but Sharrington was announced as the team Tony had chosen earlier in the day, with Paul Cracknell at outside right in place of the injured Graham Hart.

'I can't understand why Leighton's out again. I don't know why Hart's not playing either, do you?' Eddie asked Frank and Bob as they settled down in their stand seats.

'No, nothing official has come from the manager. Perhaps they are both injured,' questioned Frank.

'Could it be that Hart has gone to Cotterton as rumoured,' said Bob.

'I hope not. We would miss him. I like Paul Cracknell but he lacks Harty's skill and acceleration,' replied Frank lighting another tipped cigarette. The game started quickly with Harloft in control. They pushed forward quickly and the midfield players supported the forwards very well. Whitehouse the tall centre-forward was beating Stephen Holland in the air. Paul Brooke was having difficulty with the elusive Greg Booth, and Graham Bond was equally foxed by the speed and control of John Thompson, Booth's left wing partner.

'I keep thinking Harloft are us with their kit,' mumbled Bob.

'I wish they were. They're playing us off the park,' said Frank anxiously.

'We are not in it. We are not playing as a team. They're outclassing us,' remarked Eddie straightening his scarf.

The Harloft defence were untroubled, Sharrington weren't getting the ball out to the wing men or up to Alf Henning, and Neil Baynes was bogged down in defence.

On the half hour Harloft took a well-deserved lead. A shot by Sturgeon, the No. 6, was helped on delicately by Pinner the No. 8 to lanky Mike Whitehouse who tucked the orange ball over the outstretched arms of Alan Hawkins who had been left uncovered by the re-arranged defence.

The goal against Sharrington did not produce any retaliation from them. The nearest they came to a goal was a 30 yard shot by Simon Docker which weakly went outside the far post of the home team goal. Harloft continued with the pressure but they didn't improve on their 1-0 lead by half-time.

'Poor show, very poor performance,' exclaimed Bob.

'Pathetic really. We are very disappointing today,' stressed Eddie fumbling with the programme.

'We are missing the three regulars definitely. Brooke's out of position and Holland's short of match practice. Apart from that it is another of those lack-lustre performances,' said Frank.

'Looks like too much Christmas puddin' to me mate,' yelled a home team supporter.

'We have three regular players out today buddy and its upset our balance,' retorted Eddie.

'You can say that again. You've never got to joint second place with the team that's been out there this afternoon surely,' replied the brusque supporter.

Eddie was lost for words. He pretended he'd not heard the Harloft man.

Straight from the re-start the game continued in the same vein as the first half. The three supporters couldn't believe the difference in their team's performance from the recent games.

Harloft were so much on top that they forced six corners, one after the other. Sharrington were defending stoutly but Greg Booth, the home team No. 10, settled the result with a simple goal after a mix up between Holland and Baynes. The ball was taken from a bad pass and Booth shot passed Alan Hawkins in the easiest of ways. That goal came with only seven minutes remaining. Tony White was sent on to replace Simon Docker but it was too late for the youngster to make any impact.

With the crowd leaving the ground in the dying minutes Sharrington's first shot on target by Micky Thomas caught Brian Hooper cold and his twenty-yard shot looped out of the goalkeeper's reach and into the net. Almost immediately the referee's whistle sounded with the final result at Harloft 2, Sharrington 1. Harloft Town went to the top of the Fourth Division.

'Well, a fair result, lads. We can't quibble at that. To be honest we didn't even deserve that late goal,' said Frank with his total honesty.

'They will have to play better than that tomorrow to beat them. They are a good side,' stated Eddie quietly.

'I hate journeys home when we've lost. Hopefully Hart and French will be back tomorrow and who knows perhaps Leighton will be fit to play as well,' remarked Bob flippantly. The three supporters trooped out of the ground in virtual silence. They were less pleased when they heard that Treecliffe had drawn 1-1 at Low Grove, which put the pressure onto Sharrington if they were to stay amongst the league leaders.

Chapter 66

'Tony, may I have a word with you please? Will you come down to the ground tonight on your return from Harloft,' asked Eddie Flannagan over the telephone.

'By all means, Mr. Flannagan. May I known what its about?' replied Tony anxiously.

'Oh, I just want to discuss one or two matters which will involve our team tomorrow,' stated the stocky director who was speaking from his home in Sharrington.

'I expect we will be arriving home about 9.30 p.m,' said Tony hopefully.

'I'll see you there, then.' The director then hung up without even talking to Tony about the defeat at Harloft. Tony hung up the receiver in the Harloft boardroom. He looked angry. He had already given his team a roasting for their half-hearted performance. The players and Barrie had not seen him look so miserable or annoyed since his arrival at the club.

When everyone had boarded the club coach Tony informed his players to report at the ground at 12.30 p.m. tomorrow afternoon. He did not say any more during the journey home. The coach arrived in Sharrington at 9.40 p.m. and Tony walked quickly into the main office block. Eddie Flannagan was sitting in Tony's office smoking a fat cigar.

Eddie spoke first. 'Sorry to hear about the defeat. I heard parts of the broadcast on local radio. Apparently the better team won on the day.'

'Yes, and they'll win again tomorrow unless our players stop hiding and begin to commit themselves to the job in hand,' replied Tony sharply.

'Well, really that's what I wanted to speak to you about.'

Tony looked at the bald man curiously.

'I understand you've personally suspended Micky Leighton for his late arrival last Saturday.'

'Aye, I have. I considered he had let the side down and it was a matter of discipline.' Tony sat in his own chair.

'I accept your reasons, Tony, but don't you think you've been a bit harsh on the lad. You've fined him haven't you?' reasoned Eddie.

'Yes, I have and the lad's paid me, but I felt I had to stand firm on this one. A ban of two games is not too harsh for a breach of the club rules,' answered Tony sensibly.

'But he missed the match on Saturday as well so that will mean if he misses the game tomorrow he will miss three games and just really when we need him the most,' smiled Eddie.

'Well, the reason he missed Saturday's game was what this all started from, isn't it?' said Tony somewhat smugly.

'Didn't you consider his excuse valid then?' asked Eddie flicking the ash from his cigar into the glass ashtray.

'I didn't think he was telling me the truth.'

'Had you any evidence to distrust his story?'

'No, none at all. It was intuition only,' replied Tony leaning back in his chair.

Eddie didn't speak immediately. He seemed to reflect on the conversation. Tony jumped in to ask a question.

'What are you suggesting Mr. Flannagan?'

'Well, Tony I was just thinking, that we have given you a free rein since you joined this club but, bearing in mind how well we have been doing and how important Leighton is to us, can I suggest you seriously re-consider the position and decide to play young Leighton tomorrow. I make the point: *seriously re-consider*,' said Eddie exaggerating the last two words.

'Is that an order?' asked Tony off hand. 'And if I do play him, just how do I explain away my reasons, and can you tell me just how the other players, not to mention Leighton will look upon the club rules in the future?'

'I am sure you can handle it all excellently, Tony. You have the knack. You always will have,' answered Eddie confidently. 'I am certain the other directors would agree with me. He's been punished enough and I think we will need him more than anything tomorrow. Just go home Tony and reason it out. I think you will agree to playing Leighton tomorrow for the best interests of the club.' Eddie stood up, put on his trilby, which had been on top of the desk, and excused himself as he and Mrs. Flannagan had an engagement.

Tony watched the ruddy-faced director leave in a trail of thick smoke. Both men said goodnight simultaneously. Tony looked somewhat blank but realised he had just been given a positive order. The question which ran through his mind was his choice of team for the visit of Harloft the next day, and how best he should cope with the problem in hand. He sat for a while before leaving his office and driving home.

The day after Boxing Day arrived. The morning newspapers were on sale for the first time since Christmas Eve morning. The people of Sharrington read the reasons for Micky Leighton's absence from the two Christmas games. The simple explanation given by the club to the press was "disciplinary reasons." No reason was given in the morning newspaper and even the *Sharrington Echo* was unable to throw any light on the cause. They were unable to report the selected team for the visit of Harloft. It was concluded that this would depend on the injury problem and internal disciplinary policy. The match report on both games suggested an "uneasy" Sharrington team from their more recent games and Grant Evans, the newspaper reporter, suggested two points were vital in today's return game to keep them in touch with the league leaders.

It was a warmer day. The clouds had gone and the wind had turned into a light breeze. During the morning Tony called round to visit Jack Elliott but he did not burden him with any problems nor did he seek his advice on the Micky Leighton affair. Tony thought his chairman was looking much better in health and more talkative; although, he noticed Jack getting out of breath quicker than he ever used to. They talked about the game generally but Tony only stayed for twenty minutes, saying he had some other calls to make before meeting up with the team. Jack wished the team all the best and asked Tony to call around soon so they could talk in more detail.

At 12.30 p.m. Tony joined the players in the changing room. All the players were on time and no injuries were reported from the game the day before. Barrie Trippett reported that Graham Hart had been under treatment during the morning but the player could still feel some pain in his ankle and didn't wish to play today. Barrie added that the swelling was still noticeable and considered Graham was not 100% fit to play.

'Right, lads, can I have your attention please. I've now decided on the team to play today. As I pointed out to you yesterday we didn't start to play at Harloft. Some of us have gone off the boil recently and whilst I would accept this does occur from time to time, I've got to stress that a win today is crucial for us and I've picked the team I think will do the best job today. We are all in this together, lads, and at the end of the day we want promotion don't we?' Some of the players nodded. 'So let's get back onto the winning way, playing for each other and fighting for possession right from the start. O.K, the team today will be in goal Alan Hawkins, 2 Graham Bond, 3 Allan Smith, 4 Micky Leighton.' The player looked up in amazement. The other players glanced at each other in surprise. Tony paused slightly after announcing his No. 4. He had already sensed the disturbance his announcement would create.

'No. 5 Tommy French, 6 Micky Thomas, 7 Paul Cracknell, 8 Neil Baynes, 9 Alf Henning, 10 Tony White and 11 Sammy Chaddock. Substitute will be Paul Brooke.'

'I'm sorry Simon and Steve, but I have to try for a change from yesterday's game. Micky I've put you back to No. 4 because I think you're the type of player we need for today's game. I've thought about my original decision to suspend you for the two games against Harloft but maybe that was too harsh, bearing in mind that you missed Saturday's game as well,' said Tony quietly. 'Now then, lads,' he continued, 'I think they will be playing the same team if I'm not mistaken so let's surprise them with plenty of effort and some sharp attacking football.'

'How do you want me to play, boss?' asked young Tony White.

'Push up with Alf, Tony, for the first twenty minutes or so. I want to see you looking for the early ball from Mick Thomas or Allan Smith down that left flank. Bring Sammy into the game wherever you can and link up with Alf but don't be afraid to take their defence on,' replied Tony adamantly.

'We will have to watch their two full-backs overlapping. We got caught too many times with that yesterday,' said Neil Baynes.

'Yes, we did. We were at sixes and sevens weren't we?' agreed Barrie.

'That was basically due to us not picking them up and marking them tightly. Having said that, we were on the rack so much yesterday their confidence was sky high and they were simply taking it in turns to come forward. Likewise, we weren't confident in our own ability and as the match progressed we were just standing around and not even thinking about how to cope with the problem.

'We did have several team changes on the day and it was difficult to adjust to each other,' remarked Sammy Chaddock.

'I would agree with that to some extent but as I have always said we want to be in a position where we can replace one player for another without any noticeable problems. I know there is a long way to go yet, but I think we are on the right lines and a win today will help to strengthen our confidence,' replied Tony sensibly.

The players felt Tony had mellowed considerably since his awkward mood over the past week. He smiled more and did not have that aggressive look about him. He seemed to reassure the players more today than he had done for some time. The players had all wondered why he had not been his normal self, but although Tony now seemed more at ease, they didn't know what had caused his anxiety. Some of them wondered if it was just another one of his plays in human psychology. The twelve chosen players changed into the familiar red shirts and Tony passed amongst them individually telling them how he wanted them to play and trying to build up their confidence. Simon Docker appeared disheartened about being dropped from the team. Stephen Holland seemed used to the idea.

The kick-off was at 2.15 p.m. The crowd was recorded at 7,250 which was disappointing for a Christmas fixture against the league leaders. Sharrington chose to kick towards the main roadway end after winning the toss. Harloft who had selected the same team, were kitted in an all white strip.

The game opened cautiously, with both sides loosening up their muscles after the Boxing Day fixture. Sharrington were more involved in the game and Leighton was prominent in the early attacking moves. After 14 minutes and against the run of play, a move involving Bryant, Turner, Pinner and Grant ended with the winger crossing from the right and the big centre-forward Mike Whitehouse popping up from behind Tommy French to get to the ball first and steer it inside Alan Hawkins' far post. The move was one-touch football just like Tony loved to see but it put the league leaders 1-0 in the lead. The visiting supporters, who were behind that goal, cheered incessantly. To Sharrington's credit they hit back straight away with some enterprising football and hard challenging. Harloft hadn't time to settle on their lead before Neil Baynes dribbled his way into the Harloft penalty area, dummied as if he was about to shoot and side-footed the ball into the path of young Paul Cracknell who raced onto the ball and fired in the perfect equaliser. It was 1-1 after only 22 minutes. To Harloft Town's credit, also, they didn't let the goal upset them. They stood firm and continued to go forward. Sharrington were being marked out of taking any further advantage of the equaliser. The visitors always looked dangerous when in the Sharrington penalty box. With only seven minutes remaining of the first half, the confident Pinner, the No. 8, raced onto a pass from centre-half Welch and beat the challenges of Thomas and French before drawing Hawkins off his line and lobbing the ball over him into the empty net. Harloft led 2-1 at half-time.

'It's all right, lads. Don't be dismayed. They're a good side. They play very well together. Get your heads up. We are not playing too badly,' urged Tony as he talked to his demoralised team in the dressing room.

'We are still in this. We've just got to plug away at their defence. Alf's not seeing enough of the ball and in my opinion he's causing them so many problems in the air when he does get it. Good goal Paul, nicely taken. Fine play Neil, excellent.' Tony continued to reassure his team to build up their confidence. Barrie was also urging the players to stick at the task in hand.

'Whatever happens, lads, you've just got to keep going. They're the best team we've met this season but they're not unbeatable. Now come on let's shake them up. Get to the ball first. Make good use of it. Help each other. Get involved right from the start,' stressed Tony.

Straight from the kick-off the red shirts tried to take the game to Harloft but try as they may the white-shirted league leaders just seemed to have the edge in skill and experience. On the hour the dangerous Whitehouse shot Harloft 3-1 in the lead from out of the blue. All the Sharrington defenders were waiting for him to cross the ball but taking a leaf out of Baynes' book he dummied and raced around Allan Smith before prodding the ball underneath Hawkins. Harloft, team and supporters, were thrilled. Everything the skilful team attempted seemed to pay dividends.

Fortunately, and to Tony's delight, Sharrington didn't let their heads drop. They fought more keenly and gradually worked their way back into the game. Harloft were, at times, having to resort to fouling to keep the eager and angry Sharrington players at bay. The home crowd were also getting some vocal support behind their team for the first time. As the game wore on into the last fifteen minutes, and with darkness settling around the ground, Alf Henning won a tackle from left back Sinclair and shot ferociously at goal. His shot was deflected past the goalkeeper, Hooper, and into the path of Neil Baynes who didn't make any mistake. It was 2-3.

The crowd went wild. This pepped up the home team who seemed as keen as ever to get possession and take the ball back up field. Tony White, who had had a quiet game suddenly took on a tigerish manner and flitted all over the field. Baynes, Leighton and Cracknell were linking well and Henning and Chaddock were causing problems for the visitors. Tommy French was pushing up at corners and after he was seemingly nudged off the ball by a Harloft defender all penalty appeals were turned down. Still Sharrington didn't give up and Harloft were finding it increasingly more difficult to solve the fresh problems created by the more determined home side. One corner came after the other as the game wore on. After Sharrington's fifth corner in the space of as many minutes, Tommy French glanced a header onto the crossbar, Alf Henning raced in to follow the ball up but a Harloft defender got there first and cleared the ball to the edge of the penalty area. It dropped at Micky Leighton's feet. He controlled it and drove it straight back, into the congested penalty area in a flash. The next thing was an uproar behind the goal as the ball settled into the net. The ball had passed by everyone and nuzzled itself into the bottom corner. The Sharrington players mobbed Micky Leighton. The referee pointed to the centre to indicate a goal. It was 3-3 with four minutes remaining but Harloft manage to weather the repeated Sharrington attacks up to the final whistle.

It had been an exciting game and entertaining. The Harloft manager, Mason, congratulated the Sharrington players after the game and wished them well for the rest of the season. Tony was delighted with his team's second half performance and wondered how he would respond to Eddie Flannagan and vice versa the next time they both met. It was certainly ironic that Leighton should have scored the equaliser when all looked lost.

Chapter 67

Tony didn't have to wait long before meeting up with Eddie Flannagan. The two men met during the weekly board meeting, which was held on the following evening after the 3-3 draw against Harloft Town.

'Good result in the end yesterday, Tony,' smirked Eddie as he entered the boardroom. 'I didn't think we were going to do it.'

'Neither did I. It was a better performance all round. I hope we are over the bad patch now,' said Tony trying not to dwell on the importance of Leighton's equalising goal.

The meeting opened with the up to date medical situation on Chairman Jack Elliott. He was convalescing and much improved according to Bill Boothroyd who had visited him on his way to the meeting.

The accounts were looked at and the financial situation was so healthy that a sum of £18,000 was to be repaid to the bank at the end of the year. This left an outstanding amount of £7,320 owing to the bank, which pleased the three directors enormously. They congratulated Tony, in turn, for the way he had handled the financial side of the club since his arrival as manager some five months ago. They were particularly pleased with his introduction of the club lottery, which had brought in £2,400 in the four weeks since it was introduced. A statement from the bank was read out and they concluded that the club was on the right course of clearing its debt and, in the circumstances, they would be happy to look at any future loans or funding which was required to improve the status of Sharrington F.C.

Tony talked on the footballing side of the club. He was delighted with how the season had gone so far and also with his current squad of players. There were 8 league games to play, which were stretched out over the next 12 weeks. The next two league games were Seamingway at home, in two week's time and then local neighbours, Treecliffe, away from home on the following Friday evening. There was then another two week's gap before a home game against Braman. There were two further home games against Crookaby and Rallingborough, then another two week gap to an away game at Ellistart followed by a further two week gap before a home game against Verrington and finally an away game at much improved Warworth on March 17th 1978. Tony appreciated that the two week gaps at this stage of the season were to help Cup games and replays in addition to re-arranged fixtures due to postponed matches but he said he would prefer the games to continue on a weekly basis and fit in any backlog of games at the end of the normal season. Tony thought that twelve points from the remaining eight games would give the club promotion to Division Three. This would give the club a total of 40 points. Tony felt that there were three other teams, apart from Sharrington, which were in with a chance for promotion. They were Seamingway, Harloft and neighbours Treecliffe. He added that in his opinion the first two teams had the easier fixture list of the group, but he was optimistic Sharrington could pip Treecliffe for the third spot.

When Tony had finished his summing up everyone joined in a Christmas drink. The atmosphere was very relaxed. Tony's uneasiness of recent weeks seemed to have passed but Barrie Trippett who had worked closely with him since his arrival at the club knew that two bad results against Seamingway and Treecliffe would end Sharrington's hopes of promotion and more than likely see a return of Tony's frustrations. He still did not know why Tony had been particularly difficult to work with since the 4-0 defeat of Prent Park. He had never asked him nor felt it any of his business to ask.

The major talking points amongst the men was Seamingway's 4th round F.A. Cup game against First Division neighbours Brampforth and Treecliffe's 5-0 thrashing of Low Grove. Three of those goals were scored by Bob Villers, who after the game was quoted as saying that he was flattered with the Crest Utd's offer of £100,000. Eddie Flannagan said he had heard on the grapevine that the Crest Utd Manager was keen to get Villers signature and he had also heard that the board of directors had given the O.K. to increase the offer up to £120,000. Sam Dyson, the Treecliffe Manager, was playing down the whole affair but Eddie knew that the Treecliffe board would agree to the increased amount to help them with their financial difficulties. Villers transfer would be a great blow to Treecliffe's promotion hopes. Eddie had also been led to understand that Villers would be watched against Verrington and that, if he impressed, the Crest Utd representatives £120,000 offer would be made again and more than likely go through. His transfer would certainly be a help to Sharrington's chances of promotion. The position would be watched closely by the Sharrington management and Directors.

Chapter 68

Seamingway had drawn 2-2 against Brampforth in the 4th round of the F.A. Cup and amazingly won the replay at Brampforth 1-0 after extra time to go through to the fifth round tie against Andlerstone Utd of the Second Division, away from home. As Seamingway were Sharrington's next league opponents the prospects of coping with a confident and on form team were daunting, to say the least, for Tony and his team. Everyone was now fully fit and, during the ten days since the Harloft game, training had been kept up on every day except the Sunday, which was New Year's day.

The Seamingway cup victory had attracted much interest in Sharrington and the surrounding district and in view of the two clubs being on the same points, although Seamingway had a match in hand, a large crowd was anticipated. The visitors had arrived in Sharrington on Friday afternoon and by courtesy of the home club, trained at the ground.

Tony watched their training routine from a distance, and noted how confident and sharp they looked. He knew the cup victory at Brampforth would give them the impetus to maintain their consistent league form. He could see that their manager, Paul Royston, would prevent them from being over confident. Their forward line of Ashton, Fox, Lincoln, Swift and Sergeant were known for their goalscoring ability. They had scored 39 league goals between them during the season, 13 of which had been notched by Lincoln and 11 by Fox, Lincoln had also scored 7 cup goals including the extra time winner at Brampforth. Three of four clubs had offered between £80,000 – £110,000 for his signature, but the Seamingway club had turned all the offers down.

Tony had selected the team of Hawkins, Bond, Smith, Leighton, French, Thomas, Hart, Baynes, Henning, White, and Chaddock, with substitute Brooke. Although Sharrington had lost 3-2 to Seamingway earlier in the season, Tony knew that his team had matched them at times for skill and determination and stressed this to the players during the pre-match talk. He told them to play as they had done during the second half against Harloft and impressed upon them not to feel in awe of the fact that Seamingway had progressed to the 5th round of the F.A. Cup by disposing of a First Division outfit. The Sharrington players ran out onto the pitch to a great response from the crowd of over 11,000. Due to Seamingway being above 370 miles away there were not many of their supporters. The visitors were already on the pitch when Sharrington ran out. They were kitted in their normal all blue kit. It was another cold afternoon. The wind was sharp and the smell of rubbing oils drifted from the playing area. The stand was full and as Alf Henning kicked off there was an air of excitement around the ground.

Seamingway were soon on the attack and creating havoc in the home defence. Lincoln tested Hawkins at the first opportunity with a 30-yard drive, which the goalkeeper just managed to flick around the goalpost. The corner was cleared easily by French.

Fox and Swift linked well in the early stages and seemed to have plenty of room to work in. The Sharrington team were, once again, slow to start but like in so many of their games they were not punished for early errors. Alf Henning and Graham Hart were trying to run at the Seamingway defence but they always had sufficient men behind the ball to cope with the problem. Sammy Chaddock looked to be pushed off the ball after a good run down the left wing but the referee chose not to award a free kick to Sharrington, much to the home crowd's disapproval.

Ten minutes from half-time the rain started to fall which made the surface sticky. The crowd on the open three sides reluctantly had to stand where they were as there was no cover available for them. The game drifted towards half-time with little interest. Leighton and Baynes were being checked and marked well by Collins and captain Powers. Apart from the odd shot at goal by Lincoln the game was bogged down in midfield, 0-0 at half-time.

The second half opened cautiously. Seamingway seemed to be content to keep the score at 0-0. Sharrington played the ball more out to the wings where Hart and Chaddock were looking dangerous. Any passes through the middle at both defences were being handled efficiently.

Tony couldn't put his finger on why the Sharrington team were failing to create any goalscoring chances. Barrie Trippett felt Tony White and Neil Baynes weren't taking on the Seamingway defenders. On occasions there were smatterings of the slow handclap from various sections of the crowd. They were fortunately not prolonged.

With sixteen minutes remaining, a hard clearance by centre-half Elton went high into the Sharrington goalmouth. As the ball fell, Micky Thomas attempted to trap the ball, but although he controlled it admirably he slipped on the greasy surface and let in No 10 Swift, who was following up. The skilful forward wasted no time in stroking the ball passed Alan Hawkins and into the net. It was an opportunist goal for Seamingway but cruel luck for Sharrington. The crowd was shocked. The silence in the ground, apart from the handful of jubilant visiting supporters, seemed to be in sympathy for young Thomas.

The goal gave Seamingway the upper hand, and seven minutes later on, the Southern team had another stroke of good fortune when Graham Bond twisted his ankle while attempting to tackle left winger Sergeant. He tried to put weight on his injured ankle but fell back to the ground immediately. This left the tall, slim winger with plenty of room. He crossed to the far post where the ball deflected off the right-winger Aston's left boot and into the net. Aston had not meant to play the ball. It was another fluke goal but it put Sharrington 0-2 down.

Tony was totally dismayed. Just what could his team do to avoid a defeat in the remaining nine minutes? Graham Bond was helped off the field by Barrie Trippett. Paul Brooke was sent on in his familiar role of right full-back. Sharrington were shocked but still they fought hard but against such an experienced and professional team as Seamingway they constantly came up against a brick wall.

Paul Brooke added an extra dimension to the Sharrington play. He was quick in the tackle and adventurous in attack. The crowd were quick to give the youngster plenty of confidence.

Still Sharrington pushed forward and for the first time in the game Neil Baynes shook of his marker, jinked to his right before shooting hard and low. The goalkeeper, Delglish, palmed the ball out but Alf Henning was given a little too much space and prodded the loose ball underneath the advancing keeper to reduce the scoreline to 1-2. There were four minutes remaining but this was insufficient time for the home team to get back on level terms. Sharrington had left it too late again and were beaten by two lucky breaks against them. Seamingway were happy with the two points. It had been an exceptionally good week for them. As the crowd left the ground the loudspeaker announced a 5-1 victory for Treecliffe over Verrington and a 2-1 defeat for Harloft at Warworth.

Tony began to feel all was lost. He was easy on the players. The two goals were harsh and Graham Bond's left ankle was swollen up to twice its size. Every player was quiet and tired. The dressing room was littered with wet and dirty kit. Barrie hated the sight of a defeated team's dressing room. He and Tony made every effort to make the place as cheerful as possible but the disappointment of another home defeat was a cruel blow and meant that Sharrington had only gained two points from a possible eight in the Christmas and New Year games.

Sharrington's best crowd of the season had not seen anything to give them hope of promotion.

Chapter 69

On the following Tuesday, Eddie Flannagan was on edge as he spoke in the board meeting. 'Tony,' he said. 'What's gone wrong? Is time running out on us? We have only seven matches left and if Seamingway beat Warworth tonight, as I expect they will, we will be in fourth position and drifting away from the front three. There are also three other clubs only three points behind us,' he continued before giving Tony a chance to answer. 'Have we sufficient good players to get us promotion? Do you feel that we ought to buy a striker or two before the deadline a week today? Let's not let it slip now, for goodness' sake. We've got Treecliffe away on Friday, you know, and the way they've been banging them in lately are we fully prepared for them?'

Tony looked at his board of directors carefully before replying. 'I've thought about it obviously, but I can't see the point of buying in some more players now. Basically we've hit a bad patch and just at the time when we played against the top clubs. It's taking longer to get out of the rut than I anticipated but the players are sound enough to pull us through.' He paused briefly. 'Although Graham Bond is likely to be out for some weeks, I am confident young Paul Brooke will not let us down, in fact I am hopeful that his style of play may give us more alternatives in attack. The defence have only conceded 27 goals and I don't think we can fault them for our downfall. It is just that our goals have dried up, but I am certain that if we can get a good result from the Treecliffe game our confidence and, of course, the goals will come back. I don't think we can change the forward line drastically, in fact I propose to bring Simon Docker back in on Friday night and make Tony White sub.' Tony awaited more questions from the directors.

'If we blow it at Treecliffe I think promotion will be out of our grasp,' commented Steve King as he twiddled with his silver fountain pen.

'I hope we don't lose there, Steve, but if we do I don't think anyone can say with any certainty that we will still not get promotion. I mean–', stressed Tony, '– if we did lose we would be five points behind Treecliffe with six matches to play and who knows what could happen in six matches, and, as you know, of their last six matches four of them are away from home and one of the two home games is against Seamingway. Our six games are against the lower clubs and four of those are at home.'

'Well, I hope it doesn't have to be decided by the last match because as we all know Harloft Town play Seamingway and they could get their heads together to sort out that one but we have to travel to Warworth who won five of their last six games, and Treecliffe visit Mannish who are no great shakes,' said Eddie sternly.

'Its certainly an anxious time for us all. In any event its got to be preferable to fighting off re-election again,' replied Bill Boothroyd in his usual matter of fact manner.

'I agree, Bill, but when we are this close to promotion it's unthinkable to consider we might have to spend another season down here in the doldrums,' answered Eddie, puffing on his fat cigar.

'How do you honestly rate our chances on Friday night, Tony?' enquired Steve King.

'I am hopeful, Steve. The lads are working well together in training and, to say the results have not been good for us recently, their confidence is pretty high. A local derby always breeds excitement and it goes without saying that we want to beat them, badly. The papers favour Treecliffe in view of their recent form but if we can get a quick break or the run of the ball I am sure the ability of the lads will be good enough to do the rest', replied Tony confidently.

'Why do you want to bring Docker back in?' asked Eddie.

'Well, he shows well in training but sometimes he can not produce the goods in a game, but he links up better with Sammy than young Whitey does and I am hopeful the needle of a derby will bring that little bit extra out of him,' stated Tony.

The meeting ended at 9.30pm. Tony got into his car to make his journey home. The first thing he heard on the car radio was that Seamingway had defeated Warworth 2-0 to go back to the top of the Fourth Division on 32 points.

The local radio news also gave out a piece of sensational news. The newscaster spoke urgently. Tony listened carefully. '... *and a shock for Treecliffe supporters. News just to hand says that Bob Villers the 25 year old Treecliffe centre-forward has signed for Crest Utd, the Second Division club, for £120,000 tonight...*' The reporter paused momentarily. '*This is certainly a surprise especially on the eve of the local derby game with neighbours Sharrington. We have no comment available at the moment from either the player or the club. We will of course bring this to you as soon as we receive it.*' The reporter moved on to another subject.

Tony smiled to himself. It appeared to him that Crest Utd would not wait until after the Friday game before signing Villers. They would want him available for their Saturday game, particularly when they were splashing out such a large sum on Villers. Was this a lifeline for Sharrington to hold on to? Tony hoped his team could take full advantage of the blunted Treecliffe strike force.

Chapter 70

Friday evening arrived. It was a Black Friday: 13th January 1978. It was a clear but cold night. The atmosphere inside the Treecliffe ground was electric. It was not an all-ticket game but the crowd was 16,500. It was Treecliffe's best league crowd of the season. They had scored more goals than anyone in the Fourth Division and in their last four games scored twenty goals. It was however extremely disappointing for many of the Treecliffe supporters that the club had been forced to sell their leading scorer, of 16 goals, Bob Villers, to Crest Utd before the end of the season. He was a favourite with large sections of the supporters and his bustling aggressive style of play made him a feared opponent for many centre-halves. Tommy French compared him and Lincoln of Seamingway as the best centre-forwards in the 4th Division. Crest Utd had insisted Villers was available for their Saturday game against Brookhouse as they were in need of points to get them away from the lower region of the division.

A small core of Treecliffe supporters were demonstrating outside the ground before the kick-off, with placards suggesting the chairman Frank Hood resigned. There was local talk that as the Treecliffe forward line revolved around Villers the other forwards would fail miserably. Many thought Treecliffe should have held onto Villers until the end of the season so they could get promotion to Division Three. The club had announced that the sum of £120,000 was impossible for a club like Treecliffe to turn down. They regretted the departure of Villers but wished him well in the 2nd Division. No comment was given by Villers himself. There was only a picture in the *Sharrington Echo* of him smiling at the photographer and signing the contract. The money would certainly be useful to Treecliffe.

Villers replacement, young Mark Towns, was making his first team debut. He was 19 years of age and had come up through the local teams. He had only scored seven goals for the Treecliffe junior side but although manager Sam Dyson was full of praise for the youngster many people attached to the club knew he would be replaced shortly, and probably before the following Tuesday transfer deadline, by a new signing. It was rumoured that Dyson had enquired about Deighton of Ellistart and Whitehouse of Harloft but nothing had been officially confirmed. Grant Evans told Tony Davidson he had heard that someone connected to the club suggesting Lincoln of Seamingway was unsettled and a figure of

£100,000 may lure him away.

Tony was unconcerned about the Treecliffe's problem. He was more concerned about getting his team in the right frame of mind to win the game. The team were all changed, in red shirts, white shorts and white socks listening intently to Tony talking. It was only ten minutes to the 7.30 kick-off. 'They are going to miss Villers tonight. He was their target man up front and as you know he caused us so many problems in our three games against them this season. Tommy –' he said pointing to the Sharrington No 5. 'It's imperative that you stamp your authority on young Towns as soon as is practical to do so. He will be nervous and will be under a great deal of pressure, so use your experience and play him hard.' Tony paused. 'As I have said to you in training, lads, let's go at them from the start. I think I have asked you to play too carefully at times because once we get into our stride when going forwards we certainly look good. Don't leave ourselves short at the back though. We all know how to cover. I have no qualms about how Paul Brooke will fit into the right back spot. It is his normal position and I was pleased with his performance when he came on as sub last Saturday. Don't leave yourself too far upfront with too much ground for you or the other defenders to cover if Treecliffe break quickly,' he said, looking towards Brooke who was limbering up in the corner of the changing room. 'Always be on your guard to check you are not leaving a Treecliffe man unmarked, and that goes for all of you when they are attacking'. The bell to warn the players to go out onto the pitch rang out aloud. Some of the players visibly jolted at this sound as if every muscle in their body tightened up with nerves. 'O.K, lads we all know this game is a 4 pointer. Let's rally round and get back into the top three places.' The players danced up and down shaking their legs and arms. They were doing knee bends, leg jerks, and neck stretches as they filed towards the changing room door. 'Best of luck, lads, and listen to Neil for any instructions. Its the first time he's captained us so give him your total support,' said Tony finally, as the players trooped passed him.

Treecliffe were playing in their customary yellow shirts and black shorts. Young Towns was the first man to touch the ball as he kicked off. He didn't look too overawed by the occasion. The home team strung three or four passes together in their first attack but it ended with a good interception by Allan Smith who set up a left wing counter attack for Sharrington. Sammy Chaddock crossed high and deep but the ball ran harmlessly over the goal line before Alf Henning could reach it.

Treecliffe were being cheered on by their supporters but, as Tony had predicted, they were getting bogged down with how to go forward, as the few balls which had been passed to Towns were being laid off backwards by the youngster, instead of forwards in the style the others were used to, after playing with Villers. Tommy French was marking Towns so closely the debutant was unable to turn and as French was tackling him hard the youngster was getting rid of the ball as soon as he could.

Baynes and Leighton were linking well together and the former had gone close in the fourteenth minute with a chipped shot, from the edge of the penalty area. Docker was also playing well and had created a fine chance for Alf Henning ten minutes after, but the centre-forward put his shot wide.

The home team were attacking mainly down the wings but the Sharrington defence were coping admirably and Paul Brooke was faultless. His tackling was sharp and his distribution was accurate.

Tony was extremely pleased with the first 30 minutes but he was delighted in the 33rd minute when a move involving Thomas, Smith, Docker and Chaddock had ended with the left-winger's centre being scrambled into the Treecliffe goal by a determined Graham Hart. The crowd were stunned into silence. Sharrington led 1-0 and did so up to half-time. Treecliffe were attacking in vain as the Sharrington defence were totally in command or, alternatively, the home team were finding it difficult to get to the visitors' goal now they were without the swashbuckling style of Villers.

During half-time Tony and Barrie showed their enthusiasm and congratulated the team on their first half performance. The players appeared satisfied themselves. Tony only asked his team to carry on with the same tactics in the second half.

The second half opened with Hope, the No 8, moving to centre-forward and Towns to No 8, but both French and Thomas were handling the revised situation admirably. Sharrington were still looking dangerous as they went forward. Baynes, the new captain, was looking sharper than usual and Henning was causing many problems in the Treecliffe defence.

In the 60th minute the visitors' supremacy was rewarded again with an exceptional goal by veteran Henning. He received a pass from Hart, turned like quicksilver, pushed the ball passed his marker, Paul Simpson, the Treecliffe captain, and raced onto it and fired a powerful shot with his right foot over the goalkeeper, Hemmingway, and into the roof of the net. Tony and Barrie jumped up out of the dugout and punched the air in delight. It was the best goal they'd seen Alf Henning score since his arrival at Sharrington.

The stuffing had been knocked out of Treecliffe. The Sharrington supporters were making their voices heard above the home fans.

Sharrington were still attacking although they were 2-0 in the lead, and, after a move involving six Sharrington players in sixteen passes of the ball in which it was not touched by a Treecliffe player, as Micky Leighton juggled the ball on his right foot, he was struck from behind with a frustrated tackle by Bell, the No 6. The handsome No 4 rolled over in agony. The Sharrington players rushed to his assistance and also to remonstrate with Bell. There was a fracas but the referee quickly had it under control. After 2 minutes Bell had been booked and Leighton carried from the field by Barrie Trippett and Tommy French. Tony White was sent onto the field to replace him. Only nine minutes remained.

Treecliffe took advantage of the re-organisation in the Sharrington defence and almost reduced the scoreline to 2-1, but Alan Hawkins saved well at the feet of Mexiban, the home team's No 10. However, two minutes later, a fierce shot by Tyke was deflected away from Hawkins by a jubilant Hope who leapt in the air when he saw the ball hit the back stanchion in the Sharrington net.

Try as they did in the remaining few minutes, Sharrington's defence impressed everyone as they coped with everything Treecliffe threw at them. Even young Towns looked set to equalise but a timely tackle by Micky Thomas took the ball off his toe. Brooke also won an important challenge with left-winger Bass when the Treecliffe player looked like getting to the ball first. French and Smith were always in the thick of things offering their experience to the other younger defenders around them. Even Baynes, Docker and Henning were helping out to strengthen the defence and make it more difficult for Treecliffe to score.

As the game wore on, Sharrington broke quickly from defence and the ball was played out to Sammy Chaddock. The winger sped towards the Treecliffe goal but a timely tackle by defender, Stuart Angel, sent Chaddock tumbling awkwardly and hitting the ground with his head. He lay motionless and appeared to be unconscious. Barrie Trippett was quickly onto the field followed by Tony Davidson. After another brief hold-up of play the winger was stretched off towards the dressing room, looking pale and holding his neck.

Sharrington were reduced to ten men but they didn't have to hold on for long to their 2-1 lead. With five minutes injury time allowed, the referee blew his whistle, bringing the local derby game to an end. Sharrington had done it and moved to within one point of Treecliffe and level on points with Harloft Town, but the latter had a game in hand. The last six matches were for the taking now that the better teams of the league had all been played, but with Bond, Leighton and Chaddock all injured it looked as though Tony would be unable to field his strongest squad at home against Braman a week on Saturday. One thing was for sure it had not been a black Friday night for Sharrington F.C.

Chapter 71

'Sharrington's first league win over Treecliffe.' 'Super Henning sends Treecliffe reeling.' "H' Bombs destroy Treecliffe's home record.'

These were some of the newspaper headlines on the Saturday morning. It had been an excellent result for Sharrington, and after the game Alf Henning told Barrie Trippett and his playing colleagues that it was the best goal he had ever scored when he put the second goal in. Jack Elliott's wife also phoned her husband's congratulations to Tony after the match with a message of thanks to the team as the result had given him a new lease of life. It had always been one of Jack's ambitions to put one over on Treecliffe. His only disappointment was that he was unable to witness the memorable victory.

Tony was overjoyed with the result also. He thought his team's performance was the finest he'd seen since he had been in charge. His satisfaction was unfortunately cut short when Doctor Ericson announced to Tony that Micky Leighton had broken his left ankle and would be out of action for the remainder of the season. This was a tragic blow to Sharrington. Leighton was a fine player with great ability and, although Tony had trouble with the lad's flair for the nightlife and reliability, he had certainly proved an excellent signing and helped Sharrington to be promotion contenders for Division Three. His position would be difficult to fill as he was the driving force from the middle of the field. It was another headache on the injury front, for Tony. Doctor Ericson also told him that Sammy Chaddock had badly ricked his neck and could be out of action for one or two weeks, depending upon the effect of heat treatment and rest the winger received. The injury problem would affect the team's confidence and as the squad was at the bare minimum, Tony wondered how he would have to reshape the team for the next game against Braman.

The Saturday league results filtered in by 4.45 pm. Seamingway had beaten Crookaby 2-0, Harloft had also won 3-1 against Holydice-on-Sea and the team making a late run, Dabrook, had scored a 2-1 home win over Ellistart. They were now three points behind Sharrington in fifth place. Braman had defeated Low Grove 3-0 in a rare victory for them. They were still languishing third from the bottom of the league.

By the following Tuesday the only other Fourth Division striker to be sold was Jacques, of Aldway, to Third Division Collingwood for £40,000. The signing sensation, however, for the local area was Treecliffe's Sam

Dyson splashing out £50,000 for Third Division centre-forward Paul Gregory of Billingborough. No one had heard of this player but Dyson was quoted as saying "no one had heard of Alf Henning either but look what he did to us the other night." Tony thought that was one of Sam's better quotes. It amused him and gave him a warm feeling. Gregory was 29 years of age and had scored 8 goals for Billingborough in the season but only 7 the season before when they were relegated from Division Two.

Tony had contemplated signing a temporary replacement for Leighton but his secret mission for a possible player was to no avail. The only quote in the newspaper was that the player, who remained anonymous, failed to agree the terms offered by Sharrington. No fee had been disclosed.

A record transfer fee of £400,000 had been paid for Sprannon Albion's star midfield player, Ronny Stuart, the international starlet. He was signed by the First Division high fliers of the season, Rondale Rovers.

Seamingway had received an offer of £90,000 for Lincoln from Second Division Nottingvale but it was flatly refused. It was also quoted by the newspapers that the player would be unlikely to consider the move as it would have meant him moving approximately 500 miles from the far south west to the north east town.

During the week after the victory at Treecliffe the fit players had trained as hard as usual. Micky Leighton hobbled around the ground with a plaster cast on his left ankle. He was generally in the way but Peggy Hollingsworth, like all the other females in the town had fallen for his looks and good humour. She literally waited on him hand and foot. He teased her playfully and she lapped up his flattery. The other players smiled genially at Peggy's trance-like expression when Leighton asked her to do something for him. Mrs Maxwell was not as easy to fool as Peggy, although she had once admitted to Simon Docker that she could clearly understand why the girls ran around after Micky. Docker said that Mrs M had a twinkle in her eye when she told him, but that it was only a momentary lapse before carrying on with her perpetual chores.

Sammy Chaddock was receiving infrared treatment on his injured neck but he certainly took some stick from the other players because when he walked around it looked as though he was balancing a book on the top of his head due to his neck being so stiff.

It was clear to Tony that both Chaddock and Bond, who was also hobbling around, would not be available for the forthcoming Braman match. Barrie Trippett suggested that he should be brought out of retirement to help ease the situation. He joked to the other players that he could still perform as well as most of them and, although Tony was impressed with Barrie's training stints on occasions, he did not feel as though Barrie would be up to match fitness and, fortunately, at this stage, he knew he could bring in Paul Cracknell to play in Leighton's role. It was the youngster's strongest position and Tony hoped he would perform as well at No 4 as he had done in the other roles he'd played him in during the season. He was certainly a more competent player since signing professionally and Barrie Trippett remarked to Tony how the lad had developed physically as a result of the strenuous training he was doing.

In the F.A. Cup 5th round Seamingway finally lost to Andlerstone of the Second Division but only by 2-1. There were no surprise results in the 5th round and the favourites and current First Division leaders Trackerton Rovers beat Second Division Miltern Rovers 3-0. Second in the First Division Rondale Rovers won 2-1 at First Division Fillingway, and last season's cup winners Cotterton City scored 5 against Third Division Evercroft without conceding a goal. Last season's defeated finalists, Ashton, drew 1-1 at First Division Stanton Villa. Last season's league champions who were struggling somewhat this season did manage to draw 2-2 at near neighbours Allton. Second Division Ravenhead Athletic lost 1-0 at Torchester of the First Division. Finally the eighth team through to the 6th round were First Division Parringway, who won easily at home to Second Division Woodville, who had knocked Sharrington out in the 3rd round, by 4-1.

On the Wednesday after the 5th round F.A. Cup, Tony and Barrie went to watch the replay game between Passondale and Allton Utd. Last season's league champions ran out 2-0 winners and were through to play in the 6th round at home against Trackerton Rovers. This would be the tie of the next round. Barrie who had once played for Trackerton still had a leaning towards them and hoped they would win through. As there was no league fixture on the day the 6th round ties were to be played, both men promised each other to get a ticket for the game.

On the same Wednesday evening, Storr Town from the Second Division had shocked everyone with a 2-1 win over First Division Afondale in the 5th round of the League Cup and were through to the semi-finals along with Rondale Rovers who had beaten fellow First Division opponents Chernwick 1-0. The other two League Cup 5th round ties were to be played in the following week due to Ashton and Allton being involved F.A. Cup 5th round replays.

Neil Baynes was more surprised than anybody with his ex-teams successful run in the League Cup and promised himself to go and watch their semi-final tie. Some of the other players said they would accompany him if Storr Town were drawn out against Rondale Rovers as they were the team everyone wanted to see. The First Division outfit were trying to obtain the treble that season which, if they did it, would make them the only team ever to do it. The draw for the semi-finals was not being made until after the next week's 5th round ties between Ashton and Torchester, and Allton United and Parringway.

Tony found the cup games exciting but on the Friday prior to the Braman game he brought his team back to earth with the realities of Fourth Division football. Sharrington had to stay on course with a win over Braman, although they were unable to field the strongest side due to the recent injuries.

Chapter 72

'How's Jack?' asked Sid Parkin as he settled down in the seat next to Eddie Flannagan.

'I saw him last night and he's much better. He hopes to be able to get to our last home game of the season against Verrington. He's just as excited as ever. I'll tell you what, Sid, the win at Treecliffe did him wonders,' laughed Eddie pulling a car blanket over his legs.

Steven King had just arrived and apologised to everyone for being late. Bill Boothroyd was sat to the left of Eddie, on his usual seat in the directors' box at Sharrington. He was flicking anxiously through the club's programme. 'I see we've only got 12 fit, full-time professionals, and the part-time goalkeeper, Bates. If we get any more injuries we will be in all sorts of trouble. Perhaps we should have splashed out and bought a couple of players before the deadline, to help us out.'

'Don't worry, man, it's only Leighton's injury that is serious. Good player that. We will miss him badly. We'll get by to the end of the season, Bill, don't worry about that. We've managed on one of the smallest squads in the division so far and I've got a feeling we will be in the top three by the end of the season. You mark my words,' replied Eddie.

'We shouldn't have any trouble today with Braman particularly after the victory over Treecliffe the other week. The lads confidence must be sky high,' remarked Steve King, casting his eye over the good crowd which had gathered all around the ground. 'How many would you say are here today, Bill?'

'It's another good gate. We've certainly had much more support here than I've ever known before,' said the mild-mannered fruitier.

'About 10,000, I would say,' answered Sid Parkin as if he had counted them in detail.

'More like 15,000, I'd say,' shouted Eddie raucously.

Both men were incorrect. They're were 12,000 supporters and, as Braman were not doing well and its town was over 130 miles away, there was very little sign of their blue and white-scarfed supporters. It was Sharrington's best league crowd of the season. The game started at 2.15.

The Sharrington team was full of running in the early stages and the visitors were rarely out of their own half of the field.

Baynes, who made his debut for Sharrington against Braman, was having a good game. His tackling, control and distribution was faultless. Henning was superior in the mid-air battles with the Braman centre-half

Monks. Hart was his usual menacing self, and White and Docker were surprisingly linking together as though they were the regular left wing partnership.

It was, however, a deep run by young Paul Cracknell, who was deputising for Leighton, which created the first goal. In the 15th minute he robbed centre-forward Simonsway of the ball ran 20 yards, shaking off three tackles, before neatly laying the ball into the path of Graham Hart who struck the perfectly passed ball crisply and high into the Braman net out of their goalkeeper's reach. The rest of the first half continued with Sharrington holding the upper hand. At half-time they led by the single goal but should have had more to their name. Braman did not create one chance. Although the margin between the two teams was slight there seemed little doubt that Sharrington would end up with two more, valuable points.

Of the other promotion matches, the half-time scores would not be known until near the end of the game due to Sharrington kicking off 45 minutes earlier than anyone else. However, the directors were informed that Treecliffe had gone into an early lead at Prent Park, as they gathered in the refreshment room during the half-time interval.

The second half Braman started to attack but, fortunately for Sharrington, French and Thomas were cutting out the visitors' moves with ease. Only Earnshaw, Braman's No 8, looked like equalising and he went close when he struck the foot of Hawkin's right hand post, from a shot 15 yards out. The loose ball was pounced on by the goalkeeper and the danger stopped. Braman never got closer to scoring than that moment.

As the second half wore on, Sharrington began to take over again and the blue-shirted opponents were tiring quickly. The Sharrington forwards were starting to run the defence ragged but were unable to add to their lead, although Henning and Docker both went close with shots from inside the penalty area. Tony White also had a short range shot-cum-centre cleared from underneath the far post by an acrobatic save from the goalkeeper, Dawson.

In the 63rd minute the home supporters were finally rewarded with another goal. Corner after corner had been taken on both sides of the pitch and, when a high floated cross was put over by Graham Hart, centre-half Tommy French ran in from the blind side of the Braman defence to thunder the ball into the net, with his forehead. The supporters went wild. Three or four young schoolboys ran onto the pitch to cheer French and join in with the players' celebrations.

The game fizzled out as far as any action was concerned but

Sharrington played out time comfortably and held onto their 2-0 lead.

The surprise for the Sharrington supporters was that Braman's star right-winger, Oakes, was substituted twenty minutes from time, much to the delight of Allan Smith, who had marked him superbly throughout the game. He was their leading scorer but his heart didn't appear to be in it and the substitute Cooper ran about more in the remaining 20 minutes than Oakes had done in the first seventy minutes.

Just before the end of the game the half-time scores were put up on the board opposite from the stand. The crowd seemed more concerned with these results that in the state of the game, probably as Sharrington had done enough to win the game. The half-time scores effecting promotion in Division Three were:

Seamingway 1 v 0 Rallingborough,

Prent Park 1 v 2 Treecliffe,

Dabrook 2 v 2 Harloft.

All the results were greeted with jeers but the saving grace was that Sharrington won their game 2-0.

Tony was delighted with his team's performance and the way in which they had achieved the victory. The players were given the following Monday off as a reward.

As the players left the ground they were told that Seamingway had won 3-1.

Treecliffe had beaten Prent Park 3-2 and Dabrook had successfully disposed of Harloft by the odd goal in seven. Sharrington were still in third place but only by a better goal difference than Harloft. The pressure was still on.

In the 5th round League Cup ties on the Monday, Torchester won 3-2 at Ashton and Allton Utd defeated Parringway 4-2. The draw for the semi-finals brought together Storr Town against the favourites Rondale Rovers and the two newly promoted teams to Division One, Torchester and Allton Utd. Both games were to be played on a neutral ground and the venue for the first game was at Sprannan Albion and the second game was to be staged at Passondale.

Chapter 73

'Keep the ball moving, lads. Don't hold on to it. It's two touch only. If you have touched it twice leave the ball alone. Sammy, get to the ball. You had a half-yard start on Micky then and he beat you to it. You've got to get there,' shouted Tony from the touchline, during the Wednesday morning training session. 'That's better, Simon, give it and go and keep looking at the ball. Nice try, Alf, but it's a bit too fancy. Keep it going, lads. About ten minutes more then we will call it a day.'

After the training had finished, Tony called to Barrie Trippett and asked the trainer to join him after the players had left. About an hour later Barrie arrived in the manager's office. Tony was speaking on the telephone. Barrie sat down and waited patiently. After a few minutes Tony hung up the receiver without speaking more than a dozen words to the person on the other end of the phone. He looked puzzled. 'Anything wrong, Tony?' enquired the curly-haired trainer.

'That was Crookaby manager, Bryant. He is getting in touch with the League to ask for a postponement of our game on Saturday,' replied Tony quietly.

'What on earth for?'

'He says that they have got a flu bug up at Crookaby, which has affected about five of his players and, in addition to that, he has two others down with injuries. It only leaves him with nine fit men. I was going to tell him that I only had thirteen players to pick from and that two of them were goalkeepers, but I held it back. I don't want them to cancel the game. We need to keep in match practice and cannot let the other promotion contenders get one over on us psychologically by winning next Saturday,' stated Tony categorically.

'He's got a bigger squad than we have then, Tony. I hope the League make them play the game. When will we find out if its still on?' asked Barrie.

'I would think the League's decision will have to be as quickly as possible bearing in mind all the arrangements that have to be made for the game. He said he will ask the League to come back to us both once they have made their decision,' replied Tony as he paced up and down his office.

'Did you find out whether Collin Bird was one the players down with flu?' enquired Barrie.

'Bryant told me that Bird was still injured. Apparently he got a knock on his knee against Babrook over Christmas and is not expected to play for the remainder of the season,' said Tony cheerfully.

'Well, at least that's some good news. I didn't fancy him coming down here and kicking lumps off everybody like he tried to do up at Crookaby earlier on in the season.' Barrie got up out of his chair and looked out of the office window. 'Did you want me for anything specifically, Tony?'

'Yes, Barrie, two things really. The first thing is to tell you that I've arranged another week's training for the junior teams, starting week after next. I will make the arrangements with you shortly, but the other thing I wanted to speak to you about is more important at this stage'. Tony paused slightly before continuing. 'I need your advice, Barrie.' The trainer looked surprised. He sensed Tony was anxious about something. 'I suppose on reflection I should have spoken to you before about it but…' He paused. 'I've been bottling it up unnecessarily.'

'What on earth's the matter?' asked Barrie.

'Well…' Tony paused again as if thinking seriously about what he was going to say. 'Do you remember the press back in December?' Barrie nodded. 'Well, remember us discussing the rumour offer of £60,000 for young Graham Hart?'

'Yes. Some rumour that was,' replied Barrie as he smiled pleasantly.

'Well, it wasn't a rumour, Barrie. That's just it. It was for real. Cotterton got me on the phone on the following Monday and offered me £50,000, not £60,000, there and then and asked me to put it to the board of directors.' Barrie looked at Tony open-mouthed.

'What did the directors say?' he enquired.

'That's just it Barrie I didn't put the offer to them,' said Tony sadly.

'You what!' exclaimed Barrie. 'I couldn't, Barrie! I just couldn't do it. I thought they might decide we should sell, particularly for that sort of money,' reflected Tony.

After a brief moment's silence Barrie spoke again. 'What did you tell Cotterton then?'

'Good question, Barrie. Now here comes the crunch. I phoned them back on the following Wednesday and simply said "no" to the deal. They immediately upped their offer to £60,000 as originally rumoured but I gave them the thumbs down,' answered Tony hesitantly.

There was another silence between the two men. Barrie spoke first again. 'Well, who knows it may blow over and perhaps next year they will come back with twice the offer'.

'I am afraid it wasn't the end of it when I told them he wasn't for sale. They have been onto me every week right up to the deadline and, Barrie, between you and me they finally offered £75,000, plus Billy Cooper, their experienced winger, as an exchange to complete the deal.'

'And you didn't tell the board about that either, I gather?' stated Barrie quite matter-of-factly.

'You guessed it. I couldn't let Harty go. He's important to us and I don't want other clubs cast-offs. I've cleared out the dead wood. I don't want to have to start doing it again,' replied Tony, more confidently.

'Did you tell Cotterton no to the new deal? I guess you did,' said Barrie without waiting for Tony to reply. Tony nodded.

There was yet another silence. 'I had a funny feeling the board would accept the new offer,' stressed Tony.

'I think they would have done too, but perhaps, as I said before, it may blow over,' said Barrie sympathetically.

'Now that's what I thought, Barrie. But next Monday, the chairmen of the league clubs are having their annual general get together and, I heard last night, Eddie will be going in place of Jack,' stammered Tony.

'And you feel something might be said to him by the Cotterton City chairman'.

'Right again. If he does, I think I will be for the high jump and rightly so,' murmured Tony.

'You'd better tell him then beforehand, hadn't you?' stated Barrie feeling as a mentor to Tony for the first time since he had taken over as manager. 'Does that explain your bad moods over the past few weeks as well?' Tony nodded again slowly.

'I think I'll leave it until after the match on Saturday. If we get a good result it will certainly ease the situation,' commented Tony.

'Yes, I agree but make sure you do tell him before he leaves for the meeting,' said Barrie seriously. Tony looked absolutely shattered. 'Do I take it that you've not told Penny either?'

'No, you're the only person I've told, Barrie'.

'Why not get on off home and tell her. I am sure you'll feel much better and if we do win on Saturday, that is if we play at all, old Eddie will only reprimand you in his usual way and then forget the incident. He knows he can't afford to lose you now. Don't worry,' said Barrie compassionately.

Tony looked pale and after finishing off one or two pieces of paperwork he left his office to go home as Barrie had suggested. He thanked Barrie by shaking his hand. Barrie joked that they could both move to bottom of the table Verrington if things turned out for the worst. Tony smiled briefly and winked to Barrie as he drove off in his car.

Chapter 74

The League insisted that the game was played. They apparently did not think the flu bug was so serious. This information was announced to the Sharrington and Crookaby clubs by Thursday lunchtime.

Saturday arrived and so did the poorly-looking Crookaby team. Three or four of their players who got off the team coach looked anaemic and drained. Bryant, the manager, announced his team as the side which had beaten Low Grove 3-0 the week before, but instead of eleven fit men, three of them were still suffering from the flu bug, although better than they were three days before, and one player was still injured. Grant Evans was amazed with the honesty of the man. He had never know a manger inform the opposition and the press of how weakened his team were before a match.

They were an inconsistent team. They had beaten Sharrington earlier on in the season 1-0. They had also beaten Treecliffe 2-1 and Seamingway 3-1 at home, drawn at Harloft Town 2-2 but lost heavily at Rallingborough 4-1, Treecliffe 5-1 and at Low Grove 5-2. They were currently positioned in 11th place, winning 9, losing 11 and drawing 4. They had 24 points, 8 less than Sharrington.

During the season they had not sold anyone and only bought Collin Bird from Sharrington, ironically. Their manager, Bryant, and his directors were quite happy with the first season. They had progressed to the 2nd round of the League Cup after beating Third Division Varsity Town 3-2 on aggregate, but to everyone's surprise they had got as far as the third round of the F.A. Cup only to lose 2-1 to Evercroft of Division Three, after drawing 2-2 on aggregate. In round one Crookaby won 3-2 against Farringstone Athletic a non-league team at home and then in the second round they defeated Alderwalk Bridge, also of the Third Division 2-1 away from home. This, apart from the home victory over Seamingway, was Bryant's highlight of the season. He told Grant Evans that his side would go for promotion next season with the possibility of two or three new signings to help them.

Sharrington's team was also the same as the previous week. Graham Bond was not quite fit and Sammy Chaddock was left out to rest. It was raining steadily at the kick-off. Crookaby looked even paler in their changed strip of all white. There was a crowd of 9,200.

Right from the kick-off the home team attacked their visitors. They simply took up from where they had left off against Braman. The Crookaby team looked well organised but they were being beaten for pace and flair. It was clear that their No 2, No 4 and No 8 were suffering from the flu bug but they were putting on a brave performance. The injured player was more difficult to distinguish. Tony though it was No 11, Lazackerlick, who scored the only goal against Sharrington in the first game but Barrie sensed it was No 6, Ellis, who he thought looked sluggish.

After 16 minutes Crookaby were out of luck because in a ten minute spell Sharrington crashed three goals against them. Neil Baynes, who was playing better than ever cracked in a volley from the edge of the penalty area after a bad clearance by a Crookaby defender. Alf Henning added number 2 five minutes later, after Graham Hart had laid it on a plate for him, and four minutes after that, Neil Baynes added his second and Sharrington's third with a rocket shot from 30 yards.

Tony was delirious and in his excitement he said it was perhaps their goalkeeper who was injured by the way he never moved to Baynes' long-range shot. He felt it would be easier for Eddie to forgive him if Sharrington won by a convincing margin and if Hart continued to dominate the right wing play. He simply told his team to carry on playing as they were, during the half-time break.

Straight from the restart Alf Henning made it 4-0. He pounced upon an error in the stationary Crookaby defence to shoot hard and low past Jacks, the stranded goalkeeper. The crowd were delighted with Sharrington's performance.

Sharrington continued with the upper hand and after 82 minutes Simon Docker beat off two challenges before planting the orange ball out of Jacks' reach and into the corner of the net. It was now 5-0.

The Crookaby side looked demoralised but with only seconds remaining they grasped a consolation goal when Anderson, the No 8, stabbed a loose ball into the empty net following a corner by Simms which was not cleared by the home team defence.

The score at the end of the game was a convincing 5-1 win for Sharrington. It was such a good victory, Tony did not remonstrate with his defence about the late goal they had conceded. The scoreline made it much easier for him to now talk to Eddie Flannagan.

The Crookaby side left Sharrington looking much worse than they did when they arrived but their manager, Bryant, smiled as he boarded the coach, hunched his shoulders and said to the group of children who had been obtaining autographs: 'At least, kids, we will have a good journey now that we have swallowed our medicine good and proper'. The coach doors closed and the bus slowly left the car park in front of the ground. The Sharrington kids were left chanting 5-1, 5-1, 5-1 as the bus drove onto the main road.

Chapter 75

As the Fourth Division full time results filtered in, Tony was trying to get Eddie Flannagan's attention in the directors' team room, so he could ask him if he could see him privately in his office before they went home.

Eddie was in a jubilant mood. He had just seen his team beat Crookaby Town by 5 goals to 1 and had just heard on the radio that Treecliffe had lost 1-0 at Aldway. 'Sensational news. That's terrific. That will put us one point above Treecliffe. Anybody heard the Harloft and Seamingway results?' shouted Eddie joyfully.

'No, not yet, Eddie. They should be finished by now. We will have to wait for the classified check,' replied Steve King, looking at his wristwatch.

'What about Dabrook? They could be a danger to us if they keep winning their matches,' said Bill Boothroyd quietly.

'No fear. I think they've left it too late now although I noticed they were leading 1-0 at half-time today in their game at Verrington,' answered Eddie as he drank from his mug of tea.

'Hold on everybody,' shouted Steve King. Everyone listened to the radio presenter's voice. He announced that the top two clubs in Division Four, Seamingway and Harloft had both drawn. There was uproar in the Directors' room. Eddie Flannagan spilled some of his tea as he heard the news. Steve King shook both his fists in delight and even Bill Boothroyd cheered. Tony was also pleased with those two results but he didn't let his excitement show to the others present. Sid Parkin was also laughing along with the others as Steve King shouted out that Sharrington were now next to the top of the league, only 3 points behind Seamingway.

'Fancy Harloft dropping a home point to Prent Park? Goodness gracious me. Wonders will never cease,' boomed Eddie over the noise of everyone else.

'Yes, and I am surprised Ellistart held the leaders as well. All the top teams seem to be going through a nervous time at the moment,' retorted Steve King.

During the classified check they heard that Dabrook had won 2-1 at Verrington and had moved up to 5th place, with only 3 points less than Sharrington and 2 points behind Harloft and Treecliffe.

On the whole the scores were good for Sharrington and, in particular, Tony Davidson who had finally caught Eddie's eye and arranged the meeting with him for 5.30 in the manager's office. Eddie was so taken up with the results of the other teams that he never asked Tony what he wanted to seem him about.

At 5.30 prompt, Eddie walked into Tony's office. He had his usual long, fat cigar sticking out of the side of his mouth. His trilby was perched precariously on the top of his head and his complexion was as scarlet as Tony had ever seen it before. He guessed that the redness in his face was due to the excitement of the promotion games and possibly a little due to some whisky that the stocky director freely poured into his tea during match days. He seemed very cheerful as he dropped unceremoniously into the chair opposite Tony's.

'What's the matter then, Tony? Do you want more money?' asked Eddie out of the blue. Tony was completely taken aback. He hadn't predicted the meeting would open like this.

'No, not at all, Mr Flannagan,' replied Tony.

'Call me, Eddie, man,' resounded the relaxed director.

'Well, Eddie!' Tony started, 'it's a bit of a problem I've got myself in and I am afraid I've got some apologising to do to you and the other board members.' This opening line was not as Tony had planned it but Eddie's expression never altered. He continued to smile as Tony carried on: 'To cut a long story short, Eddie, I've not been totally honest with you. I received a sizeable offer for young Graham Hart, about three or four weeks ago from Cotterton City, plus one of their wingers thrown in as part exchange and although I rejected the deal I now realise I should have discussed it with you before I allowed myself to do such a thing.' Tony felt subservient.

Eddie still sat with the fixed smile on his face. He never moved. Tony wondered if he was drunk. Suddenly he spoke. 'How much did they offer?'

'£50,000 to start with, then £60,000 and finally £75,000 plus their man in exchange, Cooper, I think his name was,' stammered Tony as he fiddled with his watch strap.

'Cooper, Billy Cooper. He's not worth a light. Never has been and never will be, weedy little winger. Don't know how he ever made Division One in the first place,' shouted Eddie. Tony didn't know the player but he was glad to hear Eddie didn't rate him. 'He's a good player, young Hart. I like him and to say you brought him here for nothing, £75,000 is a quick profit for a club like ours,' continued Eddie in the same tone of voice. Tony wondered what he was going to hear next, 'but what would we have spent it on? We can't get in the transfer market now and although we could do with some floodlights and better accommodation for the supporters we won't need either if we stay in Division Four. I am certainly disappointed that you didn't mention it to us, Tony, but you have built this club up out of the doldrums and put us on the map for the first time for many years.' Tony saw Eddie visibly mellow in front of his eyes. 'We put faith in your ability right from the start and you have repaid us with your judgement and fine footballing brain. Once again, it is sad that you didn't feel we could discuss the transfer proposals with you before replying to Cotterton. I am sure we would have been sympathetic with your reasons for holding onto Hart, but, as I am sure you will appreciate now, that sort of money to us is a lifeline,' concluded Eddie. He immediately changed his frowning expression to that of the fixed smile as if he had just remembered Sharrington's League position again.

'I am sorry for what I've done obviously but I felt Graham Hart was too important a player for me to lose at this stage of the season and like you said, Eddie, we need him more than the money,' said Tony assuredly.

'True, Tony, very true, but in future let's know all the details, eh?' replied the trilby-headed director.

'I didn't want to let it go unmentioned because I thought that if the Cotterton City Chairman said anything to you next Monday you would be most embarrassed, not to mention furious with me,' said Tony.

'Well, I am glad you finally did tell me, Tony. I will of course mention it to Steve and Bill in my own discreet way but don't forget let's have all the facts as and when they arise from here on,' stressed Eddie.

'Certainly. Once again I offer my apologies to the Board,' confessed Tony.

'Look, let's forget it now, eh? Let's get on with winning promotion. We've played well enough all season to get it and after today's first class display you've certainly given us pride, Tony. That's what we want now. Promotion. So take it from me, don't worry any more about this Cotterton matter, just worry about keeping us in the top three,' said Eddie bluntly. He puffed on his cigar vigorously, stood up, smiled at Tony and departed without saying anything else. Tony felt relieved. He admired Eddie for his honesty and advice and only hoped he could take the club to promotion for the likes of Eddie and Jack in particular. Tony quickly told Barrie the good news before he left the ground.

The Sunday morning newspapers gave a list of the Division's five leading teams, following games and assessments made by experts as to who would gain promotion. All six newspapers Tony read predicted Seamingway and Harloft Town would get promotion but only three of them thought Sharrington would be the other club to join them. Two thought Treecliffe would make it and one newspaper thought Dabrook would pip Sharrington and Treecliffe to 3rd place.

The remaining fixtures were shown as follows:

SEAMINGWAY
v Braman (a)
v Verrington (h)
v Treecliffe (a)
v Harloft Town (a)

SHARRINGTON F.C.
v Rallingborough (h)
v Ellistart (a)
v Verrington (h)
v Warworth (a)

HARLOFT TOWN
v Aldway (h)
v Low Grove (a)
v Mannish (h)
v Seamingway (h)

TREECLIFFE
v Holydice (h)
v Dabrook (a)
v Seamingway (h)
v Mannish (a)

DABROOK
v Warworth (a)
v Treecliffe (h)
v Braman (a)
v Rallingborough (h)

<h1 style="text-align:center">Chapter 76</h1>

During the following week the Chairmen's meeting had passed off without incident. They had agreed that they would like to see the Third and Fourth Division clubs split into local areas so that travelling expenses could be cut down and attendances improved. They had also asked for a fairer distribution of gate receipts from cup matches. It was, however, unlikely that these changes would be implemented by the League Association, but they had at least made their voices heard in the right direction.

Eddie Flannagan told Tony on his return from the A.G.M that the Cotterton City chairman had snubbed him throughout the entire meeting although he did confess that the chairmen tended to stick together with other chairmen from the same division.

It had snowed lightly in Sharrington and surrounding districts. It had snowed heavier further south and on Thursday, the Low Grove home game against Ellistart had been called off. The other two games in danger in Division Four were Braman v Seamingway and Mannish v Crookaby. Decisions on these two games were to be made nearer Saturday.

The snow had covered the Sharrington pitch to a depth of 2 feet. It had drifted in the strong winds to about 4 feet down the touchline at the stand side but Eddie Connolly and a number of volunteers had cleared the greater deposits of snow and lined the pitch in blue emulsion during Thursday afternoon. The local referee had passed the pitch but everyone was watching the weather forecasts for frost.

The players, including a completely fit Sammy Chaddock, trained underneath the stand for three days. They had worked very hard on exercises, running, shooting, heading and five-a-side games but the limited space for manoeuvre was a problem. Tony had instructed the players to take the Friday off before the game at home against Rallingborough.

Tony and Barrie decided upon the same team, which beat Crookaby, but chose Sammy Chaddock as substitute in place of Steve Holland. Tony fell sorry for Steve Holland as he had been unable to gain a regular place in the team due to the sound performances of Tommy French and Micky Thomas. He was pleased, however, with the young centre-half's attitude and the manner in which he trained as hard as his team mates. He had time on his side and had made a big impression upon Alf Henning who regularly worked with the central defenders on heading skills. The veteran centre-forward had tried to get the young player to play with more aggression and not to be so casual but the more he worked with him the more he valued the young player's ability to remain cool under pressure. Alf Henning admitted to Tony that Steve Holland was a good prospect for the future and a potential captain.

Saturday came and, as there had not been an overnight frost or any further snow, the ground was passed fit by match referee, Bill McLeod. Sharrington were happy that the ground had been passed as playable but they were not in the least happy with the referee. They all remembered McLeod from the first leg League Cup game against Treecliffe and he had a reputation of being a strict but sometime inconsistent decision maker.

Rallingborough had had a poor season and were struggling 3rd from bottom of the league. After being relegated from Division Three the season before there was little support for them at Sharrington. The town of Rallingborough had become disillusioned with their team. They had only won five games, drawn 10 and lost 11 with 20 points. They had started the season with 10 points from a possible 14 points but they had slumped considerably since then due to a run of injuries and bad luck.

A crowd of 10,000 turned out to brave the cold, wintry weather and the only green they saw was the Rallingborough players' shirts.

Sharrington started the game building patiently from the back and looking for a break either wide or down the centre of the Rallingborough defence. Their defence was being excellently marshalled by Summerton, the No 4, who was constantly shouting orders to his teammates. They were a hard team and some of their tackles seemed late and on one occasion, after Graham Hart, the nippy winger sped away from his marker, the full-back Wellings chopped him down quite deliberately and was booked by referee McLeod after a moment's deliberation on the official's part. Hart received treatment for a shin injury. He hobbled on bravely only to be tackled to the ground three minutes later by the same player. The crowd demanded that Wellings should be sent off but the referee was not of the same opinion and simply gave a free kick to Sharrington.

There was a lot of nasty, niggly play by Rallingborough, and, when the Sharrington attackers made them look cumbersome, they pulled, pushed and fouled to keep themselves still in the game. The centre-half, Grimes, was having a word or two with Alf Henning and the referee had warned them both to stop the arguing.

Paul Brooke had been judged to have pushed right-winger Fanthom over the touchline and, to the players and crowds amazement, McLeod booked him for the offence.

Sharrington had come closest to scoring when a shot by Paul Cracknell had goalkeeper, Tye, palming the ball out from underneath the cross bar.

The snow was holding the ball when it was being passed on the floor and right on half-time Tommy French mis-kicked his clearance and due to the ball sticking in the snow he was able to turn and chase after centre-forward Bright, robbing him of the change to put the visitors 1-0 in the lead.

At half-time it remained goalless.

'We've got to work harder, lads. I know its difficult out there but they are coping with everything we've done so far. They are a hard side and don't mess about and you can all forget getting any help from this referee today,' stressed Tony. 'We are playing it far too much on the deck. Let's lob them occasionally. Get some high crosses into the box. We've not tested them in the air yet.' The players were seated drinking from enamel mugs full of piping hot tea. Tony continued his half-time talk. 'Simon and Tony you've got to switch the ball to the right from time to time. You are both getting caught trying to work something down the left hand side all the time. O.K?' The two left hand side forwards nodded. 'Neil run at them to make them commit themselves. Alf keep it going. Their no. 5 will weaken before you do and who knows he may do it in the box. Defence, it looks tight but watch that you don't leave a forward unmarked when we are pushing forward into their half. No complaints, lads. Just up the work rate a bit more and fight for possession. Its 2 points we need not 1,' said Tony, clapping his hands together. The players limbered up and left the dressing for the second half.

Five minutes passed, then ten, then fifteen and still Rallingborough were preventing Sharrington from getting into a scoring position. They were clearly playing for a 0-0 draw to try and keep them from having to apply for re-election or relegation for the first time in the club's history. They were even harder in the second half than in the first half. No 5 and No 6 had been booked during the first fifteen minutes of the restart for deliberate tackles on Hart and Docker. The young winger was limping quite badly and Tony was contemplating bringing him off and moving Tony White to right wing and putting Sammy Chaddock onto the left wing.

Just before he was about to do so the little winger managed to squeeze his way passed Wellings near the right wing corner flag. He played the ball back into the path of Paul Brooke who centred the ball high to the far post. The heads went up and as the ball dropped to the floor Simon Docker gently steered the ball wide of Tye in the goal to put Sharrington 1-0 in the lead. The visiting defenders appealed to the referee that Alf Henning had been pushing but fortunately for Sharrington he waved their appeals away and the goal stood.

The crowd cheered and shouted with relief. One or two poorly made snowballs were thrown at the Rallingborough defenders who were still complaining about the goal but no one was hurt.

Graham Hart continued to limp but Tony was keen to replace the winger; his injury prevented him from playing a useful role in the game.

Rallingborough came out of their defence more after the goal against them and on two occasions looked dangerous. Their front three forwards, Greene, Bright and Solley, were running and working harder.

Sharrington's play seemed to ease fractionally as Rallingborough changed their tactics, and, in the 73rd minute, No 10 Solley took advantage of a bit of space, gave a body swerve to Paul Cracknell which had the youngster falling away into the snow and chipped the orange ball as though he was using a golf wedge. Alan Hawkins frantically reached for the ball but the shot came as such a surprise to him that he was not properly balanced and the ball entered the net with hardly a sound coming from any spectator. It was 1-1 with 17 minutes remaining.

Tony immediately brought Graham Hart off and directed his forwards as planned. Rallingborough, who had looked impressive when going forward, went back onto the defensive. This tactic amazed Tony and Barrie as they were getting worried that Rallingborough looked strong enough to win the game. The visitors clam-like attitude helped bring Sharrington back into the game. Admittedly they fought harder to gain possession but they were given the incentive back by their generous near neighbours.

Chaddock was a quick-footed player on the snowy surface and created some good openings for the other forwards. Baynes got back into the driving seat and motivated his colleagues to do better. White was checked fairly and unfairly by Wellings but the aggression he received seemed to inspire him all the more. Henning, and Docker, who was still confident from his goal, were a handful for the Rallingborough defenders. The crowd were now, once again, right behind Sharrington.

In the 80th minute Baynes was brought down in the penalty area but McLeod waved on play. 2 minutes later their No 2, Baxter, handled the ball and was booked and 45 seconds after that the free kick was taken. Allan Smith charged after a loose ball and met it at the same time as No 6, Sinclair, of Rallingborough. The ball looped across the visitors' penalty area. The two players fell to the ground in pain. Sammy Chaddock was first onto the crossed ball and with his back to the goal he kicked the ball over his head and high into the six-yard box. Tye, the goalkeeper, was looking for a challenge from Alf Henning which never came but he took his eye off the ball for a second and his punch landed at the feet of Tony White who gratefully lunged at the ball and sent it, snow and all, into the unguarded net. Sharrington had gone back into the lead.

There was confusion all around. Barrie Trippett and Micky Thomas were assisting Allan Smith and the remainder of the outfield players mobbed young Tony White. The Rallingborough defenders were shouting at their goalkeeper and the forwards and trainer were treating Sinclair.

After a stoppage of three minutes Smith and Sinclair hobbled into action but both looked in more pain than they were ready to admit to their respective team trainers.

The game ended with another home victory for Sharrington but to what extent the injuries to Hart and Smith were for the remainder of the season was difficult to assess straight away

Chapter 77

'BITTER-SWEET WIN FOR SHARRINGTON' was the headline in the Monday edition of the *Sharrington Echo*. Grant Evans confirmed to the eagerly awaiting Sharrington supporters that Allan Smith had badly injured the tendon in the back of his left leg and was likely to be out for the rest of the season. The news became worse as the article stated that young Graham Hart had a badly bruised right leg and would definitely miss the game at Ellistart a week on Saturday.

'It's getting worse, Sid, isn't it?' said Peggy seriously. 'What is, Peg?' asked Sid Parkin who was reading from another newspaper and was only half listening to Peggy Hollingsworth.

'The injury situation. If it wasn't bad enough having Graham and Micky out it looks as though Allan Smith will be out for the remainder of the season and little Graham Hart looks like missing our next game,' exclaimed Peggy as she read from the back page of the *Sharrington Echo*.

'Oh that. Yes. It's all part and parcel of the game. We've been fortunate so far this season so I suppose it's the law of averages we should suffer from injuries during some part of the season,' replied Sid still reading from his paper.

'I know that, Sid, but isn't it a stroke of bad luck. I mean why did it have to come at the end of the season, just when we really needed a full squad to pick from in our last three important games?' commented Peggy as she finally put the paper down and started her work.

'I feel sorry for Mr. Davidson, especially when he's worked so hard.'

'The players have worked hard as well, Peg. They must have done to be challenging for promotion. I agree its a shame but it will certainly test the character of the other players now,' said Sid also starting his work.

'It would be a shame to lose the chance of going up into Division Three now. It would destroy everything if we had to spend another season in this division,' remarked Peggy as she typed onto a blank piece of paper.

'Aye well, we shall just have to see, won't we?' stated the greasy-haired secretary.

'That's typical of you, Sid Parkin. Apathy rules. You're predictable. Why don't you show a bit of excitement and commitment once in a while,' snarled Peggy loudly.

'That'll do, Peg. Let's get on with some work,' mumbled Sid.

'Well, you haven't even commented about the game on Saturday or the other promotion results have you? It's as though you don't want us to get promotion.'

Sid never looked at Peggy.

'Well do you?' shouted Peggy.

Sid carried on with his work.

'I don't know why I bother talking to you'.

'Good idea, Peg, my girl. Just don't bother,' said Sid abruptly. Peggy snubbed her nose at him and they both carried on working in silence.

Tony and Barrie were busy taking the junior team's coaching session. The first team squad had been given the day off. Graham Bond, Neil Baynes, Alf Henning and Sammy Chaddock all attended the ground to help out with the youngsters.

There were some fine players amongst the twenty-four juniors. Tony particularly was impressed with centre-half, Alan Benjemin, inside right, Brian Seacroft, centre-forward, Jimmy Wilde, and inside left, Ronny Banks.

Ray Walton, the local youth coach, agreed with Tony and Barrie that these four players would make good prospects for professional footballers. He said that he had received numerous enquiries from other professional clubs about Alan Benjemin and Jimmy Wilde and he told Tony that both players were going for trials to Allton United and Passondale of the First Division, respectively.

The coaching continued until 3 p.m. and all the boys were asked to attend for training on the following day at 10 a.m. It had been a good work out and the four Sharrington players had enjoyed coaching the youngsters and were delighted with the response.

'How's Graham's injury, Doctor?' asked Barrie Trippett after everyone had left the ground.

'It's a very badly bruised leg. So much so that he was having difficulty walking when I saw him this morning,' replied Doctor Ericson.

'I've taken an x-ray of the leg just to be on the safe side, but there is too much bruising to see if he has suffered any other damage just now.

'It's his calf mainly, isn't it?' asked Barrie.

'Mmm, but there is a bit of a swelling behind the knee which looks tender to me. Young Graham takes so many knocks he could not tell me how long the swelling had been there. He said it had been there for 3 or 4 weeks at least. I will see him again on Thursday to see how he is getting on but I don't recommend he trains before then, in fact I doubt if he could attempt to train with this type of injury,' answered the grey-haired Doctor.

'I gather Allan Smith has pulled a tendon in his left leg?'

'Yes, he's in a bad way. It will be long job and I think I can say with certainty that he will be unable to play in the remaining three games,' said Doctor Ericson as he stroked his jawline beard.

'That's bad luck for him. I know he was anxious to be the only player to play in every game. It's a shame because he is such a good lad to have in the team. He keeps everything nice and relaxed but he has the ability to concentrate and play his heart out for us,' commented Barrie.

'He's a pleasant young man. I know he will want to get back in action quickly but, with this type of injury, I'm afraid he won't be able to,' said the Doctor sadly.

'I suppose the only consolation about Saturday is two more points, eh, Barrie?'

'Yes, it was good to keep the victory up but it's so tight at the top we can never pull clear. With Treecliffe and Harloft Town both winning as well we are still only one point up on them,' stated Barrie as he tidied up the home team dressing room.

'Wasn't Seamingway's match postponed due to the snow?' asked Doctor Ericson.

'Yes, they are hoping to play the match at Braman tomorrow night but if the ground is still too bad they will probably play it next Saturday, which is a free date for Third and Fourth Division clubs. At least we are only one point behind the leaders but they do, of course, have this game in hand,' stressed Barrie jovially.

The juniors trained along with the professionals for the remainder of the week and as a highlight for the youth team Tony organised a Saturday afternoon game: Professionals v Youth team, on the Sharrington pitch, behind closed doors. It was an interesting game although the professionals ran out comfortable winners by 4-1, the two sensational features of the match was that Graham Bond had made a good recovery and scored a goal and the youth team centre-forward Jimmy Wilde, who only played the second half, had the Sharrington defence in all sorts of trouble with his attacking flair and, on the hour, beat Cracknell, Bond and French to unselfishly pass to No. 8 Seacroft to score.

Tony was so impressed with Wilde that he spoke to the boy's father immediately after the game with a view of signing the lad on as an apprentice player but his offer was flatly rejected on the basis that the young striker preferred to go to Passondale. Tony knew that it was Wilde's father who had laid the terms down and whilst he could accept the player was good enough to join a First Division club he hoped the boy wouldn't be too frustrated if Passondale turned him down after the trials. Tony was not put off so easily, and, although he didn't say as much to the father, he intended to follow the progression of Wilde in the immediate future, just in case he failed to make the grade for the top club.

Seamingway defeated Braman 1-0 in the re-arranged league game and stayed three points clear at the top of the league. Passondale, Cotterton City and Torchester progressed to the semi-final of the F.A. Cup with Ashton and Rondale Rovers to replay for the fourth place.

Chapter 78

The following week's training had gone smoothly but due to the number of injured players there had not been much variety. Graham Hart was still having trouble with his right leg and had been unable to train since the Rallingborough game. Allan Smith had his left leg plastered and he and Micky Leighton looked like book-ends. Graham Bond was feeling no after effects from two week's hard training or from the game against the juniors.

Tony was in consultation with Barrie Trippett for hours over the team selection during the week but by Thursday the team was announced as:

1.	Hawkins	
2.	Bond (Captain)	
3.	Brooke	
4.	Cracknell	
5.	French	
6.	Thomas	
7.	White	
8.	Baynes	
9.	Henning	
10.	Docker	
11.	Chaddock	
12.	Sub. Holland	

The journey to Ellistart was made during the Saturday morning. The snow had cleared and the 52-mile trip to Ellistart was completed after 2 hours. The three injured players travelled with the team. Eddie Flannagan and Steve King were also in attendance as was Doctor Ericson and Grant Evans.

It was a dull day and the Ellistart ground of Gregg Road loomed high over the Sharrington coach, their floodlights illuminating the playing area.

Ellistart had slipped in the league after making an impressive start to the season. They were currently in seventh position and out of the running for promotion. They had, however, only lost seven games but likewise only won seven as well. They had only lost once at Gregg Road in the league. Ellistart had suffered from injuries in the middle of the season and this, according to their manager, George Tranter, was the reason for the slump.

The crowd was a miserable 5,135. Seemingly, not many Sharrington supporters had bothered to make the trip. It was a disappointing attendance.

Tony's instructions to the players before the game were to play themselves in slowly but support each other at all times. He told them to keep the marking tight and be on the look out for a quick break but be extra careful to cover the Ellistart unmarked players. As it was a re-shuffled team yet again he knew it would be difficult to expect the team to go out and attack and play with confidence. He did not, however, say this to the players.

The injury hit Sharrington team were kitted in red shirts, white shorts and red socks. Ellistart were in their home colours of white shirts, black shorts and white socks.

The ground had two stands, one along each touchline. At the Gregg Road end of the ground was covered terracing, but at the opposite end it was uncovered and sparse of spectators.

The game got off to a slow start, Sharrington were very defence-minded and rarely on the attack. Graham Bond seemed more forceful than ever as a captain and was having a solid and reliable opening to his comeback after a four match lay off.

Ellistart had not won for four games and were a much poorer team than the side they were earlier on in the season at Sharrington, where they had lost to the only goal of the game by Tony White. The last team they had beaten at Gregg Road were Harloft Town some thirteen weeks previous. They lacked any attacking ideas and failed to put one accurate shot on target.

Sharrington came nearest to scoring in the first half when Paul Cracknell found himself in oceans of room and ran 20 yards before squaring a pass to Alf Henning whose shot was pushed behind for a corner by goalkeeper Bernards. The visitors failed to press home the advantage of a ten-minute period near half-time. The first half ended goalless.

In the second half Sharrington opened brightly with another good ten-minute period but the play became bogged down in the centre of the pitch which got more and more cut up as the game progressed.

Ellistart's game improved only slightly and within two minutes they had two separate chances when they could have gone in the lead. In the 68th minute Deighton, the centre-forward, fluffed what seemed an easy chance only 10 yards out from in front of the goal and in the 69th minute Brand, the No. 8, headed straight into Alan Hawkins' hands when it appeared easier for him to score from just inside the 6-yard box.

These two scares put a jolt on the Sharrington game and, from the moment Hawkins cleared the danger, they became tighter in defence and less adventurous. Alf Henning and the two wingers were rarely involved in the game from this stage of the game.

French, Thomas and Baynes defended soundly and Docker and Cracknell worked hard to win the ball from the Ellistart forwards. Bond, and Brooke, who took time to settle in the unfamiliar role of left full-back, slowly had the better of wingers Smith and Turpin.

The crowd from each part of the ground started to leave slowly, some as early as fifteen minutes from the full-time whistle. The last part of the match was an advert to keep people away from football. It was dour, defensive and dull. The weather was as drab as the game and the interest or excitement was nil. Both teams refused to take chances near the end and it was a foregone conclusion the result would be the same as it was at the start of the game.

The referee finally blew the full-time whistle and to the few spectators that remained in the ground it came as a relief. Ellistart had nothing to lose but they weren't adventurous on the day and Sharrington opted to keep it tight and settle for a 0-0 draw and a point. Ellistart had failed to score in the 2 games against Sharrington.

It was a game to forget and although Tony felt sorry that his team had had to play for a point, he knew that with his recent injuries and re-shuffled side, at the end of the day, another valuable point towards promotion was more important that an attacking display and ending up with nothing. He deeply regretted this approach to the game but promotion was a must for Sharrington and with the players at his disposal a point was very welcome indeed.

As the players were bathing in the giant white tiled bath after the game they were told that Dabrook had thrashed Treecliffe 4-0. Harloft Town had won by 2-0 at Low Grove and leaders Seamingway had defeated bottom club Verrington 3-0. Although everyone was pleased to hear of Treecliffe's defeat the victors, Dabrook, were now becoming a danger to Sharrington F.C. The league table, with two matches to play was:

	PL	W	L	D	F	A	PTS
Seamingway	28	17	4	7	58	28	41
Sharrington	28	14	5	9	51	30	37
Harloft Town	28	14	5	9	51	35	37
Treecliffe	28	14	7	7	58	41	35
Dabrook	28	13	6	9	43	34	35

If only Sharrington could get two points at home to Verrington in two week's time they would almost certainly clinch promotion in view of their better goal difference but the only thing that was settled at this stage was that Seamingway had won promotion to Division Three and more than likely as champions. They had successfully managed to get back to Division Three at the first attempt.

Chapter 79

'Well, Eddie if they don't beat Verrington now that they are definitely relegated we don't deserve to go up,' said Bob Bennett throwing his first dart of the night in the Village Arms' tap room on the Wednesday after Sharrington's goalless draw at Ellistart.

'If Saturday's performance is anything to go on and Davidson chooses the same team again, I think Verrington will give us a run for our money,' interrupted Frank Sneddon who was waiting for his throw.

'Rubbish, Frank. Rubbish. I thought we were pretty composed at all times on Saturday especially in defence. If we get the break and the crowd get behind the lads I think we will be in here a week on Saturday celebrating. The game at Warworth will be a formality,' answered Eddie Fisher confidently.

'Don't be so sure, Eddie. We've certainly got a serious injury problem and with the pressure on the young lads in particular it won't be as easy as you are making out,' added Frank in his usual reasonable manner.

'But Verrington are down and out, Frank. They won't have any confidence at all. Let's face it, they haven't won away this season and I don't know how long ago it is since they last won a match. They've only won three all season in the league. We've got to get two points against them,' snapped Eddie as he threw his darts firmly towards the dartboard.

'I agree, Eddie,' said Bob 'I heard young Hart ought to be fit again by then and he's just the player we need to put pressure onto the Verrington defence.'

'I hope he is fit by a week on Saturday. I agree he is a good young winger and has done exceptionally well this season but I heard from a certain source that his leg injury was causing some concern. I understood it was possibly more serious than first thought,' said Frank.

'He only got a few kicks on his leg in the Rallingborough game. I know he was struggling a bit but they said it was only bruising didn't they?' asked Bob as he chalked the scores on the blackboard.

'I don't know exactly, Bob. That's all I heard. It'll be a shame if he does miss the Verrington game,' mused Frank.

'Anyway, lads, let's look on the bright side. I think Treecliffe have blown it now. What a pasting they got a Dabrook, eh?' laughed Eddie.

'Yes, they were two down after the first five minutes, weren't they?' shouted Bob before drinking from his pint glass of beer.

'That's as may be, but I think we should look closely at Dabrook.

They are coming with a late run and they have done so well since Christmas. They are still in with a chance you know, men. It's so tight at the top,' reasoned Frank.

'Oh, Frank, why are you so cautious all the time?' joked Eddie as he collected his darts from the board.

'I'll tell you why, Eddie. For a start they are only 2 points behind us and then, secondly, they've got two games against two lowly clubs, Braman and Rallingborough, and thirdly–'

Before Frank could continue Bob butted in. 'But so have we, Frank, and let's face it, who are lower than Verrington?'

Bob and Eddie laughed out aloud. Frank ignored them both and threw his darts. The two friends tried to cheek him. 'Go on Frank, and thirdly what?' They both sneered. Frank finished throwing his dart. He smiled to himself and turned to Eddie and Bob and quite matter-of-factly said: 'And, thirdly, lads, you owe me 50 pence each. I've just won the game.'

Both men looked at the dartboard, then at each other in amazement. Frank had finished on double 10 and won the darts match. Frank laughed out loudly as Eddie and Bob dug deep into their pockets for the money to pay up.

Tony Davidson was working at his desk on the Saturday morning. As there was no game for Sharrington, he and Barrie were going to Sprannon to watch the League Cup semi-final between Storr Town and Rondale Rovers. Neil Baynes and Micky Thomas were also going with them. As he was attending to some paperwork he heard a knock on his door. He shouted "come in" without looking up. The door opened and the visitor entered the office. Tony then looked up to see who it was.

'Well, what a great surprise indeed?' exclaimed Tony as he saw Jack Elliott standing in the doorway. 'Come in, Jack, and sit down will you?' said Tony, getting up from his seat to escort the club chairman inside.

'Thanks, Tony. How are you?' asked the much slimmer Jack Elliott. He was uneasy on his feet as he walked forwards to the chair.

'Why didn't you give me a call and say you were coming, Jack?' asked Tony.

'Oh, it's all right, Tony. Eddie Flannagan dropped me off outside. He said you would be here until about 12 o'clock,' said Jack quietly and slightly out of breath.

'The doctor told me a couple of weeks ago to start engaging my mind in something again, as long as it was not too strenuous. So I thought as it was a better day today, weather-wise, I would come down to the ground and have a chat with you on how things are going.'

'Oh, fine really, Jack. We've got one or two problems with injuries but all in all the results have been as well as can be expected,' answered Tony pleasantly.

Jack made himself comfortable in the chair. He put his hat and gloves on top of the table in front of him.

'You have done incredibly well, Tony, in your first season. The lads have also done magnificently. I am very proud of the way everyone bedded down to their job since you came here. It's a delight to be up at the top of the league pressing for promotion instead of floundering at the bottom. I'll tell you this, Tony, some of the recent results and, in particular the win at Treecliffe, have helped with my recovery,' said the old Chairman joyfully. His smile was re-assuring to Tony. The Chairman appeared relaxed and in much better health than when Tony had previously seen him.

'Tell me, Tony, what's all the speculation about Hart being more seriously injured than first thought?'

Tony leaned back in his chair and raised his hands behind his head. His expression darkened.

'It's strange really, Jack. We thought at first that it was just bad bruising but it looks as though he has developed a blood clot in the back of his knee which is going to require some intensive treatment before he is fit to play,' stressed Tony.

'That's a shame for the lad and for the club as well. He has been playing really well apparently, hasn't he?' asked Jack Elliott.

'Yes, he has. He's a good player and I've been absolutely thrilled with his performances this season and it could be that he will be out for the rest of the season now, that is unless he responds dramatically in the next week or two,' reflected Tony.

Jack Elliott slowly crossed his right leg over his left knee before continuing the conversation.

'I know you were confident we could get promotion, Tony, but how do you feel now? Do you think we can do it?'

'It's tight at the top, Jack, as you know, but I don't see any reason why we shouldn't get promotion now. I think Treecliffe have lost their way of late and they might have blown it. Dabrook are on top form at the moment and they may get maximum points from their remaining games, which means we will have to get at least two points to clinch promotion as we have a much better goal difference than them,' stated Tony seriously.

'Having said that, if Treecliffe get four points and we only manage two points it will be a toss up as to who gets promotion on goal difference.' Tony continued: 'I can't see Harloft Town losing out now, but you never know in this game do you, Jack?'

'No, that's true, Tony. There is never a dead certainty in football. The tables have been turned on so many occasions in the past,' replied Jack Elliott.

'Our match against Verrington next Saturday is crucial for us. Admittedly, we are struggling a bit with injuries and in our last two games we've lacked the consistency we had earlier in the season. Probably the lads are feeling the nerves a bit but I've tried to concentrate on goal scoring again during training as we need goals now as we've never needed them before. They win your games for you and I feel that we must score early doors, against Verrington especially, when we have to go to Warworth for the last match.' Tony leant forward and rested his forearms on the table top.

'I know Verrington are down now but I'm sure they will be fighting and trying to go out in style,' concluded Tony.

'It should be a big crowd on Saturday,' commented Jack uncrossing his legs.

'I hope so. If we get the support we deserve then who knows, Jack? We might be celebrating a week tonight,' laughed Tony.

'I'd like to be here, but I'll leave it up to the doctor and quite probably Mrs. Elliott,' joked Jack. He smiled to himself.

'I would love you to be here. I really would. It would be a historical occasion for us all, wouldn't it?' exclaimed Tony.

'It sure would, Tony. It would be the highlight of my career as Chairman,' said Jack dreamily.

The two men continued to talk for a further half an hour before Eddie Flannagan pipped his car hooter outside the office block for the Chairman's journey home. Tony shook Jack's hand and they parted company.

Tony left ten minutes later to pick up his passengers for the journey to Sprannon.

It was a drab semi-final game. The First Division Rondale Rovers won by the only goal, which was scored only seven minutes from time when it looked as though Storr Town were going to cause an upset by taking the favourites to a replay.

The other semi-final was a draw, 1-1, and was to be replayed at Stanton Villa's ground on the following Saturday.

Chapter 80

The following week was an agonising time for the Sharrington F.C. The Monday brought a deep freeze to the club. There had been a very heavy overnight frost, which caused a number of frozen pipes, and the electricity supply had been affected somehow and the problem was not restored until mid-afternoon.

The players trained but had to go home to bath.

On Tuesday, Alan Hawkins slipped on his way into the ground and fell onto his left arm. He was left grazed from his elbow to his wrist. He was not happy.

On Wednesday Grant Evans was becoming such a thorn in Tony's side with his build up to the Verrington game that the manager lost his temper with him and the reporter foolishly quoted the evening headline as: 'Is the pressure too much for Sharrington?' Tony was not happy and neither were the directors when they read the article.

Thursday afternoon saw a thaw in the weather and the frozen pipes of three or four days ago turned into burst pipes. There was floodwater everywhere and also a leak in the home team dressing room ceiling. The training sessions continued, but in a five-a-side match, Alf Henning struck a full-blooded shot on the volley and the training ball cannoned into Simon Docker's face. The quiet inside forward was stunned. The surface of the ball had cut him on the nose and he was not too pleased with the experience.

Friday morning's training session and team talk went by without incident but the bad news for the play was that Graham Hart was not considered fit enough to play against Verrington. The team was announced as the same as had played at Ellistart. Stephen Holland was named as substitute again.

Tony was relaxing at home on Friday evening with his wife, Penny, but his quiet was disturbed with a telephone call from Barrie Trippett who informed him that his wife had been involved in a motor accident and, although she was all right, his car was considered a write-off. He asked Tony if he could pick him up on the way to the ground on Saturday morning.

It had been one of those weeks. Tony hoped it wouldn't extend itself to a poor result against Verrington.

'Come on the stripes. Show 'em what we can do,' shouted the small band of Verrington supporters as they congregated behind the bottom goal, where their team were kicking in before the game.

The Sharrington supporters all laughed and jeered in contempt. It was a good crowd of 10,750. Jack Elliott was not amongst the crowd. His wife had preferred him to stay at home. She didn't think the excitement would have been too good for him so soon after his heart-attack. The doctor had not advised against it but he had stressed that if Jack did go to the game he should remain as calm as possible. However, Mrs. Elliott didn't think Jack could keep calm and asked him to stay at home. He reluctantly did as she had asked. The Verrington team in their blue and white striped shirts kicked off and in the early stages looked a reasonable side, considering that they were doomed to the part-time league next season. Tony Braddock, ex-Sharrington keeper, was unfit for the game.

After eleven minutes Basil Sanders, the ex-Sharrington winger, crossed to the far post only to see Bullivant, the burly visitors' centre-forward, head over the cross bar when unmarked.

Sharrington were slow off the mark. They seemed startled by Verrington's approach to the game. Tony had warned them not to be too complacent but the younger players in particular were easily brushed off the ball.

Neil Baynes and Alf Henning were restricted to shooting from long-range as the visiting defenders were remarkably quick at recovering and tackling.

Tony and Barrie were also surprised with the doomed Verrington's performance. To say they had only won three matches during the season was a complete mystery on this form. Admittedly, they had only conceded 42 goals which suggested that if they weren't scoring goals their defence couldn't have performed too badly to keep the "goals against" so low.

The home crowd tried to lift their team and for a ten-minute spell Sharrington moved up a gear and played sensibly but they couldn't find a way through the often-packed Verrington defence. Near half-time Sammy Chaddock flicked a quick ball to Simon Docker who twisted half a circle and curled his shot just past the visitors' goalkeeper's right hand post.

At half-time it was 0-0.

'Come on, lads. This won't do. It's a bit half-hearted, isn't it?' stressed Tony. 'What's wrong with us. There's no fire in our bellies. I told you before the game and during training that you would have to force the pace.' Suddenly he raised his voice. 'Now let's get it straight, the first half was poor. People have paid to see you and we are hiding again, aren't we?

It's really not good enough, lads. They're showing you up. Any stranger to football out there must think you lot are Verrington.' He eased up fractionally.

'So, come on, let's show everybody what we can do. Let's take the game to them. We've got the skill haven't we? Run at them. Take them on. Use a few one-twos. We've not played one so far.' Tony started to pace up and down. Whitey: get on the inside of this full-back. He's rubbish on his right side.' The winger nodded.

'Sammy: you've got the other full-back where you want him, but you've not tested him for pace yet. Give him a run, eh?' The left-winger smiled and flashed his eyelids.

'Alf: get amongst them. Use your weight a lot more. Put yourself about.' The stocky forward smirked and pushed his hair out of his eyes. Simon: not bad… not bad at all. A little more running and get yourself in that penalty area with the ball. OK?' The quite No.10 drank from his mug of tea in the corner of the dressing room. Tony urged his players forward for the second half. Paul Cracknell was the last player out of the dressing room after receiving treatment for a cut on his right shin.

Sharrington started the second half with more determination. Neil Baynes and Graham Bond were rallying the team for more positive action. On the 50th minute Alf Henning and centre-half Knaves were booked for squaring up to each other. Five minutes later Simon Docker ran free from his marker but fluffed his shot. In the 59th minute Sammy Chaddock crossed into a packed goalmouth and the ball looped over the goalkeeper from a crowd of heads and bounced on top of the crossbar and out of play. The crowd were breathless. It was so near to a goal. The referee gave a goalkick but how he decided the effort on goal was made by a Sharrington player was not clear.

Verrington rarely came out of defence but in the 67th minute Phelps, their No.10, drove a long-range shot only to see Alan Hawkins dive and clutch the ball safely.

Sharrington were so much on top now that a goal seemed inevitable. Baynes, White and French went close and in the 78th minute Alf Henning saw his shot beat the visitors' goalkeeper, Swales, only to agonisingly watch it strike the far post and land at a Verrington defender's feet and be cleared. The players, crowd and Tony and Barrie all jumped up in the air only to be disappointed at the outcome of the centre-forward's shot.

Verrington defenders were fouling freely, and Maddison, Grant and Potter were all booked. The crowd were right behind Sharrington and baying for a goal but the visitors' defence were thwarting every attack.

Everyone in the ground finally thought the winning goal had come when Paul Cracknell lobbed a ball into the heart of the Verrington penalty area. The ball bounced once and Alf Henning was there to head the ball as the defence stood transfixed but Swales tipped the ball out from underneath the crossbar. There was a scramble following the excellent save and in the melee the crowd roared for a penalty kick when Neil Baynes was sent sprawling but the referee awarded a free kick to Verrington. The reason was not given. The Sharrington players protested briefly until Verrington took the free kick quickly.

Sharrington had been close on several occasions but as the full-time whistle blew they remained on level terms with relegated Verrington. The visitors seemed excited but the Sharrington players trooped off the pitch wondering just what they could have done to score. It was another 0-0 draw and only one point. Many of the crowd stayed to applaud their team off the pitch as it was the last home match for the season. They had also waited for the half-time results of the other matches. When the results were put up it appeared all the top teams were suffering from the same problems. All other half-time results were goalless.

'Hard luck, lads. Hard luck. You produced enough effort in that half to win the game. It's a shame you didn't play that way in the first half, but we can only wait and see how the others have gone on today to see how this point affects things at the top,' said Tony sadly.

The players all aired their views on the referee's decisions and the close scrapes of the second half as they bathed in the communal tub.

'It's a shame that shot of Alf's hit the bar,' commented Barrie, cleaning up the muddied kit.

'Yes, I thought it was in. I suppose it's just been one of those weeks when everything has gone wrong, but at least it's another point,' added Tony ruefully. 'Aye, it looks as though it's going to go right to the end. And what a place to go to, to have to get a result: Warworth. It's right up on the north west coast and at this time of the year it will be freezing cold, believe you me. I only hope Dabrook and Treecliffe lose today because it will not be a trip to cherish up there if we have to win the game to make certain,' stressed Barrie emotionally.

Chapter 81

When all the players had changed and the dressing room was cleared up, the results started to channel through. Since the end of the Sharrington game the messages had filtered through on the various stages of the three important Fourth Division games.

First someone said Treecliffe were leading Seamingway 1-0, another said it was 1-1. Another message was that Mannish led 1-0 at Harloft Town but that was contradicted when someone shouted that they'd heard it was 2-0 to Harloft. No second half results had been heard from Braman where Dabrook were playing.

Eventually the results were confirmed to the waiting players and management. Surprisingly, and coincidentally, the other top three teams challenging Sharrington for a promotion spot had all won by 2-1. The stories behind the results leaked out. Treecliffe's No.8, Hope, scored twice to rock the top club, Dabrook went into an early second half lead of 2-0 and held on to win 2-1, and finally Harloft Town had won their game in the last six minutes after Mannish, the draw experts, looked as though they were heading for their 17th draw of the season.

The league tables revealed that Sharrington had dropped to third place, one point behind Harloft Town, and only one point in front of Treecliffe and Dabrook. Sharrington would have to win to be sure of promotion without having to rely on Treecliffe's result, but if Treecliffe lost, drew or won by less than 3 clear goals they could afford only to draw themselves to pip Dabrook, as their goal difference was superior.

Harloft Town were not exactly safe, since if Sharrington and Treecliffe both won and Harloft lost, they would go down to 4th position as their goal difference was not as good as the 2 local teams by far.

Dabrook would only gain a promotion place if Sharrington lost and Treecliffe got, at the most, a point.

As Barrie Trippett had said, it would be decided by the last league matches of the season.

The stage was set for a thrilling final week to the season.

The Sunday newspapers were full of all the four leagues' promotion and relegation battles.

In Division One any one of four teams could win the league, although they had three games remaining. The teams involved were Rondale Rovers, Stanton Villa, Ashton and Trackerton Rovers.

Two of the three places for relegation were already decided. They were newly promoted Steeple Bay F.C. and Fillingway. The other position was to be fought out between Parringway and Trendale Park.

In Division Two, with two games remaining for the promotion contenders, five teams were challenging for the top three spots. In league order they were Ravenhead Athletic, Woodville, Blackway, Hambridge and Brookhouse Athletic. The clubs relegated were Sherman City, Billingbridge and bottom club Glassingborough.

In Division Three, Trandon Rovers and Ranchley Athletic were already promoted after both clubs had been relegated the season before and Hillwade United, Evercroft, Beckham Town and Summerstone Albion were battling it out for the remaining place.

The three relegated teams were to be decided between Billingborough, Alderwalk Bridge, Danningway and Leston United. With only two games left to play in that league it looked as though Paul Brooke's old club would be relegated as both their matches were away to Trandon Rovers and Beckham Town.

The League Cup semi-final replay between Allton United and Torchester had been played and the outcome was a 2-0 victory for the northern club Torchester. The reporters were predicting a classic final between Rondale Rovers and Torchester in three weeks' time in the national stadium. The two teams had met in the league during the season and the game at Torchester was drawn 0-0 but Rondale won their home game 3-1. There was, of course, a possibility that both teams would meet in the F.A. Cup Final.

On Monday morning training re-commenced at Sharrington. Tony talked with his players about the Verrington game and impressed upon them how important the lead up was to Saturday's game at Warworth. He had explicitly informed all the players of the week's programme:

	A.M.	P.M.
MONDAY	Training (short sprints, 5-a-side lapping)	Training (practising throw ins free-kicks)
TUESDAY	(weight training exercises understand shooting)	Off
WEDNESDAY	Team Selection (Working together as a team in defence and attacking units)	Repeat of a.m. session
THURSDAY	(exercises, sprints ball work, lapping	Swimming Baths

	shooting)	
FRIDAY	(repeating Monday a.m./p.m.) Hot Bath Team Talk Lunch at Ground	Travel to Warworth 2 p.m. by coach. Stay overnight in St. Thomas Hotel in Bringley (4 miles outside Warworth).
SATURDAY	Breakfast 8.30 Stroll on sea front lunch 12.30	THE MATCH 2.45 p.m. KICK-OFF

Tony had arranged for Bob Vincent, his old friend, to watch the Warworth v Low Grove game which had ended in a 2-2 draw. He phoned Tony to say that the Warworth team were very workmanlike and their defence were terriers in the tackle, particularly No.2, Daniels, and No.4, Mahoney. The goalkeeper, Clubb, left a lot to be desired and was at fault for one of the Low Grove goals. He was poor on crosses and weak on goalkicks. Bob informed Tony that Turner, the ex-Sharrington centre-forward, was used as a target man but was still useful in the air and in fact made both the Warworth goals for No.11, Danderville, and No.10, Garner. He thought No.7, Hardy, could be a danger man if he was given the ball more often but that the team seemed to play to the left hand side most of the time. The two goals Low Grove scored were well taken but Bob thought their equalising goal was given away by some poor marking. Tony heard that the ground was tiny but compact and the crowd was loud and partisan. The playing area was well-grassed, for the end of the season, but very bumpy. Bob concluded his telephone call with a rude comment about the wind which blows in from off the sea but Tony hoped it wouldn't be as cold by the time next Saturday arrived. It was a good and helpful report, which he hoped would stand him and the team in good stead.

On the Tuesday evening Tony met the board of directors for their customary weekly meeting. Everyone was a little tense at the prospect of Saturday's result but the normal business was passed over quickly before any other business and manager's report. Tony, as usual, got to his feet to talk.

'Gentlemen, as we all know, Saturday's game at Warworth is crucial. It shouldn't have got to this stage because I feel we should have taken maximum points from the last two games but, regrettably, we have had to settle for half that amount. I was disappointed in particular at last Saturday's result. We are struggling to get a settled side together, admittedly, but without making excuses we should be scoring with the number of chances we are creating.' Tony adjusted his shirt cuffs before carrying on. 'I have had the players practising hard on this aspect of the game but without the luck going our way. I cannot see what more we can do to find the net'.

'As you know there are a number of combinations available to get promotion but I don't want to rely on the other teams' results and whilst it would be silly and unprofessional for me to say we will be going all out to win the game we will not be going to Warworth to defend and hold out for a draw. That would be too much of a risk and one which we shouldn't take in any circumstances.' Tony cleared his throat. 'The team Barrie and I have selected for the game is the same as played here last Saturday.'

The three directors had a look of surprise on their faces.

'I have spoken to Doctor Ericson who has recently examined Graham Hart and he tells me that it would be unwise to play the young lad because the blood clot behind his knee has not cleared. This does affect the movement of his leg and should the lad get another kick in the same area he would be a liability to the rest of the team.' Eddie Flannagan and Steve King nodded. Bill Boothroyd simply stared into mid-air as though he was thinking of something else.

'Strangely enough,' continued Tony, 'this is only the second time this season that I have been able to field the same twelve players as a consistent unit. Hopefully, with the training we have done together so far this week, by Saturday we should have a side representing us who are raring to go and get us promotion. The lads seem all right at the moment but I expect three of four of the younger players will be understandably suffering from nerves by Saturday. I don't think the occasion will get top side of them though due to the game being played away from home,' Tony paused briefly. The directors were content to listen to him.

'I appreciate Warworth are not involved in either promotion or relegation and that there is nothing at stake for them, but the report I received on them suggests that they are a tigerish team full of tryers. They have had a good season to say this is their first year in league football and they have consolidated their position well. Don't forget they had a great run just recently and I see from the league tables they have only lost three times at home and, as a reminder to everyone, they have beaten both Seamingway and Harloft Town up there in the league. Also they defeated Sherman City of Division Two in the first leg of the 2nd round of the League Cup. They are clearly a team who do well at home but with a little bit of luck and a workmanlike performance from us I think we can get the right result to settle the issue once and for all without having to wait and see how Harloft, Treecliffe and Dabrook have faired.' Tony smiled and sat down.

'I'd settle for the score-line we beat them by down here earlier on in the season, 5-2 wasn't it?' asked Eddie Flannagan.

'Yes, we did well that day. I didn't rate them on that performance but they will probably be a different team on their own ground,' answered Steve King as he made an entry into his pocket diary. 'I heard it's a small ground and it has the most difficult camber on it.'

'I'd heard that it was small but I don't know of the camber. I was told it was well-grassed but bumpy,' replied Tony straightening his papers on the table.

'A couple of early goals is what I'm praying for because if it stays at 0-0 I don't know how I will manage to survive to the final whistle,' admitted Bill Boothroyd.

'I hope you mean a couple of early goals for us, eh?' asked Eddie promptly.

'Of course I do. Don't be silly,' snapped Bill.

'Oh, even Bill's getting touchy. You see, Tony, the nerves are even getting to us and we won't be playing,' grumbled Eddie as he studied the ash on the end of his cigar.

The three directors confirmed they would be travelling with the team on Friday afternoon. They had originally thought it would be best to travel to Warworth separately but basically they didn't want to change the habit of a lifetime. Tony felt that they may have decided to travel by car, or rather he felt Eddie might have decided just in case at the end of the day, Sharrington missed out on promotion, then they could return home without having to share in the misery of a long coach trip. Tony was, however, pleased the directors had opted to travel in the coach. Regrettably Jack Elliot had left word that he would stay in Sharrington, albeit close to his radio.

Chapter 82

Wednesday and Thursday passed by with everything going to plan. The team was announced and training had been carried out without incident. On Thursday afternoon the players had the private use of the public baths for 4 hours. They swam, saunaed and rested.

Friday arrived and after a stimulating training session between 9.30am and 11.30am, the players bathed and got together for a team talk at 12.30pm. Tony repeated the importance of Saturday's game. They discussed tactics and planned moves before going for lunch, which had been prepared for them by Peggy Hollingsworth and a part-time assistant. The players appeared calm and relaxed during lunch. Peggy commented later to Sid Parkin that the players dress sense and manners had improved 100% since Tony Davidson had become manager. Sid was not too bothered, in fact, in his usual whining way, he told Peggy that the only thing which concerned him was to have a relaxing time now that the season had almost finished.

Peggy was amazed at Sid's apathetic approach and had to hold back from shouting at him just in case they were heard by Tony. After the coach had left she laced into Sid but it was to no avail as Sid picked up his newspaper and briefcase and went home. Peggy was so keen for the club to get promotion that she couldn't understand why Sid didn't show any interest in whether the team got promotion or not. She found him most frustrating to work with and had on occasions thought about informing the manager of Sid's attitude to his work, but she had managed to put up with him and plod on.

The journey to Bringley took 5 hours with the coach arriving at St. Thomas' Hotel at 7pm. The party had their evening meal before relaxing in the grounds of the old hotel. At 10 p.m. the players were despatched off to their rooms after a few drinks; Tony was a firm believer that alcohol helped the players relax sufficiently to make them sleep quicker than they would have done without it.

Grant Evans had made up to Tony after pestering him on the question of promotion and, along with Barrie Trippett and Steve King, they spoke about some of the incidents of the season before retiring to bed. Eddie Flannagan and Bill Boothroyd had opted for the main hotel bar to ease their nerves.

For many of the players and other members of the Sharrington party, the night passed slowly. The hotel was just inland from the coast, and the wind, which Bob Vincent had spoken to Tony about, rattled all the windows and doors incessantly. It was such an old building that the wooden floor on the stairs and in the bedrooms creaked agonisingly at every movement. The players all shared a room but the atmosphere was as Tony White recounted "spooky to say the least."

During breakfast at 8.30am, only Alf Henning and Tommy French claimed they slept right through without interruption but as they had roomed together their story couldn't be confirmed or otherwise.

Tony thought some of the players were using the wind and creaking floorboards as an excuse to cover up the thoughts and nerves about the game but he wasn't worried that a few of them had lost some sleep. He had not slept too badly himself and felt remarkably fit and well as he sat down for breakfast.

The players all ate well. Eddie Flannagan failed to be up on time for breakfast but Barrie Trippett said he had seen him earlier that morning tiptoeing back from the lavatory looking pale and tired. Bill Boothroyd who had shared the room with Eddie announced to everyone that the acting Chairman had drunk too much during the evening to face up to a cooked breakfast.

Paul Brooke remarked over breakfast that when he played for Leston United at Warworth, they had stayed at a hotel about 10 miles from Warworth which, in his opinion, was far worse than St. Thomas'. He said the beds were uncomfortable and the food was deplorable. He joked that the latter was probably the reason why they lost 3-0 and that it had all been a plot against them. Paul Brooke also told the breakfast party that the changing and washing facilities at Warworth's ground left a lot to be desired.

Everyone felt that they were cut off from the rest of the football in the country by staying in such a little outpost of Bringley but after Tony and Barrie had escorted the players and a very delicate Eddie Flannagan along the sea front for a three quarter of an hour's stroll, it was a rejuvenated party which returned to the hotel. The walk had been invigorating as the now fresh wind had blown some life back into them.

It was a mild day but the wind was gusty at times. There was a thick expanse of grey cloud with the occasional flash of sun. The main problem for footballers was the wind. It was not a cold wind but it was troublesome and would cause havoc with the ball unless it dropped before the game started.

By 12.30 the players were more relaxed as they tucked into their steak lunch. At 1.15 p.m. Tony once again called the players together to give them a final pre-match talk. The players settled down in the hotel's main lounge.

'All right, this is it then, lads. This is what the season is all about. I think we can all agree we should have had it wrapped up by now and in fact we are giving the likes of Treecliffe and Dabrook a second bite at the cherry. One point today should be good enough, but I'd hate for us to have to rely on it. You know what I mean. We've discussed it many times this week. We will play our normal pattern of football but, and I stress this, this is now the time when you have all got to work as you've never worked before. I want 100% effort from each and every one of you out there this afternoon. I don't want to see players hiding. I want everyone working for each other. Let's do the simple things well. It's not a day for showing off because Warworth will punish you, I'm sure of that, if they see we have one or two prima-donnas.' Tony leant against the arm of the luxurious settee. 'It's an easy game if we play it as a team. We are used to each other's style of play and if we can rally round and sweat blood for this club you can bet your life that we will be celebrating in style tonight. I'm not going to harp on about it, lads, but it will be so disappointing if we let it slip away now when you have all worked so hard to get us into this position throughout the season,' Tony paused. The players looked on, awaiting his next words. 'I agree that if we can grasp promotion today it will be a bit of a fairy tale ending for each and every one of us but let's give it some serious thought and get in the right frame of mind before we go out there, because the hour and half you are out on that pitch is what we have worked for all season and you must on all occasions commit yourself fully to the job in hand.

'We have been through the tactics, you are all good players and although we've not found the net during the last two games, let's make a point of scoring today. I don't mean selfish play. I mean dedication and endeavour. It will come good if we stick at it. Listen to Graham for his instructions and it'll end up okay. Right, lads, that's enough talk. Go and prove to me and the directors and, most of all, our travelling supporters, that we are worthy of Division Three football next season. Any questions?' asked Tony.

No one spoke. There were a few nervous coughs and whistles but without any further delay Tony told the players to board the coach.

The journey to the ground was soon over. They arrived at the tiny Warworth ground at 1.45pm, one hour before the kick-off. There were a number of Sharrington supporters already outside the ground and they cheered their team into the players' entrance and wished them well.

Bob, Eddie and Frank had just arrived in Warworth and were busy looking for a car parking space. They had set off at 8.30am and had a trouble free journey.

'Get in there,' shouted Bob Bennett from the back seat and pointing to a space in front of an advertising billboard.

'Ah yes, well spotted Bob,' chortled Frank Sneddon as he indicated to turn the car into the welcomed gap.

'The ground is only just down that road I think. Well, at least that's the direction where all the supporters are heading in,' stated Eddie Fisher nodding his head in the direction he was referring to.

The car was eventually parked satisfactorily and locked up before the three men made their way to the ground.

'I am getting nervous,' stammered Bob Bennett as he wrapped his red and black scarf tightly around his neck to help keep the wind out.

'Me too. In fact I think we all are. I've never known us have such a quiet car journey to an away game,' commented Eddie Fisher.

'Looks like we've got a good following today. Have you seen all the coaches from Sharrington?' asked Bob hesitantly.

'Yes. It's not before time either. The more support today, the more confidence our lads will have,' replied Eddie, looking around him as though to get his bearings.

'Oh come on, let's nip in here for a drink before the game. It might help to take a few of the nerves away,' said Bob quickly rushing into the entrance of a public house. The other two men followed him in.

Back in Sharrington, Penny Davidson was just finishing her ironing before settling down to tune into the local radio station for the match reports from Warworth. She was also keen to hear the reports from Mannish where Treecliffe were the visitors, and Dabrook where the other local club, Rallingborough, were playing. The top game in the Fourth Division was between Harloft and Seamingway but for Penny her number one priority was Sharrington's game.

Eddie Flannagan, Bill Boothroyd and Steve King were guests of the Warworth Board of Directors. They were all discussing the season in general and the possible outcome of today's game as they drank from the cut glass goblets. The Warworth Chairman, Alwyn Sanderson, who looked as though he had just come off the set of an old RAF movie with his long, greying handlebar moustache and posh accent, predicted Warworth would end the season with Sharrington's scalp. He was an arrogant man and Eddie Flannagan was on the verge of telling him to shut his mouth but after thinking better of it he made the excuse that he wanted to go to his seat in the stand and soak up the atmosphere.

On his way to the director's box he met up with Grant Evans who was complaining about the dilapidated condition of the press box. Grant was also having problems with the telephone and was seeking out Philip Rawson, a sports reporter from Sharrington, who was covering the match for local radio, to warn him of the difficulties.

Jack Elliott was eagerly awaiting the start of the game. He was sitting in his favourite chair. His wife was sitting across from him, anxiously watching the grandfather clock as it ticked on to 2.30. She hoped deep down that the Sharrington team would win because she felt that by the club getting promotion, it would help to ease her husband's worries and make him relax properly. The radio presenter was announcing the formula for the afternoon's listening. Once again, Sharrington were kicking off before the other local teams, albeit today, it was only 15 minutes before the other games.

Warworth's ground, Burns Way, did not have floodlights but inside the ground with only 15 minutes to kick-off, there was sufficient electricity being provided by the Sharrington supporters. Grant Evans and Eddie Flannagan had never seen such support for Sharrington at an away game. The supporters, who made up for about one third of the 7,500 gate, were in good voice. They chanted songs and shouted slogans continuously to set the scene for Sharrington's vital game.

Bob, Eddie and Frank had taken up their positions on the terracing in front of the main stand. Behind each goal were two old and broken down shed-like constructions and on the opposite side to the stand and players' tunnel was a barren section of steps and just beyond that was the sea with its waves crashing against the surrounding rocks.

The atmosphere was good but the setting seemed strange for such an important game. The wind had dropped slightly but now the grey clouds were heavier and they filled the whole of the sky.

The teams were announced and within two minutes the Warworth team ran out onto the pitch to a loud cheer. Their blue and white striped shirts were darting all over the pitch as they limbered up.

About 30 seconds later Sharrington were greeted on the pitch to a crescendo of applause, cheers, whistles and a few boos. They were kitted in red shirts, white shorts and black and red stockings. They had changed from their customary black shorts so as not to clash with the home team. The team were warming up at the end of the ground which housed the majority of Sharrington supporters.

'Here goes then, Tony. Nothing more we can do now for the next forty-five minutes,' said Barrie Trippett as he put the sponge into the bucket of cold water.

The dugout was simply a hole in the ground with three pieces of black corrugated sheet on top of it which made up the two sides and top. There was some sand and gravel scattered in the bottom and what looked like an old bucket handle half buried amongst it.

'You're dead right, Barrie. It's at times like this when I wish I was playing again,' replied Tony as he settled into the makeshift dugout.

'Me too. At least when you're on the pitch you can do something about it if things aren't going right,' stated Barrie settling down alongside Tony. Tony nodded. 'Looks like we've won the toss any way, Graham's opted to stay as we are'.

'I don't think it makes a lot of difference on this pitch which way you kick but I think he's chosen to kick towards our supporters in the second half and rightly so. They are in good voice. It's a good following today. I hope we do well for them,' stressed Tony as Warworth centre-forward, John Turner, prepared to kick off against his old team mates.

'Do they look confident do you think, Frank?' asked Bob Bennett above the noise of the terracing crowd.

'We will soon see, won't we. The ref's ready to blow to get the game underway. They look okay to me, that is with the exception of young Cracknell. He does look nervous. He's been hopping from foot to foot for ages,' replied Frank Sneddon, drawing in a mouthful of smoke from his burnt down, tipped cigarette.

'They're off!' yelled Eddie Fisher. 'Get stuck in lads. Make it count from the kick-off!' His voice pierced over the crowd around him. It was a typical Eddie comment. Finesse wasn't his style. Sometimes Frank thought that Eddie lacked the basic knowledge of the game of football.

It was a careful start by the Sharrington team. They were cautious in defence and built the first few attacks steadily. Warworth were as tigerish as Bob Vincent had explained. Both teams were hard into the tackle and as a result of this no one seemed over keen to hold onto the ball for any length of time. For all Paul Cracknell may have looked nervous before the start in the 4th minute he had controlled a loose ball and accurately passed to Tony White some 25 yards away with the coolness of an old professional.

'Neil Baynes is working hard today, isn't he?' asked Bill Boothroyd nervously.

'Great player. Oh good ball, Docker. Yes, he seems back to his best form today,' answered Eddie Flannagan who was totally immersed in the action.

'They are playing much better today. Tony's got them in top form. They just need an early goal to build on,' reflected Steve King. Before he could say any more Eddie Flannagan interrupted and got hold of Steve's left arm.

'Good pass, lad. Sammy's away.' He paused momentarily. 'Good cross. Get in Alf… Oh… Yes. Oh, what a save! Did you see that? The goalkeeper stopped a certain goal then.' He turned to the young director. The crowd applauded the Sharrington's veteran centre-forward header and the agile goalkeepers acrobatic save.

'And now it's over for our first visit of the afternoon to Burn's Way, where Sharrington are playing in their vital league game against Warworth. It was a 2.45 p.m. kick-off remember, so the game should be 15 minutes old by now. Are you there Philip Rawson, our man at the game, and is there any good news?' asked the sports presenter on the local radio station, David Cassidy. There was a slight silence.

Both Jack Elliott and Penny Davidson were tuned in listening separately for some good news.

'Hello, David, Phil Rawson here. Well, no goals as yet but Sharrington have just come the nearest to scoring through Alf Henning but he was thwarted by a great save from the home goalkeeper, Clubb.

'It's a good, entertaining and positive game with Sharrington just having the edge so far.'

'Thank you Philip, we will join you at about 3.15 p.m. for the next report' said David Cassidy.

Jack Elliott smiled at his wife. 'So far so good. It seems like they are playing well. Hope they keep it up.'

Penny Davidson turned down the sound slightly before picking up her knitting again.

After 19 minutes, a throw in by No. 3 Seekard found No. 4 Mahoney who screened the ball from Simon Docker and then turned before putting a long pass down the Warworth right wing for No. 7 Hardy. The winger checked and then like greased lightning he was into his stride. He left Paul Brooke floundering and was two yards in front of the full-back. Hardy looked up and crossed with his right foot perfectly for No. 8 Williamson to race onto a head towards goal.

Alan Hawkins moved quickly to his left and palmed the ball against the post. As the ball came back into play it landed perfectly for the same striker to volley it into the net before Tommy French could challenge him. It was a sensational goal. It stunned the Sharrington supporters. The Warworth team were cock-a-hoop.

'On no, I don't believe it. Did you see how that ball came back to him!' yelled Barrie Trippett.

'I know but really we shouldn't have let them get that far,' said Tony miserably.

'They'll need lifting now. That was a fatal blow,' murmured Barrie. Tony didn't answer.

'Can you believe that. Just what have we got to do to get the run of the ball like that' said Steve King in disbelief.

'I don't believe it. I just don't believe it. How are we going to get back into this game now,' muttered Eddie with his head in his hands.

'No we are not too good at coming back from behind, are we?' shouted Bill Boothroyd over the noise of the Warworth supporters in the stand.

'And now let's go straight over to Warworth. There's been a goal apparently,' said David Cassidy.

'Yes, there has, but I'm afraid it's bad news for Sharrington supporters. A good move by Warworth brought an excellent goal, at the second attempt, by Williamson. For the last two minutes since going a goal down, Sharrington have been rushed to clear from a strong Warworth line up. They are going to have to re-organise and work their way back into the game if they are to hold on to their promotion chance,' said Phil Rawson.

Jack Elliott shook his head from side to side. It was not the result he had wanted to hear. Mrs. Elliott quickly told her husband not to worry as she said she had a feeling they would come out of it all right. Jack just stared in disbelief at the scoreline.

Penny Davidson squealed when she heard the radio. There was no one for her to speak to. She felt shattered. She wondered what Tony was thinking.

'Ian Gilmarsh here, David. I was just about to give the Treecliffe fans some good news about being 1-0 in the lead from a goal by that man Hope again but just as I came onto the air Toddy snatched an equaliser for Mannish out of the blue. So it's one-all here, David, after twenty-five minutes play'.

'Now let's go to Steve Jones at Dabrook. Are you there, Steve?' asked David Cassidy

'Yes David. It's 1-0 here to Dabrook. A goal by Salmon after 20 minutes. And what a beauty it was. He bent a direct free kick around the Kallingborough defensive

wall and it curled into the net. Superb goal. Dabrook are a well-balanced side and although Rallingborough are desperate to try and avoid relegation they haven't counter attacked at all and aren't troubling the accomplished Dabrook defence'.

'Thank you Steve. We will join you again at half-time. Now after the break we will go back to Warworth for the half-time report.' There was an intermission from the sports programme. It was an advertising break.

'Right let's see if Sharrington have edged their way back into the game. Are you there Phil Rawson?' asked David Cassidy eagerly.

'Yes, I hear you loud and clear. Well things have improved slightly for the Sharrington fans. Their team managed to withstand about ten minutes of pressure from Warworth and in the last ten minutes or so of the first half they played some attractive football and were creating some openings. Henning and Baynes are playing well and young Tony White is starting to get the better of his full-back Seekard. We can only hope for better things and a goal or two for Sharrington in the second half,' reported Phil Rawson.

'What do you make of the first half, men?' asked Bob Bennett.

'We are just not pressurising them enough, if you ask me. We just haven't got that extra push,' ranted Eddie Fisher.

'They have had a difficult time to my mind. Warworth are not playing badly and the tiny little ground doesn't help us. We were starting to come into it just before the break and who knows, perhaps a total assault on their goal in the second half may bring it's reward,' answered Frank sensibly.

I'd love to know how Dabrook and Treecliffe are going on,' said Eddie.

'They are letters L and T on the half-time board. L is Dabrook. The scores won't be up for about 15 minutes or so yet though,' answered Bob.

'Now let's take it up where we left off. Don't do anything too rash just because we are trailing by a goal. You've played well and the goals have got to come if we play it sensibly,' said Tony, patiently. The referee's bell sounded. 'Okay, lads, this is it. Keep it flowing. Keep up the work rate. Let's make them have it. Give it everything, right up to the final whistle, regardless of the score. Whatever you do, don't lose faith in your game. You are the better side. Now go out there and get the result to prove it!' shouted Tony.

The players wished each other luck as they tramped out of the dressing room in search of promotion.

Tony stood alongside Barrie, watching the team walk down the players' tunnel. 'You know, Barrie' murmured Tony 'Man management is an art. I seem to repeat the same things over and over again but I'm never certain I'm getting through to them all at the same time. It's funny really. I suppose it's all about performing as a collective unit but there are times when I don't feel as we are making any headway at all. Don't know why I should say that now. Maybe it's nerves or a fear of facing such a disappointment in failing at the last hurdle. It's up to them now,' reflected Tony dreamily.

Barrie looked at Tony, wondering why he should be reflecting on man management at a time like this. The manager was always full of surprises. Barrie just frowned and walked down the tunnel in front of Tony.

The Sharrington supporters got behind their team from the restart. They cheered and applauded every good thing a Sharrington player did.

After 55 minutes, Sharrington were outplaying Warworth. They were faster to the ball and more determined. They were attacking down each wing and all their efforts were being prevented from crossing the home team's goal line between the posts.

'Sorry to be the bringer of bad news men but have you seen those scores,' said Bob mournfully as he pointed to the half-time score board. The two men looked up straight away.

'Oh no, Dabrook are winning 2-0 and Treecliffe are drawing 1-1,' said Eddie angrily.

All three men turned back to watch the game and yet another midfield battle.

'We've got to run at them, as I see it,' stated Eddie Flannagan. 'All this passing is getting us nowhere.'

'It's no good losing possession, Eddie, when they are one up,' replied Steve King.

'That's as may be. But if we don't take the chances we will not get anywhere. We have the players. Look at Baynes, he's got enough skill to get through them and then come back and do it again,' said Eddie off the cuff.

'We've got only 30 minutes to do it,' urged Steve King patting his knees with the rolled up programme.

Jack Elliot was anxiously awaiting the next bulletin. He had heard the other half-time scores, which hadn't pleased him. Everyone seemed to be on course other than Sharrington. Even Harloft were drawing 0-0 to

Seamingway.

Eventually he recognised Philip Rawson's distant voice. *'Still 1-0 to Warworth but Sharrington are still on top with more possession at the moment. No clear cut chances to report though.'* He signed off and Jack felt all was beginning to fade away from Sharrington. To make matters worse for the chairman there was a rush of excitement in the studio, and presenter David Cassidy announced in an enthusiastic voice: *'and good news for Treecliffe supporters. I've just heard that new signing Gregory had put them 2-1 up after 7 minutes of the restart at Mannish.'*

Jack got more and more frustrated. He was annoyed that the voice in the little box at his side should be making him hear things he didn't want to hear. He was tempted to shut it off and just switch on for the full time results but he couldn't make himself do it.

Penny Davidson was also disappointed but knew she couldn't do anything to change the results. She forced herself to knit one row after the other.

'How long do you make left to play?' asked Eddie Fisher anxiously.

'About 14 minutes' replied Frank Sneddon apprehensively.

'Warworth are getting back into this match you know, men,' stated Bob Bennett.

'We seem to be running out of steam. It's so frustrating,' said Eddie angrily.

'They are a dogged side, Warworth. They chase and chase. Well, at least they have done this afternoon. They are a far better team than the one that we beat earlier in the season,' commented Frank.

'Even Johnny Turner's having a fine match,' remarked Eddie somewhat reluctantly.

'And now for a round up of the latest scores effecting the local teams' said David Cassidy.

The first broadcast came from Dabrook where the home side were still leading by 2-0. The second report confirmed Treecliffe were maintaining their 2-1 lead. Before going over live to the Warworth ground, David Cassidy reported that in a three minute spell at Harloft the score had moved on to 1-1. The home team striker, Pinner, had opened the scoring in the 54th minute and his opposite No. 8, Fox, had equalised for Seamingway in the 57th minute.

Finally the link was joined up to Philip Rawson. *Ten minutes remaining here and still Sharrington are trailing to that 19th minute goal by Williamson. The game is pretty level at the moment but still the Sharrington crowd are behind their team and giving them plenty of vocal support. Time is running out but Sharrington are still pressing. Back to the studio,'* reported Philip Rawson.

'Oh dear, can Sharrington do it? If they can they are leaving it to the last minute. What a disappointment if they fail now. Anyhow for the next three minutes we will listen to the No. 1 record in the area,' said David Cassidy. The music started slowly. It was a pleasant melody.

Jack Elliott was not listening to the words of the song. He stared into space. His wife had just brought him a cup of tea. He automatically picked the cup up to drink from it. Just as he got the cup to his lips he heard David Cassidy's voice break into the record. *'Sensational news Sharrington supporters.'* Jack's eyes widened, was it a goal for Sharrington or goals for Rallingborough and Mannish? The presenters voice continued *'Over to Phil Rawson'.* The line crackled slightly and the reporter's voice was shouting above the background noise. *'If you can hear me in the studio, the toast of Sharrington tonight will be big burly Alf Henning. Just after you left me a Sharrington move developed down the right wing. Tony White beat his full-back and crossed to the far post, the ball was challenged for by Simon Docker and a Warworth defender but it broke loose and, in a scramble just outside the six-yard box in front of goal, Henning stuck his boot out at the right time and sent the ball out of Clubb's reach and into the net. It's pandemonium here now. The Sharrington supporters are chanting so noisily I can hardly hear myself talk. Returning you to the studio with Sharrington on another attack, 1-1 then at Warworth.'* Philip Rawson's voice disappeared beyond the cheering.

'Oh that's fantastic isn't it, love? Just hold on, lads,' said Jack in sheer delight.

Penny Davidson dropped her knitting onto her knee and clapped upon hearing the good news. She knew there were only about 5 minutes remaining. It was so exciting. Could they do it?

Eddie Flannagan was still on his feet since the Henning goal. People from behind were shouting to him to sit down but he was living the match and going through the motions of the equalising goal.

Steve King was giggling at Eddie in his own excitement. Bill Boothroyd was flushed but in control of his emotions.

Sharrington were coming forwards in waves but Tony and Barrie were quick to shout to the defenders to maintain the cover if they ventured too far. The team's confidence was so obvious. They had broken the habit of not scoring and they were playing like a team who knew they were promotion bound. Warworth were still exchanging tackle for tackle but Sharrington had a stranglehold on the game. Right from

Alan Hawkins to Sammy Chaddock, the confidence glowed. The red shirts were enjoying the dying minutes.

'We must have done it now, surely? Come on ref, put an end to it. Let's celebrate,' rambled Eddie Fisher

'I can't stand it any longer. Every time they get the ball I feel the worse will happen,' stuttered Bob Bennett. 'The ref's looking at his watch. And again. He's putting his whistle to his lips. This is it. It must be!' screeched Frank.

Baynes juggled the ball on his right foot, controlled it on the floor and swerved a pass to Paul Cracknell. The youngster seemed shocked to receive the ball. He was standing with his back to the goal just outside the penalty area. He hastily kicked the ball high in the air. It seemed to go higher and higher. As the ball started to fall back to the ground, the referee's whistle signalled the end of the match.

Tony quickly turned to Barrie and smiled and winked at him. They shook hands. Sharrington had done it on the condition that Treecliffe had not won by 3 clear goals. The scenes were sensational. The players were hugging each other and the supporters were racing onto the ground to celebrate with their heroes.

Bob, Eddie and Frank hugged each other as they danced around in a circle on the terracing.

Eddie Flannagan finally sat down, breathed in slowly then let out the loudest yell anyone had ever heard.

Steve King shook his fists tightly in mid air.

Bill Boothroyd was all at sea. He was busily shaking hands with everyone on the Warworth Board of Directors.

Jack Elliott slumped back in his chair when he heard the result. He couldn't really believe his good fortune. Promotion for Sharrington to Division Three was almost a certainty with Treecliffe only leading Mannish Town by 2-1.

Penny Davidson sang happily: 'We are the champions.' She was thrilled and delighted for Tony.

Although everyone had assumed that Sharrington had done enough to gain promotion, it wasn't definite until 15 minutes later when the full time results of the other games were announced:

Harloft Town 1 v Seamingway 1
Mannish Town 2 v Treecliffe 2
Dabrook 2 v Rallingborough 0

Sharrington F.C. had won promotion to League Division Three. It had been a great day in the history of Sharrington F.C.

Chapter 83

Sharrington's goal difference was far superior to Dabrook's although both teams had finished the season on 39 points.

In the dressing room it was chaotic. The champagne had been opened courtesy of the three directors. The players were in great spirits. They were laughing and joking. Tony was shaking every player's hand and congratulating them individually. There was so much noise that Tony was unable to express his delight to everyone at the same time.

Apart from all the players, there were the other lads who had not played, including Leighton and Smith, hobbling over the cast-off kit and boots, the three directors, Grant Evans, Barrie Trippett, Philip Rawson and well-wishers from the Warworth staff. It was pandemonium. Some players were bathed, others had not even taken off their kit, and Henning, Hawkins and Bond were polishing off the first bottle of champagne between them.

Telegrams were flooding in from everywhere and a number of excited Sharrington fans were also trying to flood in to the dressing room to join in the celebrations.

Eddie Flannagan and Grant Evans were acting as go-betweens to the rejoicing fans and eventually the ruddy-faced directors allowed three fans into the already overcrowded dressing room so that they could obtain the Sharrington players' autographs.

Nobody seemed to mind. As the majority of the players had never experienced anything quite like the feeling that went hand in hand with success and popularity, no one objected to the attention that they were being given and Micky Thomas said that he never wanted the moment to end.

For almost an hour after the game, the festivities continued but by 6 p.m. the whole Sharrington party had left the dressing room and been cheered ecstatically onto the coach by the delirious supporters. It was a unanimous decision to return straight to Sharrington.

Sam Johnstone, the driver, made haste, as the celebrations continued on board.

Tony made his way from the front of the coach where he had been sitting, to the middle section. He leant his hand on two seats on each side of the aisle. 'Listen lads, just before you get too carried away I would just like to take this opportunity of thanking you all for not only your fantastic performance today but for all your efforts over the season. It has been a great pleasure working with you and you have all made my job so much easier. Congratulations to each and every one of you. Enjoy the success and I'll see you next Tuesday for a bit of light training, eh?'

The players all applauded Tony and, as the successful manager returned to his seat, they joined in an impromptu chorus of "For he's a jolly good fellow."

The journey was enjoyable for everyone on board. It was a day none of them would ever forget.

At 10.45 p.m. the coach pulled up outside the Sharrington ground where about two hundred supporters greeted them joyously.

Tony headed for home straight away to celebrate with his wife and family. He phoned Jack Elliott who was over the moon and admitted to celebrating the occasion with a couple of glasses of sherry. Tony was delighted that the recuperating chairman was in good spirits. He promised to call and see him on the following day.

Before the day was over there had been more telephone calls of congratulations, and by midnight, Tony was exhausted. At last he could rest and relax. The season had brought more strain than he had imagined. As he put his head onto his pillow he knew in his own mind that it was now all over. He had proved to everyone that he had made a success of the job. He was satisfied but he didn't want to think of what tomorrow might bring. The lights went out. His thoughts slowly disappeared. He fell asleep.

During the following weeks the promotion and relegation battles were sorted out in every division. The FA Cup and League Cup issues were also solved. Rondale Rovers won the League Championship and the FA Cup by beating Passondale 2-1 but they had been defeated by the same margin in the League Cup final by Torchester.

The Sharrington players continued to enjoy the popularity promotion had brought them. The directors had also given each player a £200 bonus and the mood at the club was at its peak. The players trained on every other day and Tony and Barrie kept the sessions hard and interesting as there was a possibility of an end of season tour.

After the FA Cup final, which brought the season to a close, Tony was, as usual, in his office on the Monday morning when he received a telephone call.

'Hello, Davidson here.'

'Ah, Mr. Davidson. Good morning to you. My name is John Reynolds, Chairman of Miltern Rovers of the Second Division. I was wondering if I could make an appointment to see you in the near future,' said the gruff voice on the other end of the telephone.

'May I ask what you wish to discuss?' asked Tony curiously.

'Yes, certainly you may. I want you to become our new manager before the start of next season and I think the terms I have to offer you might appeal to you.' Tony was dumbfounded. It came as such a surprise. Before he could answer the Chairman continued, 'I would prefer to discuss this matter with you privately though. Should we say next Wednesday at 8 p.m. at the Royal Hotel in Beckham? I appreciate this request may have come out of the blue but I assure you Mr. Davidson, you are the man I want to run Miltern Rovers and I would be pleased to have your company to discuss my ideas and proposals. I'll leave it with you for now but should you decide to find out what I have to offer, please let me know as soon as possible. I promise you the matter will be treated in the strictest confidence. I do hope you will, at least, listen to what I have in mind. Hope to hear favourably from you shortly. My home number is Miltern 5728.' With that the Chairman hung up and Tony, who was so surprised with the caller was left writing the telephone number down on the writing pad in front of him.

Lightning Source UK Ltd.
Milton Keynes UK
UKHW021136201020
371904UK00009B/489